CHRISTMAS

CHRISTMAS

by William Sansom

Weidenfeld and Nicolson

5 Winsley Street London W1

© 1968 by William Sansom
Designed by John Wallis for
George Weidenfeld and Nicolson Ltd, London
SBN 297 17649 8
Phototypeset by
BAS Printers Limited, Wallop, Hampshire
and printed by Jarrold and Sons Limited, Norwich

Contents

THE GOLDEN BIRTH FORESEEN

The last great Age, foretold by sacred Rimes,
Renews its finish'd course: Saturnian times
Roll round again; and mighty years, begun
From their first Orb, in radiant Circles run.
The base degenerate iron Offspring ends;
A golden Progeny from Heaven descends.
O chaste Lucina! speed the Mother's pains,
And haste the glorious Birth! thy own Apollo reigns!

. . . .

The Son shall lead the life of Gods, and be
By Gods and Heroes seen, and Gods and Heroes see.
The jarring Nations he in peace shall bind,
And with paternal Virtues rule Mankind.
Unbidden Earth shall wreathing Ivy bring
And fragrant Herbs (the promises of Spring)
As her first offerings to her infant King.

Lines written by Virgil
several decades before the
Nativity of Christ. Eclogue 4,
trans. Dryden.

1

The Great Illusion

Sommer in Winter, Day in Night
CRASHAW

What is the colour of Christmas?

Red? The red of toyshops on a dark winter's afternoon, of Father Christmas and the robin's breast?

Or green? Green of holly and spruce and mistletoe in the house, dark shadow of summer in leafless winter?

One might plainly add a romance of white, fields of frost and snow; thus white, green, red – reducing the event to the level of a Chianti bottle.

But many will say that the significant colour is gold, gold of fire and treasure, of light in the winter dark; and this gets closer.

For the true colour of Christmas is black.

Black of winter, black of night, black of frost and of the east wind, black of dangerous shadows beyond the firelight.

Darkness of the time of year hovers everywhere, there is no brightness of Christ Child, angel, holly, or toy without a dark surround somewhere about. The table yellow with electric light, the fire by which stories are told, the bright spangle of the tree – they all blaze out of shadow and out of a darkness of winter. The only exception is an expectation of Christmas morning, the optimistic image of sunlight on the snow of Christmas Day and a sparkling brisk walk through the white-breath frosty air. But it only lasts a short while, and has its own dark frame, made up of the night before and the early dark of a December afternoon.

This is, of course, no fanciful concept; it is the wholly practical reason for Christmas and for all the festivals of light which preceded Christianity. A

lighting of fires, a prayer and a feast have throughout man's existence relieved the tedium of the long dark months. Today, in an electronically stimulated metropolitan winter, when glitter and kinds of gaiety can be switched on at any time, the necessity is not so apparent: but even so, people still need an *occasion*, some agreed and communal burst of big light in the middle of the dark. To appreciate this need at its fullest, one might put oneself in the shoes of a child at school, a child for whom time in any case travels slowly, to whom three months of work is not an addition of days but a condemnation without foreseeable end. Such a boy or girl must look at the long dark sunless tunnel of the first winter months as quite intolerable without a light somewhere at the end.

Christmastide is essentially a festival of hope. It marks the time of year when the sun again gains strength. Although the new unconquered sun does not show much of itself, the slow-living countryman of old perceived it, priests and magi of many nations invoked it; everywhere a turning of the year was recognised, and fires were lit in sympathy. Impossible to do without it. The Emperor Aurelian gave it a Roman dignity: *Dies Natalis Invicti Solis*.

Pre-Christian origins   The keeping of Christmas has origins far from the image of Christ. It is an older habit caparisoned. The setting of the December date and most of its practical traditions are pre-Christian. In any case, no one knows when Christ was born; scholars are still divided even as to his birthplace, many rejecting Bethlehem as an expedient Davidian myth. The church of Rome did not establish the festival as Christian until the middle of the fourth century. Previously, in all latitudes away from the equator where the sun was more desired than rain, the solstice had been celebrated with religious service. For Son we must read sun. Not that it matters much; the symbolic presence and goodness of Christ is of more importance than any factual dating. Even in non-Christian terms, the image of a newborn child is a rather more appealing symbol of new life than a sacrificial huddle of smoking limbs.

Christmas, from whatever angle you look at it, is a complex. When the English-speaking countries sit down at lunch-time to a 'traditional Christmas dinner', they eat an Aztec bird by an Alsatian tree, followed by a pudding spiced with sub-tropical preserves, while in England itself the most popular of Christmas carols still tells of the Bohemian King Wenceslas to music taken from a Swedish spring song. And so on. Gone the boar's head, gone the yule-log, gone the Pickwickian wassail. We still have holly, mistletoe and much else – though it has taken America to send back across the Atlantic the old circular sun-symbol of the holly wreath. Meanwhile, there are always what seem to be innovations – florists and manufacturers of plastic plants now market a sophisticated parcel indeed, a crucifix of holly, birth and sacrifice in one. Yet one suddenly finds, in an American account dated 1863, that children decorated a parlour with 'evergreens, crosses, stars etc.'.

Ogden Nash wrote: 'Roses are things which Christmas is not a bed of them . . .'. Many of us might agree with him, or think we do. But a really close examination of all the facets and feelings of Christmas usually ends up by breeding not contempt but its opposite, a slow snowballing of approval and applause In spite of all our experience of commerce gone tastelessly amok, of sore feet and emptied pockets in a dictated and mainly senseless shopping chore, and of over-eating and all that – one may finally recognise what was not clear before: that it would be dangerous to do without Christmas, that a respite from winter and a sense of occasion are vitally and humanly necessary. One may wish the design to change but that is difficult, we are in the arms of usage, a fluid matter of human agreement. Like a language with its live changes, all modifications of tradition demonstrate that the whole occasion is not a dead force of habit but a lively and even creative force.

People complain of the sentimentality of Christmas. But sentimentality is an easily abused emotion – right enough abuse when it is plainly mawkish, but wrong when sentimentality is really sentiment and simply reflects a few of the illusions which embellish life. America, for instance, is much given to the idea of snow as part of the Christmas scene. Yet this is a sizeable country with a large and warm southern area. In southern California Christmas is a peak time for the blooming of roses, in Florida the nose-masks are out against the basking sun. Yet the land which invented Santa Claus and his reindeer, creatures of the snowy night, must somehow accept throughout itself these influences conceived in the north. Effigies of the snow scene penetrate the warm southern night, plaster reindeer and artificial snow illuminate with a mental rime the palmy shadows – though fingers drape grey Spanish moss as a garland, minds still yearn towards sharp nights of frost and yulish tradition far away somewhere upwards on the map. Palms may be used as Christmas trees, and excused as being closer to the reality of the Holy Land – but this does not seem to be enough; snow is somewhere at the back of the mind or tinselling the front of a shop window. It is a sentimental necessity.

Sentiment and sentimentality

Or take, for example, the concept of snow at Christmas-time in the closer confines of England. In spite of the almost celebrated three-inch icicles seen on the nose of a Nottingham horse in 1860, records show that snow itself at Christmas is unusual. But then, records do not cover all England – there is also a north and a south to the place; and different winds strike different places; and there are different land levels, even mountains. There is often mildness in one part, and frost in another; snow elsewhere. Who can tell? The one thing we know is that the illusion of snow pleases us. It looks nice, and fits the latter-day historical story. It also suggests that people will be warmer inside the house, the home – thus emphasising the family atmosphere of the occasion. The whiteness of snow has a connotation of purity. Snow with its flakes and its falling is one of childhood's greatest excitements – it changes the world, and makes magic seem really possible. And there are a thousand other associations, simple and sophisticated. Christmas cards are the better for it. Plastic frost in a shop window is not to be lightly

A Christmas card
designed by Reynolds Stone

dismissed. So, snow. And snowmen, and robins, and many of the other illusions and devices of a Victorian Christmas hovering near the mawk-line but on consideration innocent: one might look for a line to be drawn, one might draw it at the stage-coach. A man-made thing, no natural element, it has been over-used.

Victorian? Rather – late Victorian, though even this latter phrase is a vague one. It covers what – twenty, thirty years? When one examines a period of twenty years closer to today, say the twenty years which Aldous Huxley described as *Entre deux Guerres*, it becomes clear how many different atmospheres can be contained in two decades. The years of inflation and hunger; the jazz and pyjama years; the Crash and ukulele years; the rise of Fascism; the final shadow of Hitler. Also it is difficult to define exactly when this or that historical atmosphere or new custom ever becomes general for a whole country and people. Sherlock Holmes, in *The Blue Carbuncle* (1891), still chose the goose as his Christmas bird, though the turkey was by then a common enough Christmas dish. Anthony Trollope in 1870 had the north of England eating beef; and that went on for many years later. The history of the Christmas pudding takes a similar course, from frumenty and meaty porridge, and possibly also from the great sausage called hackin, to the present-day thing from a tin. The most one can do is to celebrate the best of the past that remains. And for us today the majority of this best was current at least in the last decade of Victoria's reign.

Few people now will ever remember seeing a properly round, ball-shaped Christmas pudding. Even the ample servings of the twenties were flat-bottomed as the pan they were boiled in. But the ideal Victorian affair was bound in a cloth and cooked in a clothes copper, coming out round as a football. Dark brown, alive with sixpences, hatted with holly, blue with

Overleaf
The Christmas drama of Light in the Dark. A Tyrolean crib, featuring the town of Bethlehem and the manger, built up in the early nineteenth century but using figurines from the middle of the eighteenth century

12

Opposite: *The Madonna and Child. An early fourteenth-century work in stained glass from the Schlosskirche Kappenberg in Germany*

flaming brandy – about the only natural touch of blue at all in the many-coloured festivities of Christmas –, this is the sustaining image the Victorians once spooned at, probably with chilblained fingers. Where have all the chilblains gone?

The truth about Dingley Dell

Whenever a 'Victorian' Christmas is mentioned, somebody is there to breathe 'Dingley Dell'. But how long is it since we have followed Mr Pickwick through his formidable Christmas Day, if we ever did? The truth of the book is different from the general conception. All the wassail and dance and mistletoe-kissing was finished by the end of Christmas Eve. Snapdragon, Blind-Man's-Buff, the ghost story by the fire – all were over by twelve o'clock midnight, when the company greeted the first minutes of Christmas Day and then retired to bed. But Mr Pickwick's Christmas Day itself was a very different matter. The early morning is taken with the arrival at Dingley Dell of the two trainee sawbones who begin breakfast with brandy and oysters, and later discuss human dissection as they cut up a fowl. When the ladies come, one of these medical students, Bob Sawyer, illustrates the removal of a tumour from a gentleman's head with an oyster-knife and a half-quartern loaf 'to the great edification of the assembled company'. Then the whole train goes to church. But it is after church that there comes the main blow to our reminiscent sensibilities. It is the description of the main mid-day Christmas meal, and it is thus: '... after a substantial lunch ...'.

The possibly well-remembered skating scene follows soon after this characterless meal. It records a tetchy and quarrelsome Pickwick hardly consistent with requirements of peace and goodwill and it culminates in the portly old thing falling through the ice. He is extracted, and whisked off up to bed where Sam Weller 'took up his dinner'. And that is all about our 'traditional' Christmas Day feasting.

It may be added that 'a bowl of punch was carried up afterwards, and a great carouse held in honour of his safety'. But that would have occurred on any other day of the year in similarly demanding circumstances. In those early Victorian times, there was, of course, no Christmas tree: and there were no presents to be exchanged, if one excepts a tip of five shillings to Weller. Thus before 1837. Presumably the great cod, which had been loaded on the country-bound coach with such trouble, never even belonged to Pickwick: for no further mention is made of this fish, which makes it possibly the largest red herring in narrative history. But a fish course had been usual enough in earlier years – in *The Diary of a Country Parson*, James Woodforde writes in 1773 of 'two fine codds boiled with fryed Souls round them and oyster sauce', before the beef, wild ducks etc. of a meal whose only tradition is its amplitude.

This tradition of ample feasting was naturally taken to America. So many different nationalities made up the population that any one type of meal is more than ever difficult to fix upon, except that the turkey, being an indigenous bird, comes into account more often than in Europe. The American experience was split between two realities: first the immigrants' wish to establish the customs of their parent country, and the second

Above: *How a white Christmas could have looked in Paris a century and a half ago. An anonymous print, dated 1804, of sleighs driving up and down the Champs Elysées*
Below: *'Christmas at Home', from* The Graphic *of 1881*

*'The Jolly Old Bird
of the Season'*, c. *1870*

involving new climates and new people like the Indians, and new animals
for the convivial slaughter. Thus we find a degree of convivial sophistica-
tion in the *Diary from Dixie* set down by a comparatively well-off Mary
Boykin Chesnut. Of Christmas·1863 on a South Carolina plantation she
writes: 'We had for dinner oyster soup – soup à la reine; it has so many good
things·in it -- besides boiled mutton, ham, boned turkey, wild ducks, par-
tridges, plum pudding, sauterne, burgundy, sherry and Madeira. There is
life in the old land yet!' This at a time in the Civil War when oranges were
five dollars each, and turkeys a year before had sold for eleven dollars and
were by then priced out of the market for ordinary folk. The experience,
however, of Dixie contrasts acutely with a meal recorded for miners in the
Rockies in 1858. Then, at the Platte River gold diggings, the bill of fare
began with oysters and the conventional pork, but soon went on to elk,
antelope, buffalo 'smothered' and grizzly bear à la mode. There was also
Black Mountain squirrel, prairie dog, and mountain rats – all of which
were curiously followed, in the profusion almost of a mediaeval banqueting
table, with swans, cranes and quails. Wines and whiskeys were brought
through by wagon train. They did not do themselves badly, these rough,
tough boys of the West, but at least they did themselves differently. Twelve
years later, Charles Kingsley's daughter Rose Georgina Kingsley notes in
her journal of Denver, Colorado that at Christmas-time, in a snowy scene of
sleighs and toys and Christmas trees, the butchers' shops still had buffalo,
deer and antelope meat hung up for sale. However, this is expedience, not
tradition. It was mountain country where furriers, she also noted, hung up
mink and ermine and sable coats for sale.

    Returning to Dickens, and to a Victorian England less disturbed, we
still find that tradition has not set in firmly anywhere. Pip's Christmas
dinner (pickled pork and greens, and a pair of roast stuffed fowls) was eaten
at half-past one on Christmas Day. That is about 1860. Scrooge (1843)
purchased his prize turkey on Christmas morning for Cratchit's mid-day

dinner. These and many other sources tell us only one thing – that habits change only slowly with the times, and one must wait for many years for any tradition to set solid; these also were days of much slower communication, so that country habits even near London hung a half-century and more back behind those of the capital, just as a village in the west of Ireland hangs decades behind Dublin today, or a Castilian village behind Madrid.

Any assumption that a national habit has changed plunges one into treacherous water. News of other peoples' lives comes from the Press, and it is in the nature of the Press to print a colourful story, not a national cross-section: headline photographs of some particularly garish new trend in men's clothes fade under the real evidence of ordinariness in the majority of tailors' shop-windows and behind the counters of an insurance company – a huge ordinariness compared with the bright minority noticeable in main amusement centres.

Chesterton said that tradition is merely a democracy of the dead. He was right, and the habits of such a democracy are quicker to die than to form. In the old agricultural England and elsewhere in Europe, Christmas lasted twelve and more days. There was then time to spare for so long a break during the least pressing of farming seasons. But in an industrial era, the period of feasting had to be severely shortened. The Twelve Days used to begin after Christmas Day and continued to Epiphany. Gradually these holidays, including the day after Christmas, Boxing Day in England or St Stephen's Day in Roman Catholic countries, became ordinary working days. But no factory owner could get rid of the calendar-sure date of New Year's Eve, though the daytime was absorbed and New Year's Day ceased to be a holiday. Industry just refused to afford any further occasion which prevented the wheels turning; and the poorer workers, paid by the hour or by output, were willing enough to accede.

Thus to speak of any general 'Victorian' Christmas, we are on unsure ground. But there remains a general illusion which we might as well idealise and love, since it was true of many parts and peoples towards the end of the century and on into the next. Let us recreate, then, the essential scene: set roughly between 1890 and 1914.

Cards and presents were by then accepted customs. There were not as many of either as today; but the pattern was set. The keeping of Christmas Eve and Day had in days long before been a strongly family affair and often, as in much of Europe today, of a holier nature. But by now cards, for instance, had for many years been sent to friends, and the closer friends exchanged presents. So that the days before Christmas, days of preparation, became complicated beyond the stitching of new dresses, the gathering of holly and mistletoe, and the last stirring of the pudding. Now there had to be a careful choosing of cards. Smells of paper in the stationer's, smells of ink and a scratching of nibbed pens! Now came the first involved shopping for presents, and the birth of the Christmas Eve sounds of rustling paper and scissors snapping at string, while children in bed tried to sleep and listen at the same time to all these mysterious sounds from below mingled with the landing light under the door, the guttering night-light, the dying bedroom

Presents and preparations

Nice young ladies leave no footprints.
A page from The Girl's Own Paper,
December 1882

fire. Brown or white paper in these days; smells of sealing wax; stockings hung up by the fireplace or on the bed-rail – it was an era before the large white pillowcase was substituted by those children who had their eye on the later large boxes of factory-made toys.

Midnight, and father at last off the ladder, his fingers pricked by holly. And the tree decorated. And mother flushed from a further flurry in the kitchen. And so to sleep, perhaps with a last prayer in recognition of the Birthday. Unlike other European countries whose families gave and still give presents on either St Nicholas's Day or Christmas Eve or at Epiphany, the English and most Americans waited till Christmas Day. For most children, the magic moment came at dawn – when after trying to stay awake to catch Father Christmas coming down the chimney, their over-tired deep sleep was disturbed good and early by the dreaming knowledge of that bulging stocking at the end of the bed. With some families, the main present-giving became a ritual held later in the morning, with the bigger presents set around the tree for after church.

Of course, it has snowed. And to see this idealised Christmas at its best,

The large Christmas tree erected each year in Rockefeller Centre, New York

እግዝእትነ፡ማርያም፡

የሴፍ፡

ኢየሱስ፡ስኪ፡ዮ
ውክተጎል፡

አድግ፡ወሳህም፡

የሴፍ፡

we might as well imagine ourselves out in the country. On Christmas Eve it was frosty with snow already on the ground; there was the bringing home of the holly at the purplish sharp end of the winter's afternoon, with the essential woodsmoke rising straight up and pale blue from a cottage chimney; and as we half-slid, half-walked home mufflered and mittened with cold fingers and frost-running noses, the warm yellow-lighted windows of home shone wonderfully with messages of firelight and curtains and muffins and safety. Later the disembodied voices of the carol-singers came chorusing weirdly in from the empty night: they gave us 'Nowel' and 'While Shepherds Watched', 'Good King Wenceslas' and 'Come All Ye Faithful' – no 'Silent Night' in English-speaking countries for many years to come. The handbell ringers were there too. All these stood grouped round a lantern on a pole. Afterwards they came into the hall for hot beer, punch, pennies. But while they were still singing outside we had parted the curtains to watch them and had seen above the lantern-light bare winter branches not white with snow but glassily silvered with ice and now sparkling bright in moonlight. This ice and its glittering effect of stars being, of course, the exact origin of the lights and tinsel on the Christmas tree inside.

In the night new snow fell. Christmas morning brought fresh white everywhere, thick folds of white, with spinney black and church tower grey against it; delicate arrow-flecks of birds' feet across the lawn – our robin, no doubt; and over by the snow-moussed laurel at the front gates, there lay great virgin drifts of deep white from which on the day after Christmas there would arise the annual snowman, carrot for nose, pebbles for eyes, smoking his empty pipe above the bravado muffler and beneath the battered black tall hat. In January the last stump of him would long outlive the general thaw, a sad and mudlocked little bollard of grey ice.

A traditional white Christmas

The nursery bleats music of trumpet and drum. Smells of burning paper and kindling firewood rise through the house, and then the clink of breakfast china; 'Merry Christmases' are kissed and wished, and in mid-morning the sun comes out for the walk to church. In the church, which is hollied and bayed but almost never mistletoed – for mistletoe is often forbidden as the badge of the Druid –, we sing the special service with its messages of affirmation and hope now that the Babe is born; and the full congregation, though in those days not much larger than on an ordinary Sunday, is afterwards larger with smiles than usual. Affability in the air. There is the intention, at least, of peace and goodwill, which is half the battle. And now home to the mid-day Christmas dinner, a dramatic half-an-hour or hour later than our usual lunch-time. But first there is the grown-ups' present-giving. And a glass of wine and seed-cake with old Auntie Bea up in bed among the smells of her bowl of apples and of lavender essence or burned paper (for commodious fragrance – no dearth of paper for Auntie now).

Down to a table alive with coloured crackers, and to the eating. The turkey. Or the goose. Some families had two turkeys, one roast, one boiled. Soup? Perhaps. But eventually in comes the bird propelled by a stove-red cook flushed as Father Christmas. By the way – did he really come last night? Down the chimney? Indeed he did; even the firmest non-believer

keeps quiet on this point, as if frightened of denying a kind of god: only too right, for Father Christmas can be traced back to a Carthaginian deity whose brazen fiery belly *ate* children, who were then themselves the gifts.

Father carves, and reserves for himself a drumstick. Who wants the pope's nose? Sausages, bacon, stuffing, roast potatoes and whatever vegetables are about – turnips, swedes, with luck sprouts or some cabbagey thing. Gravy. Bread sauce. The whole edifying shoot; second helpings; and a ham to help out.

Then the curtains are drawn on the low red winter sun, and in comes the pudding in its ghostly blaze of blue. Soon the chase for sixpences and silver threepenny bits – marmoset bites half fearful of breaking a tooth or swallowing the little coins. And mince-pies, brandy butter, oranges, Elvas plums, nuts and the infuriating pineapple whose interminable tuft of leaves must first be plucked and counted – he who guesses the total gets a fine silver crown. The crackers, the paper-hats, a light smell of gunpowder; and lastly the port and a gasometer of a Stilton cheese gently alive within its adobe crust.

Games, ghost stories and Christmas pudding

The fall of darkness: satin shoes glinting in firelight and the tree at its best with all the candles lit. Glass ornaments, sweets and small toys decorate it in place of our present-day fancy for tinselled bells and balls: a star or an angel or a fairy (German Christ Child? Pagan wood-spirit?) at the very top. And now games for the children and energetic aunts. Blind-Man's-Buff. Hunt-the-Slipper. All probably the residue of rites of dark and ancient origin now become innocent. And when these are ended, and most of the mistletoe kissing done, there is the Christmas cake as heavy as the pudding and thickly coated with marzipan and sugar. Laden, we group around the fire and tell stories of ghosts: a little frightening – for however much of it all

we disbelieve, the shadows away from the fire are animate and we draw nearer the light. Later, snapdragon comes to fortify our spirits: plucking a raisin from a tray of burning brandy, the room blue with strange light, hot flames scorching our fingers.

More mince-pies and cream? Chestnuts? Where does one put it all? One thing for certain – cold turkey tonight, and minced and rissolled and devilled turkey for days to come … beginning tomorrow when the village boys go out to hunt and kill a rather smaller bird, the traditional St Stephen's Day wren or sometimes a robin, ancient substitutes, they say, for human sacrifice; and the gentry leave for town and the pantomime.

That is the main gist of a turn-of-the-century Christmas; and a fair-sized remnant is much with us today. Many a modern robin-ed Christmas card is indistinguishable in lettering and layout from its late Victorian fore-bear. The handbell ringers have largely gone, some of the carols changed, the singers are usually either dedicated professionals or children out for cash and a quick get-away, the doorbell pressed before they begin to sing. In America particularly, they have the disembodied task of singing of celestial things into street-level intercoms serving rooms that scrape the very angels above.

Gone now the snapdragon; gone too, it seems, the snow. Yet, in other ways, we gain. Forgetting for a moment some of the bloated pother of too much shopping and too many advertisements, the actual ingredients of Christmastide itself are not so much spoiled, if looked at selectively. The radio pumps to us better choral singing: the atmosphere of the waits is lost, but the music much improved. Television brings a moving picture of the whole world at wassail, scenes sometimes quite touching. Broadcast church services may be of more moment than those at the local parish church.

A present-day Christmas

25

Altogether we regret the past too easily, it is a moan which must be tempered or it becomes a malaise: one lives in the present – switch-on machines like television are irreversible, part of our time and particularly important for the lonely and old, casualties of the break-up of family life, non-communicant victims of an age splintered by quicker communications. And there are other small benefits and improvements. There is the generous habit begun in America of putting the Christmas tree in a front window, so that passers-by in the street can see it. Coloured electric lights are possibly prettier than candles; the living flame and the moving shadows are gone, but colour and a longer life compensate. Another growing habit – wreaths of green with a red bow to decorate front doors. And inside, the house is much more decorated than in the past: the very amount of Christmas cards obscures the everyday look of a room, they range the chimney piece and climb up ribbons on the wall, and though the idea of plastic frost from a tube sounds at first unpalatable, it works, it embellishes. A hundred other new decorative devices do so too: as always, the result is a matter of taste. Just as the decorations of a shopping street in London or New York have often been unbelievably hideous, the main shopping street of Helsinki behind the Esplanade can be movingly beautiful in a gentle sentimental way; even a canned music of bells works well against the Finnish snow and the Finn's endemic sense of design. And even the centre of Frankfurt, commercial and concrete, blossoms in a rich but restrained artifice of mainly the traditional green and gold.

Commercialisation and nostalgia Meanwhile there are general social changes one must never forget – the automobile, for instance, has a new use in restricting drunkenness. In our longing for the Victorian past, we should remember that mittened Millicent, tripping with her gift of Christmas goodies to the cottage door, would too often be greeted by sounds of thrashing belt and screaming wife. Christmas is indivisible from the society of its time. If you want the waits back, you have to take the gruel too; and the workhouse, the mines, the mills. Probably our present situation is the best one. Looking back on a thing is often the best way of enjoying it: human instincts for survival blur the painful parts and illuminate the best. The gilded bones of the past coupled with our better associations – that is the recipe for uncritical pleasure. In not having it, we can eat our cake forever.

Thus one object of these pages will be to investigate the past, search out the teetotums, the gilded apples, the Noah's Ark peg-tops of the old-fashioned Christmas tree; to investigate wassail and lambswool, *piñatas* and *posadas*; to look everywhere in Europe for survivals of the old horned god, like the Welsh Mari Lwyd; to note how very pagan a Christian festival can be – always remembering that such disinterrments are only part of the luxury of knowledge, and that the proper Christian gifts to the world of love and gentleness outweigh any coincidental heritage of idolatry.

We shall also enquire into Christmas in other countries, envisaging a dribbling of succulent Christmas pud into the navel of a hot and bikini-ed Australian tum-tum, remarking on a Christmas palm-tree in a Liberian home, noting that in Harlem there are white golliwogs, seeing a red-robed

Santa Claus skimming a Cingalese lagoon on a catamaran, asking what happened when missionaries brought their first Christmas trees to the eskimos? They ate the candles.

We shall dissert upon the pharmacology of the big brown pudding; and see what other people eat – boiled buffalo hump in early Canada, turtle on an Australasian island, lyed cod in Norway. And notice how Christmas has stopped some battles, started others. And watch the strange ceremony of the live lamb in the church at Les Baux, and children reciting at the church of Aracoeli in Rome. And note how a bunch of mistletoe can lead to industrial strife – making momentary maenads of a group of factory girls and putting the terrified male roster to rout, down-tools with a vengeance.

The enormous literature of Christmas will be skimmed, quoting some of the major creators of atmosphere, poking into some of the odd corners, glancing at a few instances of modern writing; but leaving alone some of the giants, like Shakespeare and Wordsworth, as being rather well known. But much that is also rather well known in other spheres must be recorded again – the history of pantomime, the genesis of the great Catholic Christmas cribs, the games and foods and entertainments of Christmas, for these are all inalienable from the subject, their reminiscence is well deserved.

And the swollen facts of the Christmas economy, of the access of commercialisation. The large new plastic tree industry, the reaction to charity Christmas cards. And what else drives the great solstitial spree? In the USA there is a training school, run by psychologists, to turn out the model department store Santa Claus. Going too far? ... but surely a sight better than the usual tired and alcoholic ex-sandwich-board man?

And how other people spend their Christmases, from a lighthouse-keeper to the inmates of an old people's home. Christmas at war and Christmas in the tropics. And there will be part of a chapter describing scenes and atmospheres of Christmases this writer personally can remember: so personal an intrusion is necessary because I have found it very hard indeed to find out what other people individually can remember of their Christmas experience – it is so easy to forget the detail, the verity of the vine is lost in amiable fog. The only way is to bleat of myself – and trust that this may stimulate the reader somehow to recall something of his own.

So – on with the galanty.

Galanty? A show of moving silhouettes, once popular at Christmas-time, just prior to and put out of business by the innovation of the magic lantern in the home.

'Père Noël', by Picasso

2
Origins and Observances

Ev'n the poor Pagan's homage to the Sun
I would not harshly scorn, lest even there
I spurn'd some elements of Christian pray'r.
THOMAS HOOD

To get green food for his beasts, and later for himself when the first corn was planted, primitive man needed rain and sun. At more temperate levels, sun was always more important than rain. So with eyes on the mysterious sky, where anything could be going on, the first religious instincts prayed towards the sun.

The moment of the sun's annual rebirth, in late December, was one of the vital religious times of the year. How did people judge this subtle moment – since one does not usually notice any perceptible lengthening of the days until some time later? Living a life close to the elements, tied to one slow place and pace and one set of shadows, it would have been more easily apparent; priesthoods were interested, and made the first astronomical observations. Because living was crude, there is no reason to suppose that the primitive brain itself was not as introspective as today's – there is a parallel in the natural wisdoms of a present-day uneducated peasant.

This time of year was also the least laborious on the land. There was time for festival. Early northern peoples with no exact astronomical findings began their winter festival earlier, in November, when signs of the sun's recession and the scarcity of fodder made necessary the slaughter of a proportion of the cattle. Later, the rites moved forward to mid-December, either to satisfy whatever more sophisticated organisations built such temples as the sun-orientated Stonehenge, or in sympathy with the impor-

A Bacchanalian Christmas at Zellerfelde, by Chodowiecki, 1784

ted largesse of a richer Roman period of Saturnalia. In Roman times, a pre-Christian message of peace and goodwill accompanied the festivities; it was a practical message based on probability or possibility, for the usual farmer's battles, which are often disputes about water or cattle destroying crops, were in wintry abeyance. So the time of year was one of lighting fires, praising the new sun, relaxation and feasting.

Not until the middle of the fourth century was the birth of Christ officially celebrated at this time; first in Rome, some years later in Antioch and the East. It was a wise, if obvious decision. One cannot estimate exactly what thinking went into this: but it was probably not so wily as it sounds, for the early Christians were not puritans, and wine and rejoicing were natural concomitants of the season. If other people were worshipping their gods at that time it was only naturally competitive for the Christians to worship theirs. The general atmosphere of rebirth would suggest personal birth. Mithra already had the twenty-fifth of December as his birthday. Associations and vague transferences probably grew into belief: most things were handed down through the generations by word of mouth, little was written down. In the family circle it was often the grandmother who instructed the children and the household – and there are not only clerical but also grandmotherly errors and glosses. It may thus have been an assumption of general growth which the Church decided to formalise.

The first official celebrations

'Winter' by Arcimboldo

Certainly the official Church inspired its missionaries to make the winter feast a Christian festival. In 601, Pope Gregory instructed Augustine of Canterbury to follow the custom of decking temples with greenery by decking churches in the same manner, and to solemnise the time by Christian feasting. 'Nor let them now sacrifice animals to the Devil, but to the praise of God kill animals for their own eating, and render thanks to the Giver of all for their abundance... For from obdurate minds it is impossible to cut off everything at once ...'.

Mithraism

A most important historical fact during the Roman period was the competition with another new religion, Mithraism. Mithra came from Persia. It was an earlier religion than the Christian, but at the time of the beginning of Christianity it was spreading widely. This may have been a time when a new faith was particularly needed; it was certainly a time when Roman roads and shipping and a policy of peace within the Empire made communications quicker than ever before, so that the practical word of a religion could more easily be spread. It is a sobering thought that without the techniques of the Romans, Christianity might have subsided into parochial oblivion.

The worship of Mithra shared many similarities with the newer Christian ceremonies. There was a baptism, a sacramental meal, an observance of Sunday, and the god himself was born on the twenty-fifth of December, and out of rock. There were also many parallels in the doctrine, though Christianity was more nearly monotheistic than Mithraism; but ideas of good and evil, of the defeat of evil by moral rectitude, of sometime salvation, of a last trump and of heaven and hell were among much that was shared. Mithraism travelled by Roman roads among the soldiers and the poorer classes, consolidating itself on the way with small underground temples. Christianity also made its appeal to the poor, and on the way established itself in human cells each controlled by a bishop. Apart from the differences of teaching, and of the stimulus of persecution of Christians and

Boar-hunting scene for December, from the French calendar Les très riches heures du Duc de Berry, *1413–16*

other considerations which might have had their effect, there is little doubt that the eventual victorious emergence of Christianity from what was very like a race found its reason in women – Mithra in set oriental tradition gave no place to woman, Christ did. Women were held to have souls, women were received on a parallel with men. This meant a social dramatisation, a conscription of extra and efficient tongues, and a double source of converts.

Many Mithraic features themselves may have been adopted from earlier cult necessities – like baptism (irrigation and purification) and the eucharist (consumption of sacrifice), like the solstitial date and the emergence of Mithra from godlike, awe-inspiring rock. This latter also has a curious parallel in the legend of the birth of Christ. A manger in the Palestinian hills was usually a hole in the rock – indeed the popularly believed site of the nativity in Bethlehem is in a cave, and no cattle-shed as we know it or have seen illustrated in paintings. Whether competitive Christianity absorbed these various features from Mithra cannot be known; history only shows, with absolute definition, that Christianity succeeded and continued to succeed until now Christian areas cover a population of nearly a thousand million, twice as much as any other religion.

However, the twenty-fifth of December is our present point of issue here; and though it has changed with the calendars from the sixth of January, and earlier from the eighteenth of January, a date which the Armenian Church outside Armenia still holds to, we are within the solstice and Saturnalia-Kalendae period. The Roman Saturnalia is an important vantage point because it is recorded in writing and was the function of a highly civilised people. The first period of feasting was generally for seven days. The god celebrated was Saturn, farmer of a former golden age, eater of his own children. The festival was followed without much respite by another, the Kalendae, more mathematically concerned with the date of the New Year and the two-faced deity Janus, god of doors as two-way engines, and one who looks back on the past and forward to the future: and a god who might also be thought to express a ghost of all split intentions, shadowing the great dichotomies of Good and Evil, God and Devil.

One thinks of the Saturnalia as Roman in Rome, but of course its celebration was equally true of Bath or Colchester or any other part of occupied Europe. Nor were the Saturnalian roisterers a band of shaved and big-beaked Latins: the greater population of moustached and fair-haired Britons and the dark, more superstitious Celts, brought their own solstitial cults to join in; and such of these people who had them issued from centrally heated homes, with wine from local British vine-harvests, to dance and sing and light their candles and exchange presents, as well as the little clay dolls called *sigillaria* and the *strenae* or boughs plucked in honour of the goddess Strenia. This was a time when slaves were served by masters, and all rules were turned inside out. The Greek Libanius writes: 'The impulse to spend seizes everyone. He who the whole year through has taken pleasure in saving and piling up his pence, becomes suddenly extravagant …. From the minds of young people it removes two kinds of dread: the dread of the schoolmaster and the dread of the stern pedagogue.' But a sixth-century

33

Christian sermon sees it otherwise: 'How vile, further, it is that those who have been born men, are clothed in women's dresses ... they have bearded faces, and yet they wish to appear women ...'.

It was into the residue of such an atmosphere, which lasted for three to four hundred years of influential Roman establishment, that years after the Romans left came the Mass of Christ. When? The age was dark, in the sense that next to nothing was put down in writing. One of the first recorded Christian ceremonies at Christmas in England was the baptism of ten thousand converts in Kent at the end of the sixth century.

The Feast of Fools and the boy bishop

The mediaeval Feast of Fools, led by a Lord of Misrule, derives directly from the Saturnalia; again a somersaulting of rule was the order of the day, with the same deep wish to escape personality by masters serving servants and the sexes exchanging dress, and all disguise paramount in a general relaxation of ordinary rules. Exact traces of this turnabout impulse can still be found in military regiments where on Christmas Day the officers serve the men; and in, for instance at another time of year, the June celebrations in Belgium at Bruges, where dockers parade jovially in their wives' underwear. There was also in England and elsewhere the odd institution of a boy bishop, current until the Reformation, where a boy took over the bishop's part in church, conducting the ceremony and preaching a sermon. This might again have been a relic of the Saturnalia; or it might have been an older echo of the ancient personification of a new priest-king for the sun's rebirth. This boy bishop was taken seriously by the serious clergy; he did not share the atmosphere of misrule. Traces of him still appeared in France and Denmark centuries after the Reformation.

These are only a few of the most easily traceable elements of Christmas festivity. But what went on before the days of the Saturnalia is as important, since so much local belief and superstition lived on alongside the Roman celebrations, or were borrowed and absorbed. We enter the mysterious

The Lord of Misrule, from The Book of Days

sphere of the horned god and the ages of stone and bronze. Before the coming of iron, before anything as organised as the Druids. A time whose dying beliefs have become 'superstitions' or are docketed as witchcraft.

The last Stone Age and early Bronze Age people, small and dark, were hunters, and breeders of horses, cattle and sheep. Naturally their gods took the form of beasts, and their priests and adherents would have worn, in sympathy, horns and sacred skins. The sacred horn and the cloven hoof gave rise much later to a concept of the devil, as Christianity sought to find a means to outlaw such evidences of older religion. But the original horned god was a figment of good; and by now we may be tolerant enough to realise that the cattle-worshippers had as strong, serious, and trusting a religious instinct as we may have now. The form and the ethics were different – but the impulse to prayer the same.

Into the stone and bronze culture of cattle-breeders came immigrants with iron and corn. Corn established new people in solid, cohesive groups; iron as a weapon defeated flint. The older religion and its people were scattered, and hid themselves away in marshes, hills and forests. There the cult continued. In parts of England and north Europe, particularly in the preservative earth of Denmark, the dried bodies of strangled human sacrifices have been found at sacred points, usually near some magical atmosphere of water. Not nice, but not unusual among primitive peoples. After the small dark people had been driven 'underground' by the iron-wielders, they sallied out from time to time, probably at night, and struck back at the newcomers with flint arrows, probably poisoned. Elf-bolts; in fact, they were the fairy folk. And their horned gods persist at Christmas in such disguises as the old Abbots Bromley Horn Dance (now performed in September) and the old Christmas Bull of Wiltshire, the Welsh Mari Lwyd, and similar figures in Poland and Austria and elsewhere in Europe. To raise the skin into animal shape, a pole was needed; hence the witch's broomstick, which was carried to the sabbat. Witches, or those persisting with the old religion, used to leave the house by the big open chimney, for there were no windows in early houses, to go to a sabbat, the door being too easily watched. The door was also guarded by a symbol of iron, the horseshoe. (Santa Claus and hoary old Father Christmas use a chimney too.) The old religion, secret and relatively harmless, was not put down with any ferocity until the time of the Inquisition, when the Church pretended it to be heavily organised. It was always, of course, disapproved of. But in early days there was never much of a designed attempt by the Church to eradicate it.

After the fairy and the horned men, the Druids; with evergreen and mistletoe, with golden sickle and jealously guarded crystal, magical maker of fire with the sun's rays, which some authorities equate with the holy grail in western England. A townsman who has not seen mistletoe growing cannot realise the weird quality of this high green ball alive in the dead winter branches. It looks as if it is writhing within itself, full of a moving snaky substance, and being light-coloured, giving out its own light. With such an almost animal quality of life, little wonder that it was thought to be

The Druids and druidical survivals

35

'*The Victim*',
*Victorian romance
of a Druidic child
sacrifice from*
Good Words,
1863

connected with the skies and with lightning, and given holy importance. And this eerie quality might also be the reason that of all other pagan evergreens it is the only one persistently banned inside church. The holly, the rosemary, the bays have always been allowed, and holly and fir still furnish our Christmas houses with old sympathetic magic: but even here in the secular hall we limit mistletoe to one bunch, unique and sacred. Previous to the coming of the Christmas tree, mistletoe formed part of the kissing-bough, which was an involved contrivance of apples and candles built in the ball-form of mistletoe: the kissing is variously thought to be a legacy of human sacrifice, or of some form of sacred prostitution, or of a sacred gesture of peace.

In this devotion to the green, as with the lighting of tapers and fires to celebrate the sun, one may assume that people went about their religious task with joy as well as awe; it was hardly a penance; there would be pleasure in fire and light, and there would be pleasure in the green transformation, with much the same ambivalence as when the mouths which offered prayer above a burning sacrifice seldom wasted it but instead ate it. One must again remember that the brains of these people were neither animal nor simple, but as imaginative and complex as ours are.

In Scandinavia midsummer night is still an important event, with drinking and dancing all night long and a sun-wreath raised high in each village. Local pockets of spring and summer sunfire and floral celebration remain here and there in other countries. May Day, with its queen and garlanded pole, is better known nowadays as Labour Day. In England the autumnal need for a fire festival is surrogated to the burning of an image labelled Guy Fawkes – and how odd that this one political incident has, in name, stuck so fast, and how suspiciously coincidental it is that 'guy' forms the first syllable of 'guiser' or the old name for people who dressed up and disguised themselves to celebrate the ancient November fires, as is still the American tradition at Hallowe'en. It is noteworthy that these occasions are now not holidays, nor extend much in feeling beyond their actual celebration. Easter remains the only other important sacred holiday of the year. Taking the place of earlier spring festivals, it carries a vital spiritual message of death and resurrection, but Easter has nothing of the material presence of the Christmas festival apart from giving people a holiday; a short period of light at a time of light, it comes and goes with little preparation and no aftermath. It is no blaze of light in the dark: though of course in the Eastern Church, and in countries as Catholic as Spain, with its long and beautiful *Semana Santa*, its importance can rival Christmastide.

All in all, the disappearance of sacred holidays and the shortening of the twelve days of Christmas itself in northern countries can be put down to Protestantism and as much again to the Industrial Revolution, which soon became unwilling to spare its workers the time off. Other social changes solidified the trend: the granting much later of a summer holiday instead, a new adulation of the sea and so on. What has been ineradicable is the need for some sort of light in the long cold dark. Even in parts where Christmas itself is devalued, like Scotland, the burst is relegated to the New Year celebrations, when all commerce stops.

'*Under the Mistletoe*', *1865*

The burst of light and the need to feast permeate the annals of history. The holy revelling of King Alfred lost a key battle against the Danes at Chippenham. Henry v supplied besieged Rouen with food to celebrate Christmas Day. Historical instances of shipwreck mount suspiciously at Christmas-time, including the wreck of Columbus's *Santa Maria* in 1492. Our present-day toll of road deaths bears contemporary witness. It is a time of light.

When Christianity first came to England to take over the older celebrations, it was common to find ancient idols and new Christian images occupying the same church or temple. We find the royal temple of Roedwald of East Anglia housing altars to both the Christian and pagan gods, just as in Rome Severus had Orpheus, Christ and Abraham side by side. Meanwhile King Lucy built the first church at Canterbury, and attempts at clarification were begun.

Symbolic significance of the robin   They have never succeeded. The more excitant manifestations of the older religions, the masking and guising and mumming and waiting, the children's games and the charades are only lately disappearing, casualties of the social switch from private action to public voyeurism. Take, for one single instance, the case of that small phenomenon of Christmas display, the robin. Within living memory, and perhaps somewhere still, the wren was hunted and killed on St Stephen's Day, the day following Christmas Day. The robin became confused with the wren, a traditionally sacred bird whom no one was allowed to kill except on this one day of the year. After

Carrying round the bush in which the wren was killed on St Stephen's Day

the hunt, the body was paraded, in some places on a decorated miniature bier. It is supposed, again, that this ancient custom was a substitute for human sacrifice, for the death of the old priest-king. On some Victorian Christmas cards, the dead bird lying on its back is the sole pathetic, or triumphant, illustration. But dead or alive, such is little robin redbreast's real connection with Christmastide.

The paper hat is one of the last traces we retain of the masking of mediaeval Misrule. The giving of presents (particularly candles and dolls) was part of the Saturnalia, and the doll possibly also derives from this insistent origin of human sacrifice. Candles are a fire emblem, and so of course is the disappeared yule-log or clog, often not the neat-cut bole seen in illustrations but rather a big old root and probably introduced to England with the worship of Odin. Yule is still celebrated in old Norse fashion at Lerwick in Shetland. Guisers dressed as Vikings burn a lifesize long-boat in the night ceremony of Up-Helly-Aa, which means 'end of the holiday'. The Viking yule lasted for several weeks – up in the hard-frozen north there was no reason why not – so that Up-Helly-Aa is still celebrated at the end of January. It is one of the better-looking folk festivals of Britain, since it takes place after dark and the scene is dramatised by firelight. Darkness hides anachronism – none of the Druids' boots and striped trousers sprouting from his midsummer white robe, none of the morris-dancers' breeches and gartering against a background of little coloured motor-cars. The high horned helmets of Up-Helly-Aa look mysterious and fearful against the red firelight; and a heightening of the head always makes impressive magic, as Napoleon knew with his guards in giant bearskins, as anyone knows who has faced a woman with a bird on her hat.

Survivals of the sacrificial traditions

The Haxey hood game is still played at Haxey in Lincolnshire. This is an observance either of Twelfth Night or of Old Christmas Day on the sixth of January before the calendar change of 1752. Thirteen men take a main part in the game. They are the 'fool' and the 'lord' and eleven 'boggins' (bogies, boggarts – fairies from the bogland?), though the whole spectator crowd can take part in the game, which is a rugby-like struggle to get a series of thirteen folded canvas hoods into pre-arranged goals. The game culminates when the last hood, a roll of leather, the Haxey hood itself, must be fought towards the winning inn, where then the drinking begins. Such a skeleton description sounds pretty bald: but one must imagine the force of crowd hysteria to realise, in a good year, its full vigour. What such a hood originally represented is not exactly known ... but it is thought to have been the head of a slaughtered sacrificial bull. At the beginning of the game the fool announces that a half of a bullock is running in the next field. And in previous times the fool was also 'smoked' with burning hay – again a connection with earlier sacrifice. Then why a wrapped hood? Lincolnshire is a ghosty old county, and the ex-fairy Robin à Hood appeared and disappeared not far away. Hoods were in early days ordinary wear, much as Moor and monk today have hoods attached to jellaba and habit; but they were also factors of disguise, and thus of magic. Hoodman Blind was the old name of Blind-Man's Buff.

Another Twelfth Night ritual is the wassailing of apple trees, still observed for instance at Carhampton in Somerset on the seventeenth of January (the eve of old Twelfth Night). A libation of cider is thrown on the trunk of an old apple tree, cider-soaked toast is placed in its branches, guns are fired through the branches and an old invocation to the tree is sung. It is a straight prayer to the god of trees and fruit: the firing of blunderbusses and shot-guns is intended to frighten away evil spirits – the same is done in many other parts of Europe, from mountain tops round Berchtesgaden, for instance: and by the light of torches, with the cider barrel broached among gnarled trees, and the gnarled urr-ing and arr-ing of deep-chested West Country voices rolling time backwards, the din and the sense of old magic is considerable. Wassail derives from the Anglo-Saxon *wes hal*, 'be whole': thus, Good Health.

Sound to drive away spirits may also be behind the ringing of church bells late on Christmas Eve, though the call to midnight mass is a more immediate and practical reason. It has largely disappeared; but, for instance at Dewsbury in Yorkshire, it still takes the form of a long funeral tolling, the number of the knell matching the year since the birth of Christ, and consequently of the death of the Devil. The presence of evil spirits at this time of year is again echoed in the habitual telling of ghost stories. But there is also a parallel belief that no spirits can be potent on so gracious a night: the total impression is that the evil ones have been flushed, and are roaring about in rout, so they must be belled and banged away before they can settle again.

The Mummers
and the Wild Men

Mumming still continues in some places, as at Andover in Hampshire on the Eve, the Day, and Boxing Day; or at Marshfield in Gloucestershire on Boxing Day. In America the term signifies masquerading; but in England it usually refers to masked plays. An accompaniment once to Christmas festivities everywhere, the plays usually involve a St George and an alien knight, who was often Turkish, for these are mediaeval plays and the crusades and later the threat of the Turk covered a long and formative period. The Saint George sometimes became King George when the Hanovers arrived. Sometimes, when the Turk or evil one is slain, a doctor is called for and, curiously, the *villain* is revived. So are we back with the priest-king and his ritual death and replacement? The dress of some of these mummers is traditionally a complete disguise of ribbons from top to toe. The ribbon, and even its use in cross-gartering, is part of the magical accoutrement of the witch-survivor of the old religion. The mummers so dressed look very like the dancers, straw-decked from head to toe, in primitive African religious rites. The Wild Man of Teutonic legend is dressed in leaves from top to toe: and particularly the Wild Men of Oberstdorf, who dress in the hoary fronds of old fir-tree beards, who number thirteen, and who every seven years perform a long and intricate dance-play worked out on a complex and intricately repetitive Runic pattern. This is said to be the oldest survival of prehistoric ritual in all Europe: it is not a Christmastide occasion, but provides a chilling glimpse of the nature of such early ceremony.

Horned and animal grotesques still abound in Austria, in Poland, in

The Dreikönigssänger (*three-kings-singers, also known as star-singers*). *Crowned and dressed as the Kings and their retainers, they go from house to house on the sixth of January singing of the Journey from the East, offering incense and receiving small gifts in return*

Germany and in many other parts of Europe: the aforesaid Welsh Mari Lwyd appeared before Christmas draped in a white shroud alive with tinsel and ribbons and bells but headed with the clean skull of a horse carrying a brushlike hair-tuft stiff upon the brow. In the eye-sockets, glass bottle-ends. The man hidden inside moved the jaws of the horse up and down, snapping the teeth, a live and laughing skull snickering and snackering, darkly pleasing to children as it pranced and chased. Meanwhile, hundreds of miles away at Berry, French children at this time of year munch cakes moulded in the ancient horn-shape.

One reads an Edwardian authority stating that the Mari Lwyd was long discontinued; but one also reads a present-day writer who still remembers it in the Welsh village of his childhood. Today, it is revived. Such traditions cannot easily be pinpointed. One remote village may always continue it, unknown to the research student; or if discontinued, the old skull and dress could be found in an attic by someone interested enough to revive it – and today, in reaction to modern mechanical atmospheres, or as a result of a better distributed education and a widely distributed tourist, there is a tendency to revive old customs. So somewhere Mari Lwyd or its Kentish equivalent, the Hodening Horse, still clacks a grinning jaw. The whole celebration of Christmas suffered a marked decline in the eighteenth century: no one then would have imagined its tremendous revival a hundred years later, or its even greater proliferation today.

The Mari Lwyd ritual

President above the old Christmas revels is the new American conception of Santa Claus. He will be discussed in detail in a later chapter, but this much may be now noted. In his present red Arctic apparel he definitely derives from mid-nineteenth-century Dutch influence in America: he is a

The big-nosed mask of the terrible Frau Percht, from the Rauris Valley in Austria. She, and people masked like her, appear at the windows on the nights of the fifth and sixth of January, and must be given a small gift to go away

Left: *The Mari Lwyd ritual*
Right: *The legendary eater of children, possibly related to the Knecht Rupprecht figure*

mixed-up version of St Nicholas of Myra, with his date moved forward from the traditional sixth of December to Christmas Eve. However, quite apart from this saint, there has always been a dominant if sometimes shadowy male maestro of the solstice. A hundred years ago in England, Father Christmas wore a wreath of holly above his large bearded figure, achieving an oddly mixed Bacchic and Druidical effect, consonant perhaps with the original sacred intention of the wassail bowl. He might also contain elements of that other figure of authority, the mediaeval Lord of Misrule. His presence can thus be felt right back to the Saturnalia and further, as, indeed, Saturn himself, the very ancient agricultural god-king who ate his own children presumably to avoid regicide. And Saturn was parallel with a Carthaginian Baal, whose brazen horned effigy contained a furnace into which children were sacrificially fed. This connection with children, as themselves gifts becoming over the years the recipients of gifts, seems of likely significance.

A further connection between Christmas and pre-Christian ritual may be found in the numerical intrigue of the figure thirteen. Astronomically, thirteen is the number of lunar months in a complete cycle of sun-ruled seasons in a year. Whether this gave the figure its original importance can hardly be proved: but there has always existed in human tradition a conspiracy of twelve plus one, as with judge and jury, Robin Hood and his twelve foresters, King Arthur and his twelve or twice twelve knights, Romulus and twelve lectors, Solomon and his twelve officers and so on. Christ and his twelve disciples at the Last Supper is the paramount instance revered today: but it is a reverence which has brought in its train possibly false assumptions that the number is unlucky.

Thirteen has always had a ritual significance. Thirteen is the exact and historically proven number of the witch's coven. Witchcraft – not necessarily the black, anti-Christian affair of its decline – was the remnant of an old religious cult; Pennethorne Hughes, for instance, cites the discovery of a neolithic sepulchral cave in Granada where twelve human skeletons sat in a circle round a central skeleton dressed in a leather skin. With the Wild Men of Oberstdorf, with the Haxey hood game and much else this figuration of thirteen survives. The period of the complex of Christmas, with all its different shiftings of date and increases or decreases of attention in different societies, solidifies on the figure twelve, on the Twelve Days of Christmas. To this was usually assumed, and in many countries officially declared, a thirteenth: a baker's dozen of days to include Christmas Day itself.

These pre-Christian origins have been here stressed, apart from their intrinsic interest, for another emotional reason. Although the birth of Christ takes precedence as the centre of the Christian occasion, it is almost impossible to connect such a birth with the dark drama of evergreen and firelight and ghosts. Rationally one may equate the birth of new hope in the Saviour with the birth of a new and hopeful year. But it has nothing to do with the feelings aroused by the traditional trappings of the evergreen feast.

The two conceptions simply do not mix. We are still very much creatures of irrational thought and primitive emotion. Man's tarsial beginnings still shift him with alertness in instinctual fear of the dark, reflections of a night-hunted animal. Various kinds of intimate landscape or effects of light move us without apparent reason. Small hills presaging something behind them; the sudden light green of woodland groves in the greater shadow of tall trees; a central object, say a post, isolated in a meadow; small occasions of water, a tarn, a marshy lake. In the same way the phenomenon of evergreen inside a house has a presence far beyond its festive meaning. Innocent enough in a modern room, or in any room fully lit for the occasion, it may have quite another effect in a house not brightly lit; holly in clumps at picture level – above you, in fact – can frown darkly, gather shadows, appear to contain some sort of suspended life. Similarly, the presence of even a medium-sized Christmas tree, unlit, stands like a personage. Such impressions are not consciously welcomed, as the ghost is: but they are part of the same thing, and of a strangeness to the house with all its new reflections of tinselled glitter, its mirrors freshly alive. Nowadays few people may notice this in the crowded time before Christmas; but it can still be felt

The presence of the evergreen tree

in the quieter evenings that follow. It is a powerful time, full of ancient apprehensions. Alongside the joyful birth of the Saviour, alongside the bright toys, there rides a darkness of old instincts. Mid-winter and the world frowning. This co-existent atmosphere is perhaps best summed up in that phenomenal old ballad called *The Mistletoe Bough*. The story is an older one: but when Thomas Bayly rewrote it he put it in a Christmas setting. Why? It is a story of doom and horror, the young bride locked up to die in the old wooden chest. It was attracted to Christmas by the very atmosphere of mistletoe and holly and all the darker side of those pretty, berried things.

Christmas in the Middle Ages Resuming a fragmental look at the history of Christmas, we know that the Middle Ages celebrated the season with much energy and licence. Christmas was now long established as a sacred Christian period, solemn with Masses of rejoicing. But alongside went the feasting and dancing, and there were, of course, disagreements between Church and laity. On the whole, the two managed; but they managed side by side, rather than together. For instance, Christmas coincides with the New Year festival, and we find Chaucer referring to Christmastide as follows:

> Janus sits by the fire with double beard,
> And drinketh of his bugle horn the wine:
> Before him stands the brawn of tuskéd swine,
> And 'Nowel' cryeth every lusty man.

He thus mentions a Roman god and that ancient symbol of sacrifice the boar's head; and the cry of 'Nowel' meaning new birth refers as easily to the calendar year as to the Christ.

Nor was the period a time of sanctuary. In 1170, the Archbishop Thomas à Becket was murdered in Canterbury cathedral during the Christmas festival – while Henry II over that time consumed his boar's head and other more sophisticated Christmas fare, among them the now unknown dellegrout, maupigyrum, and karumpie, along with pigment, morat and mead to wash these down. The sanctity of Christ's birth was overshadowed by the solsticial excuse for carousal; with little exception has it ever been otherwise. However, from Advent onwards the Church was able to build up its presence by a number of special days not to culminate until Epiphany and Plough Sunday; its Roman Catholic character also fortified the recognition of saints' days, of which there were many. But other yuletide customs were not then integrated into the Christian idea. Carols, for instance, were not then of a particularly holy nature, and, as the sing-song of ring-dances, had no favour from the Church. Popular Christian verses are unrecorded until the Italian friar Jacopone wrote *Il Presèpio* (The Crib) in the thirteenth century: thereafter the spread was slow indeed, the first recorded carol-like verses in England appearing in later mediaeval plays.

The Church in mediaeval times and later was not proof against the heady atmosphere of Misrule. Dancing in the church yards was common; and even inside the church – Philip Stubbs recounts in his *Anatomie of Abuses* how bands of up to a hundred men got themselves up in liveries of 'light wanton colour' bedecked with scarves and ribons and bells, and accompanied by hobby horses and drums and pipes entered the church like devils incarnate during service time – 'their stumppes dauncying, their belles iynglyng, their handkerchiefes swyngyng about their heades like madmen'. To the evident enjoyment of the congregation and the natural censure of the Church. Yet – how serious was such censure? From time to time it was put into strong words: but tolerance tends to go unrecorded, and a genial clergy might have preferred some sort of inclusion of the church to exclusion, for in those days the church was a central meeting place; its neighbourhood attracted business and eating and drinking and the setting up of stalls, as evidenced by those shops built into church walls which can still be seen at, say, Haarlem in Holland.

The lower clergy itself instituted a Feast of Fools immediately following Christmas. Burlesques of the liturgy were performed, miming and mimicking of seniors accompanied profane singing. In France an Abbot of Ninnies and a Pope of Fools was elected even in a cathedral, with accompanying revels and grotesques: prayer-books, for instance, were read upside down by false prelates wearing cuts of orange rind for spectacles, and the tone was set for much licence and bawdy. That these revels were thus of a licentious nature is fairly plain: but would they have been generally considered outrageous in those rougher days? It is difficult to assess, it is the sober opposer of revelling of any kind who bothers to put things on paper. In most walks of life it seems to be a virtue to be able to laugh at oneself: perhaps these bursts were conducted in such an amiable spirit, with rough sympathy, involving the old distinction of laughing 'with' rather than 'at'. The question of a public bounty for Christmastide play-actors was also a matter of moment; it was a useful benefit, and the clergy became interested in performing mystery plays, competing with the popular secular mumming and juggling, and to compete well, they were tempted to mix their standards.

Royal and noble entertaining proceeded on a vast scale. One Victorian writer assumes that the Round Table of King Arthur's court at York, with its feasting and minstrelsy, was as happy by the great log fire 'as if they shone in the blaze of a thousand gas-lights'. Edward III set up a Christmastide Round Table at Windsor in imitation of Arthur's; and held a great tournament on New Year's Day 1344 where 'the fierce hacklings of men and horses, gallantly armed, were a delightful terror to the feminine beholders'. Richard II, despite money troubles, made Christmas an excuse to entertain Leon, King of Armenia, in splendid fashion at Eltham; and the rich magnificence of Henry V opened Westminster Hall to a banquet for his Queen whose astounding list of foodstuffs runs into paragraphs, each course culminating in a Subtlety, or symbolic statuary confected of paste and jelly, representing such involved set-pieces as St Katharine and a pelican on its nest, or a man on horseback and a tiger looking in a mirror: meanwhile one has the stirring picture of the Earl Marshall riding about the smoking hall on an immense charger to keep order. Edward IV fed more than two thousand people each day over the Christmastide of 1482 at Eltham. Henry VII sat down to a Christmas court dinner of a hundred and

Masques and royal entertainments

47

twenty dishes. Henry VIII tempered his splendours with private fun, once surprising the Queen in her quarters with his splendidly rumbustious figure disguised as Robin Hood. All these and so many other grand annual occasions were accompanied by masques and pageants and the ordering of much cloth of gold and jewelled drinking services, and of costly gifts to noble guests.

Colleges and the Inns of Court also put on tremendous banquets, accounts of which are larded with the fine titles of serving officers, the Panter, the Gentleman Sewer, and others. A record of the Inner Temple Christmastide of 1561–2 shows banqueting night after night, and always a breakfast of 'brawn, mustard and malmsey' – brawn made of hog's meat was a Christmas speciality and much attention was given to the mustard which invariably accompanied it, and to the necessity of wine to cool the attack of the mustard. At these revels there is mention of what present-day thinking would condemn as indeed a cruel sport. At a climactic moment there entered into the hall a huntsman in green, bearing a fox and a cat bound to a staff: then, to a blowing of horns, these animals were hunted round the hall by 'nine or ten couple of hounds' before a final killing in front of the fire. This was a ceremonial of St Stephen's Day, the day particularly observed by hunters, and of course is long abandoned. But in certain regimental messes nowadays there thrives unofficially, and not particularly at Christmastide, an unpleasant pleasure known as 'piping the cat', where an officer parades with a cat held in bagpipe position beneath his arm, the tail in his teeth as the blowing device: he bites the tail, the cat pipes loud. Coincidence or tenuous connection?

The Reformation had a certain tempering, or at any rate changing, effect on the Christmastide revels in Europe. Martin Luther certainly introduced a different spirit into the Christian celebration, a kindlier and simpler notation of 'glad tidings of great joy'; and legend for a long time attributed to him the first candle-lit Christmas tree as a device to illuminate the humblest home. There has since been found exact mention of what seem to be the earliest recorded household trees in Alsace and across the Rhine in the Black Forest – though some suggest that trees were decorated with paper flowers in many places before that. The legend of Luther's assumption of the tree might have made locally popular a habit which did not become generally accepted in Germany until very many years later.

Meanwhile in England Henry VIII broke with Rome, and his officer Thomas Cromwell dissolved the monasteries and gagged the pulpits, and during a reign of terror must certainly have limited the Church's own display at Christmastide. It took the violent Thomas's namesake Oliver Cromwell to try to abolish Christmas altogether. In 1642 the first ordinances went out, particularly directed at the performance of plays. Gradually puritan repression increased until churches were closed, and shops and offices ordered to stay open over what had hitherto been a holiday period.

The people, deprived of both Holy Day and holiday, resisted. Many kept Christmas as before and came up against the Roundhead soldiery. Records state, for instance in 1647, that 'At Oxford there was a world of skull-breaking; and at Ipswich the festival was celebrated by some loss of life'. Canterbury was the scene of a great riot where the Mayor got pummelled 'senseless as a pocket of hops' and the men of Kent publicly resolved to have the King on his throne again. The quarrel continued, both sides persisting. Ten years later Evelyn records going up to London to celebrate Christmas, and being surprised by soldiers who stuck muskets against him while he received the sacrament; he was then taken into confinement, questioned, but released the next day. Now why? The Puritans, though convinced of their rational attitude, must have recognised they were on difficult ground: as usual at Christmas time, there were economical matters involved as well – those who lived by piecework or maintained shops may have been glad to keep open, whereas the very poor without winter employment would have suffered from the abandonment of general alms-giving, and of the many seasonable customs like carol-singing or mumming which brought door-to-door money, and generally of the goodwill gifts of food from a population in festive mood.

However, on the whole Christmas went underground; the great displays were over, and perhaps here began the feeling for spending Christmas at home, with the family and particular friends. In 1660 Breda was signed and Charles II became King: but this merry Monarch never brought back the full scale merriment to Christmas as once it had been known. The repression had lasted eighteen years, in varying degree, a long enough time for a change of the generations, for people to forget, for customs to fall away. Besides, the sensuality of Charles himself was of a personal nature: he was not so much interested in reviving public display. Money, too, may have come into it: as we have seen, Christmastide previously had been a time of bounty for the poor, a matter for every man's pocket – it was a scarce time of year in most trades, how then to argue a return to the opening of pockets? Though it was a terrible season for the poor, charity had often flourished as custom rather than true sympathy for the less fortunate; the poor were a natural state of things, and, if anything else, a danger. It was a general feeling; there would have been a thousand exceptions.

The end of the repression

Yet this period, and those previous, must always be seen in a continuing garment of holly and rosemary, of the wassail bowl of hot strong Christmas ale and apples, of minced meat pies and plumb porridge and goose, of 'shooing the wild Mare, tumbling the young Wenches'. Snow too in some

Wreathed Father Christmas with wassail bowl, 1843

49

years, and many more times frost, a nip in the nose and blue hands, weather for great fires. Slow pale clouds on a slate-grey sky, and the earth hard as a rock: weather for artificial cheer. Rhyme after unexceptional rhyme echoes the feeling:

> With holly and ivy
> So green and so gay;
> We deck up our houses
> As fresh as the day,

or:

> Now enter Christmas like a man
> Armed with spit and dripping-pan,

or:

> This is Yuletide! Bring the holly boughs,
> Deck the old mansion with its berries red;

On and on they go. The keeping of yuletide or Christmas was still very much alive, if not in quite the large, showy or licentious scale of earlier years. Though many years later, another show began to be popular in England and only in England – the old Roman pantomime (all-mime) in a new and spectacular form, a creature of the early eighteenth century.

In that century people everywhere kept up Christmas, but the rich were divided between those who kept it in the old way – usually in the country – and those whose new fastidiousness of intellect and fashion found it too gross to make much of. The year 1752 saw the changing of the calendar in England, and much indignation when people were expected to observe the festival eleven days earlier than usual. Not only did this begin the quarrel between Old Christmas Day and Christmas new style, but many a simple mind felt it had somehow been robbed of eleven days and of the wages that went with them. Superstition tried to test the correctness of the day by observing whether the Glastonbury Thorn, supposed to have been planted by Joseph of Arimathaea, flowered or not on the new Christmas Day or on the old, now the sixth of January. It did and it did not, according to the weather; though on the whole it had a better chance of flowering on the later date. The years passed, the new calendar stayed. Thereafter, though Christmas was still much privately kept, the public fuss and feeling for it went on declining until its recrudescence a third of the way through the next century on a wave of new romantic feeling. The festival was now never again to suffer a general setback. It has lost a custom here and there, and altered this or that of its character, but its large tendency has been to grow and grow against all odds of criticism, to achieve the still swelling, even alarming proportions of today.

The great nineteenth-century revival Why was there so sudden a change in the nineteenth century? Certainly it was a time ripe for 'looking back' – as shown by the mood of Washington Irving and Charles Dickens, who are often cited as 'inventors' of the modern mould of Christmas. Was this partly an echo of general change, of a period

The double-edged demons or Perchten *who come screaming and drumming on one of the Advent Thursdays through Austrian villages, in this case in the Salzburg country. They are half inimical, yet half helpful if persuaded to dance on your fields to ensure a fruitful harvest*

of peace regretting all the vast changes of Europe after the Napoleonic Wars? Was it a moment when the industrial revolution was *recognised* as having taken an absolute precedence over the great agricultural past, threatening the future and thus bringing into being yet another golden age to long back for? Was it even the railway – faster postage, and the easier ability of relations to move to each other for an occasion? Was it, again, the greatly improved technique in printing and in circulation of printed matter, so that the earnest solicitude of Washington Irving and the tremendous human magic of Dickens were able to reach a totality of reader and read-to never before possible?

Whatever it was, the magic worked. And the old image of yuletide festivity and goodwill was reborn and then reshaped after a few decades into the mid-to-late Victorian Christmas of Father Christmas and the Christmas tree which is still largely ours today.

In summary, a short history of the mid-winter festival in Christian times, Christmas proper, would comprise:

First, the removed, rather enclosed nature of a monkish Church, unable to do much more than tolerate strong ancient beliefs, allowed a fusion of pagan and Christian customs which worked well until the Middle Ages. After this came a gradual strengthening of the Christian legend as the Church richened and flowered.

Secondly, the Reformation and various Puritan measures came to refine and strengthen Christian spirituality and do away with the trumpery of old and meaningless heathen traditions, what they called 'Fool-tide'. At the same time, we must remember that from another direction St Francis and Jacopone da Todi brought a fleshly love of the Child itself, a humanity to the deification. And later, there was Luther's message of a kind of *Gemüt-lichkeit*.

Thirdly, we meet the partial recovery of traditions largely forgotten during a period of repression, but which in any case could not stand against a newly rational mood among the thinking and, therefore, the formative classes – the moderns of an eighteenth century too usually misinterpreted as just so much powdered elegance and wiggery.

Fourthly, there comes the great revival in the nineteenth century, as emotion was roused for a golden past which brought a huge sentimentalism gradually up to a level of true sentiment; a sentiment of charity and of goodwill which today too many too easily feel has been spoiled by commercialism, but which, like Venice among the water-colourists and photographers, risks death by drowning but undoubtedly survives.

Generally in these later developments, one may notice two motifs reflecting exactly the early beginnings of solstitial worship. First, the entry of St Francis, whose visionary love of all nature reflects a kind of pantheism similar to the worship and wonder for nature of earlier religions. Secondly, the Victorian and again the present-day longing for the past as a time of plenty and of generous spirit – the golden age myth indeed, the original motivation of the Saturnalia. It makes an intriguingly reiterative pattern.

The burning of a Viking ship at the Up-Helly-Aa celebration towards the end of January at Lerwick in the Shetland Islands. Up-Helly-Aa signifies the 'end of the holiday', originally the very long Viking yuletide. The ship is thirty feet long, towed through the town in torchlit procession by men dressed as Vikings and a large crowd of guisers in costume

3
Words in Season

Ut hoy!
UNKNOWN

Like walking from painting to painting in a picture gallery, when each cancels out the impact of the one before, too many historical details at once cannot be properly digested. So let us leave the bulk for the flavour, and, before enquiring further into the detail of other traditions, of games and greenery and Santa Claus and all the wassailing, taste some of the general feeling and atmosphere of Christmastide; and, for this, go to literature and lyrics which can give a feeling picture of the time.

A million words and more have been written on the subject: long poems, short poems, stories, scenes in novels and plays. One can only glance at random into this tremendous album, and even then reduce it by a surgery of dots, excising dissertations alien to today's reading pace, as one may rightly cut Elizabethan drama for the quicker, though not necessarily livelier, perception of a modern audience.

Since Dickens played so large a part in the great Victorian revival of Christmas, and since his method was so rich and atmospheric, it is best to dispense with any chronological order and start with him. He first began to write of Christmas in the *Sketches by Boz* in 1836. Then, six years after the young Victoria ascended the throne, came the famous *Christmas Carol* and the beatification of bony old Scrooge, a book which sold immensely, and which was immediately dramatised on many stages at once, and which Dickens himself re-enacted year after year on his literary tours in Britain and America.

He had his effect: and this is epitomised in the words of a factory owner

A Washington Irving Christmas service, illustration by Randolph Caldecott from Old Christmas and Bracebridge Hall

from Vermont whom Gladys Storey in *Dickens and Daughter* records as saying: 'I feel that after listening to Mr Dickens's reading of *A Christmas Carol* to-night I should break the custom we have hitherto observed of opening the works on Christmas Day.' From then on, the factory was closed on the twenty-fifth of December.

Dickens also wrote Christmas stories and articles in annuals and journals as each Christmas came round again. In all this, he seldom sought to emphasise Christian aspects as such. Social altruism was his *fortissimo*. Warmth of friendship and charity and their associated feasting and simple sentiment were his jovial, tender texts. Goodwill, in fact. And rumbustious peace.

But he must speak for himself, and here he is first in reflective mood on the Christmas tree, in 1850:

I have been looking on, this evening, at a merry company of children assembled round that pretty German toy, a Christmas Tree. The tree was planted in the middle of a great round table, and towered high above their heads. It was brilliantly lighted by a multitude of little tapers; and everywhere sparkled and glittered with bright objects. There were rosy-cheeked dolls, hiding behind the green leaves; and there were real watches (with movable hands, at least, and an endless capacity of being wound up) dangling from innumerable twigs; there were French-polished tables, chairs, bedsteads, wardrobes, eight-day clocks, and various other articles of domestic furniture (wonderfully made, in tin, at Wolverhampton), perched among the boughs, as if in preparation for some fairy house-keeping; there were jolly, broad-faced little men, much more agreeable in appearance than many real men – and no wonder, for their heads took off, and showed them to be full of sugarplums; there were fiddles and drums; there were tambourines, books, work-boxes, paint-boxes, sweetmeat-boxes, peepshow-boxes, and all kinds of boxes; there were trinkets for the elder girls, far brighter than any grown-up gold and jewels; there were baskets and pin-cushions in all devices; there were guns, swords, and banners;

'*The Children's Christmas Table*', *by Chodowiecki, 1776*

there were witches standing in enchanted rings of pasteboard, to tell fortunes; there were teetotums, humming-tops, needle-cases, pen-wipers, smelling-bottles, conversation-cards, bouquet-holders; real fruit, made artificially dazzling with gold leaf; imitation apples, pears, and walnuts, crammed with surprises; in short, as a pretty child, before me, delightedly whispered to another pretty child, her bosom friend, 'There was everything, and more'. This motley collection of odd objects, clustering on the tree like magic fruit, and flashing back the bright looks directed towards it from every side – some of the diamond-eyes admiring it were hardly on a level with the table, and a few were languishing in timid wonder on the bosoms of pretty mothers, aunts, and nurses – made a lively realisation of the fancies of childhood; and set me thinking how all the trees that grow and all the things that come into existence on the earth, have their wild adornments at that well-remembered time.

Fifteen years earlier, we find the picture not of Christmas Day but Christmas Eve in the country, the scene that gave rise to the Pickwickian myth. After the mince-pies and the dancing, Mr Pickwick is found under a huge bunch of mistletoe suspended from the kitchen ceiling:

... and before Mr Pickwick distinctly knew what was the matter, he was surrounded by the whole body, and kissed by every one of them.

It was a pleasant thing to see Mr Pickwick in the centre of the group, now pulled this way, and then that, and first kissed on the chin, and then on the nose, and then on the spectacles: and to hear the peals of laughter which were raised on every side; but it was a still more pleasant thing to see Mr Pickwick, blinded shortly afterwards with a silk handkerchief, falling up against the wall, and scrambling into corners, and going through all the mysteries of blind-man's buff, with the utmost relish for the game, until at last he caught one of the poor relations, and then had to evade the blind-man himself, which he did with a nimbleness and agility that elicited the admiration and applause of all beholders. The poor relations caught the people who they thought would like it, and, when the game flagged, got caught themselves. When they were all tired of blind-man's buff, there was a great game at snap-dragon, and when fingers enough were burned with that, and all the raisins were gone, they sat down by the huge fire of blazing logs to a substantial supper, and a mighty bowl of wassail, something smaller than an ordinary wash-house copper, in which the hot apples were hissing and bubbling with a rich look, and a jolly sound, that were perfectly irresistible.

'This,' said Mr Pickwick, looking round him, 'this is, indeed, comfort.'

Another Dickensian Christmas Eve ball, given by Mr Fezziwig for the domestics, gives an interesting sidelight on what we imagine as the almost boundless amplitude of these Victorian occasions. It was indeed a jolly affair, with much jigging and 'Sir Roger de Coverley', and with the host dancing in so spritely a fashion that 'a positive light appeared to issue from Fezziwig's calves'. But – all this ended abruptly on the stroke of eleven o'clock!

Mr Fezziwig's ball

Of *A Christmas Carol* certain atmospheric passages illuminate the detailed flavour of people's lives at that time, which was taken from the author's experience before 1843. For all those who can remember that in childhood kitchens and Christmas were synonymous and particularly exciting, he brings back a lost smell that lingered well into the present century:

Hallo! A great deal of steam! The pudding was out of the copper. A smell like a washing-day! That was the cloth. A smell like an eating-house and a pastrycook's next door to each other, with a laundress's next door to that! That was the pudding! In half a minute Mrs Cratchit entered – flushed, but smiling proudly – with the pudding, like a speckled cannon-ball, so hard and firm, blazing in half of half-a-quartern of ignited brandy, and bedight with Christmas holly stuck into the top.

And there is a vivid moment of after-dark winter light in a London street:

The brightness of the shops where holly sprigs and berries crackled in the lamp heat of the windows, made pale faces ruddy as they passed. Poulterers' and grocers' trades became a splendid joke: a glorious pageant, with which it was next to impossible to believe that such dull principles as bargain and sale had anything to do.

Then there is a good deal more detail of the street-scene on Christmas morning itself, when in those days the shops still traded:

The Grocers'! oh the Grocers'! Nearly closed, with perhaps two shutters down, or one; but through those gaps such glimpses! It was not alone that the scales descending on the counter made a merry sound, or that the twine and roller parted company so briskly, or that the canisters were rattled up and down like juggling tricks, or even that the blended scents of tea and coffee were so grateful to the nose, or even that the raisins were so plentiful and rare, the almonds so extremely white, the sticks of cinnamon so long and straight, the other spices so delicious, the candied fruits so caked and spotted with molten sugar as to make the coldest lookers-on feel faint and subsequently bilious. ... But soon the steeples called good

Mr Pickwick under the mistletoe, by Thomas Nast, 1873

people all, to church and chapel, and away they came, flocking through the streets in their best clothes, and with their gayest faces. And at the same time there emerged from scores of bye-streets, lanes, and nameless turnings, innumerable people, carrying their dinners to the bakers' shops.

After Scrooge's long dark night of ghosts, and all the rest of the Christmas paraphernalia with which the *Carol* is saturated, there comes a very simple but beautifully affirmative passage epitomising our bright illusion of Christmas morning itself. Scrooge wakes up at last and:

He was checked in his transports by the churches ringing out the lustiest peals he had ever heard. Clash, clang, hammer; ding, dong, bell. Bell, dong, ding; hammer, clang, clash! Oh, glorious, glorious!

Running to the window, he opened it, and put out his head. No fog, no mist; clear, bright, jovial, stirring, cold; cold, piping for the blood to dance to; Golden sunlight; Heavenly sky; sweet fresh air; merry bells. Oh, glorious! Glorious! ... Christmas Day!

By 1861 Pip was having the dinner on Christmas Day at half-past one: 'We dined on these occasions in the kitchen, and adjourned, for the nuts and oranges and apples, to the parlour.' Pip was uncomfortable in reformatory-like clothes which might have been dictated by 'an Accoucheur Policeman', and he sat squeezed in at an acute angle of the tablecloth with the table in his chest and with a grown-up's elbow in his eye and was 'regaled with the scaly tips of the drumsticks of the fowls, and with those obscure corners of pork of which the pig, when living, had had the least reason to be vain'. He was ceaselessly rebuked and criticised by the grown-ups, whose severe talk gives a cruel impression of another side of Christmas from a child's point of view: Dickens, as one knows from certain of his descriptions of frightening toys, saw that there was this other side to the joviality of it all, to the sentimental ecstasy of a child's Christmas.

Pip's Christmas dinner

One may take a long step forward in time and find James Joyce echoing this same atmosphere of unease in his Christmas dinner in *A Portrait of the Artist as a Young Man*. It starts off fairly well, though with undertones:

... the warm heavy smell of turkey and ham and celery rose from the plates and dishes and the great fire was banked high and red in the grate and the green ivy and red holly made you feel so happy and when dinner was ended the big plum pudding would be carried in, studded with peeled almonds and sprigs of holly, with bluish fire running around it and a little green flag flying from the top.

It was his first Christmas dinner and he thought of his little brothers and sisters who were waiting in the nursery, as he had often waited, till the pudding came. The deep low collar and the Eton jacket made him feel queer and oldish: and that morning when his mother had brought him down to the parlour, dressed for mass, his father had cried. That was because he was thinking of his own father.

Then for poor young Stephen the grown-ups become involved in their long and bitter religious quarrel, with dreadful silences, with swearing and screaming and finally a slamming of doors until we find, against all the trimmings of gravy and the pope's nose: 'Stephen, raising his terror-stricken face, saw that his father's eyes were full of tears.'

However, other writers keep to a major affirmative attitude. Washington

Irving wrote much about the English Christmas, extolling all the old virtues, the feasting and the sacred singing,

... the burlesque pageants, the complete abandonment to mirth and good fellow-ship, with which this festival was celebrated ... It brought the peasant and the peer together, and blended all ranks in one warm generous flow of joy and kindness.

And while he recalls how the old halls of castles and manor-houses re-sounded with the harp and the Christmas carol, he feels keenly the winter aspect and the profound theme of summer in winter:

The pitchy gloom without makes the heart dilate on entering the room filled with the glow and warmth of the evening fire. The ruddy blaze diffuses an artificial summer and sunshine through the room, and lights up each countenance with a kindlier welcome.

Good honest sterling stuff; but based on the broad ordinary fact of this extraordinary time of year, and so must be re-stated. Keenly as Irving feels about winter, he is generous about one aspect of the middle of a Christmas-tide night which has reputedly and almost traditionally upset many another – the custom of the waits to serenade the sleeper at midnight or dawn.

Even the sound of the waits, rude as may be their minstrelsy, breaks upon the mid-watches of a winter night with the effect of perfect harmony. As I have been awakened by them in that still and solemn hour 'when deep sleep falleth upon men', I have listened with a hushed delight, and connecting them with the sacred and joyous occasion, have almost fancied them into another celestial choir, announcing peace and good-will to mankind.

A kindly thought from the days of draughts and warming-pans; and here he is again, coachbound before Christmas, casting the same benevolent eye:

The coach was crowded, both inside and out, with passengers, who, by their talk, seemed principally bound to the mansions of relations or friends, to eat the Christ-mas dinner. It was loaded also with hampers of game, and baskets and boxes of delicacies and hares hung dangling their long ears about the coachman's box – presents from distant friends for the impending feasts.

Robert Herrick is the poet of country yuletide ceremony. His are the most celebrated lines whose measured, lyrical tread bring on the yule-log, the bumpkin's good wassail:

> Come, bring with a noise,
> My merrie merrie boyes,
> The Christmas Log to the firing;
> While my good Dame, she
> Bids ye all be free;
> And drink to your hearts desiring.
>
> With the last yeares brand
> Light the new block, and
> For good success in his spending,
> On your Psaltries play,
> That sweet luck may
> Come while the log is a-teending.

Interlude at the Twelfth Night table, from Hollyleaves *of 1894, showing the cake cut but not divided up in search of the bean. By this time the old ritual was falling into disuse*

Drink now the strong Beere,
Cut the white loafe here,
The while the meat is a-shredding;
For the rare Mince-Pie,
And the Plums stand by
To fill the paste that's a-kneading.

Those are choral, gutteral lines of men singing: you can hear the thump of pewter mugs as they banged out the old truths of lighting the log from last year's wood, and of pies where hacked meat met dried plums on the long way to beginning our present-day Christmas pudding. And now here is W. M. Thackeray, who also wrote much about Christmas, in a stranger, lighter vein. Crisply he trills the first verse of that curious, breathless poem about the convivial mahogany table, huddling round the wine and wassail against cold draughts in the corners and the freezing world outside:

Christmas is here;
Winds whistle shrill,
Icy and chill,
Little care we;
Little we fear
Weather without,
Sheltered about
The Mahogany-Tree.

There is a telling passage in a story by Harriet Beecher Stowe of the first arrival of the English to the New World, and the first American Christmas: *Christmas in the New World*

The men had come back from their work on shore with branches of green pine and holly, and the women had stuck them about the ship, not without tearful thoughts of old home-places, where their childhood fathers and mothers did the same.
Bits and snatches of Christmas carols were floating all around the ship, like land-birds blown far out to sea.

Charles Reade, in *Put Yourself in His Place*, gives a long, conventional yet properly moving account of Christmas Eve as kept by a Victorian squire deep in the country and the past. The setting is a banqueting-hall, the polish and colour of the panelling are warmly described, we are in a place of traditional and benign ease; and he goes on to say:

What might be called the dining-room part, though rich, was rather sombre on ordinary occasions; but this night it was decorated gloriously. The materials were simple wax-candles and holly; the effect was produced by a magnificent use of these materials. There were eighty candles of the largest size sold in shops, and twelve wax pillars, five feet high, and the size of a man's calf; of these, four only were lighted at present. The holly was not in sprigs, but in enormous branches, that filled the eye with glistening green and red; and in the embrasure of the front window stood a young holly-tree entire, eighteen feet high, and gorgeous with five hundred branches of red berries. The tree had been dug up, and planted here in an enormous bucket, used for that purpose, and filled with mould.

John Leech's well-known illustration of Mr Fezziwig's Ball from Charles Dickens's
A Christmas Carol

Close behind this tree were placed two of the wax pillars, lighted, and their flame shone through the leaves and berries magically.

Then, when a servant announced 'The Wassailers':

'Well, let them come in,' said Mr Raby.

The schoolchildren and young people of the village trooped in and made their obeisances, and sang the Christmas Carol –

'God rest you merry, gentlemen,
Let nothing you dismay.'

Then one of the party produced an image of the Virgin and Child, and another offered comfits in a box; a third presented the wassail cup, into which Raby immediately poured some silver, and Coventry followed his example, Grace fumbled for her purse, and, when she had found it, began to fumble in it for her silver.

But Raby lost all patience, and said, 'There, I give this for the lady, and she'll pay me *next Christmas*.'

The wassailers departed, and the Squire went to say a kind word to his humbler guests....

It was nearly eleven o'clock when Mr Raby rejoined them, and they all went in to supper. There were candles lighted on the table and a few here and there upon the walls; but the room was very sombre; and Mr Raby informed them this was to remind them of the moral darkness in which the world lay before that great event they were about to celebrate.

He then helped each of them to a ladleful of frumety, remarking at the same time, with a grim smile, that they were not obliged to eat it; there would be a very different supper after midnight.

Then a black-letter Bible was brought him, and he read it all to himself at a side table.

Mr Raby and
the Noel
After an interval of silence so passed, there was a gentle tap at the bay window. Mr Raby went and threw it open, and immediately a woman's voice, clear and ringing, sang outside –

'The first Noel the angels did say,
Was to three poor shepherds in fields as they lay
In fields where they were keeping their sheep
On a cold winter's night that was so deep.'
 Chorus – 'Noel, Noel, Noel, Noel,
 Born is the King of Israel.'

As the Noel proceeded, some came in at the window, others at the doors, and the lower part of the room began to fill with singers and auditors.

The Noel ended, there was a silence, during which the organ was opened, the bellows blown, and a number of servants and others came into the room with little lighted tapers, and stood in a long row, awaiting a signal from the Squire.

He took out his watch and, finding it was close on twelve o'clock, directed the doors to be flung open, that he might hear the great clock in the hall strike the quarters.

The clock struck the first quarter – dead silence; the second – the third – dead silence.

But at the fourth, and with the first stroke of midnight, out burst the full organ and fifty voices, with the '*Gloria in excelsis Deo*'; and, as that divine hymn surged on, the lighters ran along the walls and lighted the eighty candles, and, for the first time, the twelve waxen pillars, so that, as the hymn concluded, the room was in a blaze, and it was Christmas Day.

This is one of the few literary mentions of the very large Christmas candles, relics of light and fire worship and designed to burn for a day or more; and of frumety or frumenty, an unappetising dish of hulled corn which was sometimes the accompaniment to mutton but also found a traditional place at Christmas Eve as a fasting-dish, according to the old Catholic keeping of the Eve.

This blazoning of great bunches of evergreen, this odour of old things, tempts one to look again at pre-Christian times, and to read again a famous passage from Frazer's *Golden Bough*, not indeed particularly of Christmas but specifically of the priest-king kernel of life and resurrection which was the ancient prelude to all.

In this sacred grove there grew a certain tree round which at any time of the day, and probably far into the night, a grim figure might be seen to prowl. In his hand he carried a drawn sword, and he kept peering warily about him as if at every instant he expected to be set upon by an enemy. He was a priest and a murderer; and the man for whom he looked was sooner or later to murder him and hold the priesthood in his stead. Such was the rule of the sanctuary. A candidate for the priesthood could only succeed to office by slaying the priest, and having slain him, he retained office till he was himself slain by a stronger or craftier.

The post which he held by this precarious tenure carried with it the title of king; but surely no crowned head ever lay uneasier, or was visited by more evil dreams, than his. For year in year out, in summer and winter, in fair weather and in foul, he had to keep his lonely watch, and whenever he snatched a troubled slumber it was at the peril of his life. The least relaxation of his vigilance, the smallest abatement of his strength of limb or skill of fence, put him in jeopardy; grey hairs might seal his death-warrant ... we picture to ourselves the scene as it may have been witnessed by a belated wayfarer on one of those wild autumn nights when the dead leaves are falling thick, and the winds seem to sing the dirge of the dying year. It is a sombre picture, set to melancholy music – the background of forest showing black and jagged against a lowering and stormy sky, the sighing of the wind in the branches, the rustle of the withered leaves under foot, the lapping of the cold water on the shore, and in the foreground, pacing to and fro, now in twilight and now in gloom, a dark figure with a glitter of steel at the shoulder whenever the pale moon, riding clear of the cloud-rack, peers down at him through the matted boughs.

Such a sinister picture as this is indeed relieved by the pleasant image of the birth of Christ. How prettily, and even gaily, the new and blessed event could be construed we may feel in such early English lyrics, half carol and half pastoral song, as the winking, twinkling words about Joly Wat:

> The Shepard upon a hill he sat;
> He had on him his tabard and his hat,
> His tarbox, his pipe, and his flagat;
> His name was called Joly Joly Wat,
> For he was a gud herdes boy.
> Ut hoy!
> For in his pipe he made so much joy....

Whan Wat to Bedlem cumen was,
He swet, he had gone faster than apace;
He found Jesu in a simpell place,
Between an ox and an asse.
Ut hoy!
For in his pipe he made so much joy....

'Jesu, I offer to thee here my pipe,
My skirt, my tarbox, and my scripe;
Home to my felowes now will I skipe,
And also look unto my shepe.'
Ut hoy!
For in his pipe he made so much joy....

Most early hymn and carol lyrics had none of this touching familiarity. Many are tender enough, many are portentous and laudatory; but it is worth while quoting here another exception, the lyric attributed to Jacopone da Todi, mystic and wandering ascetic, who would speak of Christ with loving diminutives – *Bambolino, Jesulino* – and whose message among the ordinary people of 'their dear little brother' did so much to humanise the story of the birth. As translated by J. A. Symonds, the verses run:

Come and look upon her child
Nestling in the hay!
See his fair arms opened wide,
On her lap to play!
And she tucks him by her side,
Cloaks him as she may:
Gives her paps unto his mouth,
Where his lips are laid.

For the little babe had drouth,
Sucked the breast she gave;
All he sought was that sweet breast,
Broth he did not crave;
With his tiny mouth he pressed
Tiny mouth that clave:
Ah, the tiny baby thing,
Mouth to bosom laid!

Little angels all around
Danced, and carols flung;
Making verselets sweet and true,
Still of love they sung;
Calling saints and sinners too
With love's tender tongue;
Now that heaven's high glory is
On this earth displayed ...

Jacopone's last observation of the nativity was to die on Christmas Day itself, in 1306.

FROZEN OUT.

Poor mother bird! thy tender brood
   In vain for aid are feebly calling;
The snow that mocked thy search for food
   Around a lifeless form is falling.

How cheerily thy wood notes rang
   In brighter days of brief duration!
Too soon they fled and left the pang
   Of nipping frost and dire starvation.

Was it for this thou kept such guard
   Upon thy nest through hours of quiet?
Ah, birdie! life is very hard
   To understand—we will not try it.

Nor lost shall be thy dying woe,
   Nor aimless quite my simple ditty,
If both but prompt some heart to show
   For all God's creatures care and pity.

                S. E. G

4

Customs and Survivals

These dances were perform'd of yore
By many worthy Elfes,
Now if you will have any more
Pray shake your heeles yourselves.
JACOBEAN MASQUE

Atmospheres of fiction breed from the facts of life, and vice versa. Religious fancies began the festival, the festivities became fact, and then fancy plays again all over the facts – which may now be recapitulated in a glance at the essential elements of Christmastide common to most parts of Europe and the Europeanised parts of other continents.

Everywhere we find a bringer of gifts – such as Father Christmas, the American Santa Claus, the Christ Child of Germany, the old woman Befana (Epiphany) who is abroad on the eve of the sixth of January in Italy, the Three Kings also Epiphanous in Spain, and so on. Some of these gift-bearers are accompanied by a separate dark devil-figure, or by a dark side of their own nature, to question children as to their past behaviour and mete out punishment to the bad: gifts only for the good.

Everywhere at Christmas we find a historical letting up of law and a popular genuflection to the idea of chance, as witnessed by the prevalence of dicing and card-playing at Christmastide, and particularly by a further and special lottery never quite explained, the choosing by lot of a leader via one small object hidden in food like a cake or a porridge – as with the Bean King chosen on Twelfth Night in England and Holland and France and elsewhere by finding the one bean hidden in the Twelfth Cake; like the one almond in the Christmas Eve rice dish in Denmark, like the sixpences in Christmas puddings and even like Little Jack Horner who pulled out a

68

plum and assumed thereby his well-known elevation. This indeed suggests the survival, again via the Roman Saturnalia, of some very ancient choosing of priest-king or sacrifice by lot.

Everywhere at Christmas there is or was the idea of fasting before feasting on special foods which vary from country to country. Everywhere houses and churches are decorated with greenery, from the fir-growths and hollies of the north to exotics like the poinsettia popular in many warmer climates and like the algaroba of Hawaii and Persia. Everywhere there is a symbolism of the re-birth of the sun's light through some fire device, as with the disappearing yule-log and French *souche de Noël*, as with candles, as with the burning of the bush of hawthorn in, for instance, Herefordshire – a custom which with so many others has crossed to America, and is celebrated in some magnitude at Rochester every Twelfth Night; and as with the candle-crowned girl representing Santa Lucia in each Swedish household on the thirteenth of December (and actually singing the Neapolitan song!).

Throughout Europe there is the belief that animals such as oxen and horses and sheep bow to the East, or make praise in human voice, at midnight on Christmas Eve. This is the moment when legend believes that rivers run with wine and great mountains open up to shine with precious stones; when church bells ring from drowned cities and trees blossom forth from their winter sleep. Everywhere, too, there is this deep wish for masking or dressing up. There are the *Krampus* and *Bartel* of Austria, with headmasks of horrible device very similar to devil-masks in Oceania or other present-day primitive communities; and there is the animalistic yule goat

The yule-log, the souche de Noël and Santa Lucia

The Befana presiding over an Italian shop

69

of Norway, and the wicked black-faced *Kallikantzaroi* of Greece: all figures of devils to drive out the devil. Very often we find the myth that not only are evil spirits roused up at this holy time, but also that the spirits or ghosts of the dead themselves rise to populate the winter's night. Everywhere too there is found the excuse to play some form of drama, from mystery or miracle plays to our present-day etiolated but derived 'charade'; and there are the star singers – boys who at Epiphany carry a lantern in the shape of a star, in Poland and Rumania and Spain and Alaska and elsewhere, to honour Bethlehem and the three Kings and sing carols and, of course, get money. In parts of Germany carols are played on brass instruments from the tops of church towers, the *Turmblasen*, dramatic muezzin music from the all-sounding heavens; and in an oily part of the USA, for instance, massed trombonists do the same from the top of a steel-girdered oil tower.

St Stephen's Day festivities   The day after Christmas Day, St Stephen's, is generally associated with hunting and with horses – there are special fox-hunt meetings in England and horse races and bull-fights in South America and, for only one European instance, a hunting of roebuck or hares in the mountains of Austria. St Stephen has, particularly in Sweden, a legendary connection with the horse: as a missionary he is supposed to have travelled with five horses, two red, two white and one dappled, mounting one steed when the next was tired; and we are reminded suspiciously of Santa Claus's hypothetical reindeer. For all these matters get much mixed up as the centuries pass, as grandmother's tongue wags vaguer, or expedience makes changes in the ritual more profitable.

All Catholic countries build Christmas cribs or manger scenes – *Krippen*, *nacimientos*, *pesebres*, *presèpios* – from the enormous affairs commanded at the Bourbon court of Naples, to the modern Brazilian and West African scenes where around the manger there may be found such modern delicacies as electric trams and racing cars, dive-bombers and atomic rockets. The whole matter has grown with man's love for model-making – but began perhaps

A uniquely short-bearded, bare-chested, Bacchic-looking conception of the Father Christmas figure as depicted by John Leech for the Ghost of Christmas Present in Charles Dickens's A Christmas Carol

not only with St Francis of Assisi, who is recorded as staging the first Christian 'nativity scene' with live people and animals, but long, long before in the making of token sacrificial puppets.

A hot wassail drink – in England, mulled and spiced beer dancing with hot apples – is common, though not only at Christmas: for instance, *glögg* in Sweden, *Glühwein* in Germanic countries; and egg-nogg, usually cold, in the United States. And as we have seen with the 'shooting' of apple trees in England, so in Tyrol the trees are embraced by maidens or knocked at and told to wake up, and there is a Slavonic habit of threatening them with a hatchet: either you bear me fruit next year, or I chop you down. Similar exhortations are performed with cattle in places as far distant from each other as Hereford and Yugoslavia. There is a baking of cakes with a hole in the centre to place on the horn of a chosen ox; and in Ireland we find a dung-cake made and set with lighted candles. The making of cakes, and biscuits stamped with holy figures, and other traditional devices is universal in the days towards Christmas; the Swedes used to confect a dough-cake in the shape of a boar, the Poles had holy wafers blessed by the priest, it was a general pattern everywhere.

The eve of the New Year is, of course, universally celebrated with a new burst of merry-making and with ritual processions. Today we feel it to be slightly apart from Christmas: but though it has no association with Christ's birth, it is properly part of the inherited sequence of festivity at this time of year, just as the Saturnalia was followed by the Kalendae. The end is usually on Twelfth Day or Night, whichever term you prefer: days were originally reckoned as and called nights, quite distinct from eves. But there is still a tendency to continue even beyond this date in some places, with Plough Sunday and Monday in England and Candlemas, the second of February, elsewhere – though these are really the first very early spring festivals. As late as the nineteenth century carnival in Tyrol began at Epiphany – making after the twelve days of Christmas a stretch of licence exhaustive as the old Viking yule.

These are some of the customs of Christmas common to most parts of Europe. Let us examine at least one of them in detail: and one which has a full dedication to Jesus Christ and a sizeable pagan element as well. The Christmas Eve mass at Les Baux, in Provence.

Les Baux is a skeleton city standing on a high white limestone ridge in this sunny region of sheep grazing on lavender and *fines herbes*. It is made up of the bony stone ruins of Angevin seignorial houses and churches, lovely architectures still half-standing, and enough of them to make the place more of an evacuated ghost town than an ankle-deep figuration of classical foundations. Les Baux still feels largely there. We can wander the streets, dreaming up an almost round-the-corner past as at Pompeii, and feel the knightly city as once it was. In summer it has become a tourist attraction, with a cinematic *exposé* of its past and with restaurants; but in winter Les Baux is mostly empty, except for such occasions as the Christmas mass at the little twelfth-century-founded church of St Vincent.

The winter cold in the *Midi* strikes in quick at afternoon sundown: after

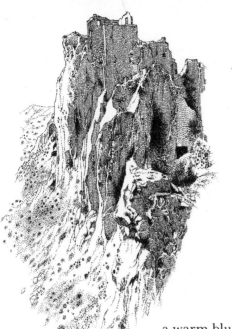

Three drawings by Robin Jacques depicting (left) *the landscape of Les Baux,* (right) *a Provençal shepherd and* (opposite) *an Arlé-sienne holding the lamb at the midnight mass*

a warm blue day, the change can be emphatic, and on the minor heights of Les Baux the more so. Weather for wool, for hot chestnuts and warm drinks – and some of the well-wrapped congregation of locals and visitors even carry thermos flasks when they begin to arrive at 7.30 p.m.

But inside the stone church the air soon warms up with so much packed human flesh, and with the hot smell of wax candles. There is a long wait; not until 10.30 does the service begin, with a solo singer of Provençal carols accompanied by *tutu-panpans*, the local name for the music of the *tambourinaires* with their long narrow drums played with the right hand as the left manipulates the *galoubet* or pipe.

Half-an-hour later the priest delivers a half-hour French sermon and then the choir, dressed in the Spanish-looking silks and shawls of the Arlésienne and glinting with gold jewellery, sing carols and hymns from the chancel. At midnight the curé places the Infant, a wax doll, in the crib set in a chapel beside the high altar. Around the crib is a *tableau vivant* impersonated by people from the parish – Mary, four grown-up adult angels and six younger ones, and Joseph. Now there begins the mass proper conducted entirely in Provençal dialect, and composed by one of the Félibrige company of Provençal poets.

Christmas Eve Mass at Les Baux, Provence

Meanwhile there comes slowly up the aisle a strange procession indeed. A shepherd in a wide cloak leads a ribboned and red-coated ram which draws a small ceremonial cart festooned with candles and greenery, some of which is a broom called 'holly' by the locals: in the cart lies a female lamb with a red ribbon round its neck. The cart is followed by sixteen pairs of shepherds and shepherdesses, all cloaked, the women wearing bright-coloured silks and patterned costume beneath.

Now the choir of Arlésiennes and the drummers leave the chancel, and the Holy Family and the angels move from the crib into the chancel and surround the curé at the communion rail: to compose a picture, the tallest angels stand behind.

74

A candle in each left hand, the procession of shepherds reaches the High Altar. The Virgin hands the Child to the curé, who shows it to the congregation. A *Gloria* is sung by the angels, to the sound again of the drummers.

The *baile pastre*, or chief shepherd, takes up the lamb under his right arm and bows his head to the curé. All the lights go out but for the candle-lit procession. The shepherd with candle and lamb kneels at the rail and kisses the foot of the Child Jesus. He steps back, bows to the curé, bows to his shepherdess and hands her the lamb – whereupon she, in the same manner with lamb and candle, goes forward to kiss the Infant's foot.

These grave and formal motions, in great cloaks by candlelight, and the women in white caps, are repeated by each shepherd and shepherdess of the procession.

Finally the chief shepherd returns to the curé, bows to him, turns and bows to the congregation; and all resume their original places, the angels and Holy Family to the crib, the choir in their Arlésiennes to the chancel, and mass is continued.

Then the chief shepherd again goes with the lamb to the rail and at the elevation, when Host and Chalice are raised and the acolyte rings his bell, gives the tail a sharp nip to make it squeal, once, twice.

And that is all.

In an ancient place, it marks the slow and formal meeting of Christian and pagan belief in adoration of the Child and supplication for the flock's fertility.

A knowledge of the living landscape, and the opportunity to examine details, always bring folklore and ritual to life. Take, for instance, Risan in South Dalmatia. One may state baldly the facts – that for instance oaks are felled at Christmas, and the women deck the trunks with red silk and gold wire, and with leaves and flowers, before seeing them carried to the houses, when a libation of corn and wine is thrown upon the male owner, and the log placed on the fire. A southern Slav yule-log, in fact. But if you know Risan, a small apricot-roofed town set by the mirror-smooth waters of the great Kotor fjord, and if you know the immense bare walls of white limestone rising hundreds of feet vertically around to cup this town and its green meadows in a resonance of peace only known to fjords, if you can see the little raft-like island opposite floating its church and cypresses like Boecklin's *Island of the Dead* – then the immense *thereness* of such a pretty ritual makes for a truer depth and beauty. One may perhaps know, too, that these same waters of Risan received the living body of the last Illyrian queen, who drowned herself there rather than become Rome's prisoner. That has nothing to do with Christmas: but it marks the fact that Christmas and the decking of logs by pretty girls happens on this precise historical piece of the earth in a place lived in minute after minute through centuries of human experience.

Or again one may envisage the midnight mass at the church in Bethlehem built above the cave where an elaborate silver star marks the supposed place of Christ's birth. In so extraordinary a place it is always a crowded ceremony. But beyond the people attending, one must remember all that is

going on outside – Bethlehem for the time has become the cynosure of a strange new traffic of processions and automobiles from Jerusalem, and there are parking problems, and a loud-voiced crowd of gapers ... matters which, spoiling or not, show that it all happens here on this tobacco-breathing earth every year: such rituals are never as dead as the list of them, in words, may make them seem.

But lists we must have: and here is a short one of games – now usually 'children's games' – which were once or are still played at Christmas-time. There was Hot Cockles, where a blindfold player holds out his hand, cries 'Hot Cockles, hot!', and receives a whack on it from another whose name he must guess. And Shoeing the Wild Mare, which involved a whack on the foot. And Puss-in-the-Corner and Hunt the Slipper and Blind-Man's Buff and Postman's Knock and Nuts in May and a host of others. All these were played at other times than at Christmas; though as a time of year when people stayed inside the house, Christmas with its air of festivity plainly offered the best conditions. There is also a longer list of forgotten games whose names defeat the antiquary – from Rowland Bo to The Parson has Lost his Cloak, from Feed the Dove to Steal the White Loaf. It all sounds very jolly, and undoubtedly was and is. But the times were once rough, and so were the games. Blind-Man's Buff used often to consist of leading the blind to trip over furniture: '... and then it is lawful to set any things in the way for folks to tumble over, whether it be to break Arms, or Legs, or Heads, 'tis no matter ...'

Christmas games through the ages

The game of Puss-in-the-Corner involved kissing of no mean intensity: '... and one may ramp at it as much as one will, when even at this game a Man Catches his Woman, he must kiss her till her Ears crack. ...' While in 1711 a letter appealed to Mr Spectator: 'I am a footman in a great Family and am in Love with the Housemaid. We were all at Hot-cockles last Night in the Hall these Holidays; when I lay down and was blinded she pull'd off her Shoe and hit me with the Heel such a Rap as almost broke my Head to Pieces. Pray, Sir, was this Love or Spite?'

It was not so in America. The early settlers brought a strong Puritan

'Cutlets', a Victorian party trick. (left) *The last man says, 'Are you a believer in the Great Mogul?' (pr. muggle = muddle), and* (right) – *'So am I', he says, suddenly getting up. From* The Diary of a Nobody, *illustrated by W. Grossmith*

influence with them. William Bradford's *Journal* for the year 1620 records a Governor in Plymouth Colony coming home from work on Christmas Day to find others 'in ye streets at play, openly; some pitching ye barr and some at stoole ball, and such like sports.' He immediately took away their implements and sent them home, 'since which time nothing hath been attempted that way, at least, openly'. Generally, this forbidding attitude towards play continued until the late nineteenth century. Not until 1856 did Massachusetts proclaim Christmas Day a legal holiday; though the first states to do so were in the easier South, in the 1830s, while the last was Oklahoma in 1890. Though Dutch settlers had always held a festive Christmas, the English Puritans set a definite code for work on that day: in 1959, for instance, five shillings was the then heavy fine for observing Christmas Day in any way whatsoever.

One must best imagine the party games in England and Europe as being played by the light of a fire, and once by the light of the traditional yule-log, that great root of a thing which with its many twisted wooden tentacles must have sat in the flames like a grotesque devil-figure itself. The yule-log is thought to have come to England via the Vikings. In France there is the *souche de Noël* and in Slav countries there are similar logs and even so far south as Greece a cedar log was burned. Almost everywhere some sort of sacred fire and vegetation emblem, usually appealed to with a libation of wine or corn, was lit at this time of solstice – and invariably it had to be lit from a brand kept from the previous year's log. It is, of course, possible that this whole ritual was spread by the Norsemen, who sailed so far down rivers and round distant coasts: according to Rudbeck, and since to a fraternity of modern anthropologists, they began many things if not everything. Others believe that Mediterranean man spread these or similar customs from south to north. And there is the further argument that such matters did not need anyone to spread them, but occurred spontaneously here and there as man's mind developed.

The yule-log and the fire were to honour the need for the sun: but as we go further south to hotter and drier countries more attention is paid to

Origins of the yule-log

water, as an irrigation factor or as an agent of ritual cleansing. One finds the Greek Church continuing a special ceremony at Epiphany. The priest goes to the nearest water with a cross of metal or wood, throws it in, and young men dive to retrieve it. For the Church, it represents the baptism of Christ: for others earlier it was a propitiation of storm-rich sea-gods or rain and river-water gods. The ceremony has long crossed a most sizeable stretch of water, the Atlantic, and continues among a settlement of Greek sponge-fishers at Tarpon Springs, Florida: and among Bulgarians in Pennsylvania; and on the Californian coast and elsewhere.

Twelfth Night and the Bean King

In parts of France and Spain – and in Mexico also – the eating of a Twelfth Night cake with its secret bean still goes on: but in England the habit has gone and with it the final burst of Christmas jollity, often recorded as the merriest of the whole Christmas season, when the world was alive with practical jokes and boys on the street might, for instance, pin people's coat-tails and dresses together. As we have seen, a single bean was hidden in the cake: and the finder became Bean King, a straight derivative of the Saturnalian King chosen by lot. The sole survival of the Twelfth-cake in England occurs each year in the green-room of Drury Lane Theatre, among actors and actresses, to whom a cake is carried by the wigged and liveried theatre servants according to a bequest made in 1794 by a chef-actor. The bequest was of a hundred pounds in 3% funds, the interest to be used for preparing a cake.

A further Twelfth Night tradition now gone with the growth of industry and its shortening of holidays is that of the Twelfth Night characters. These were painted cards – the king, the queen, the dandy, the captain etc. – and the number proliferated to include such as Patrick O'Tater, Monsieur François Parlez-Vous, and Farmer Mangelwurzel, all attendants of the court of the Bean King. Each of the company drew an illustrated card and had to act that person until the Bean King should order a change. Shades of charades again. All forgotten. As indeed is the origin of the song-game of gifts, 'A Partridge in a Pear-Tree'. This has now been sanctified into a carol or hymn and is sung sometimes in church. As from *perdrix* and older English spellings like *pertrych*, it all possibly began from a simple pun and the need for a game of word-skill.

Hogmanay or New Year's Eve in Scotland still sees a fair amount of first-footing, the tradition that the first person to cross the threshold of a house should bear gifts of food or coal and receive a hospitable drink in return. Once there was great competition, and they ran races from door to door, in one house and out and into another. The characteristics of the first-footer are of great importance. A woman first-footer means bad luck for the year. Especially prized is the man known to have been born feet foremost. Dark men are often preferred to fair – possibly a hangover from early solidarities of the dark Celt against the red invader. Bank clerks coming home late after balancing the end-year books used to be convenient first-footers. Similar first-footing traditions occur in many other places, as far distant as Macedonia and China. The derivation of the word 'hogmanay' is undecided: but in Normandy the word *hogninane* is used by the *quêteurs*, and in Guernsey *hognihannen*. In Guernsey the whole period from St Thomas's Day to New Year's Eve is a tricky one, the powers of darkness are out *en masse* and white rabbits pop up beneath the feet of anyone out after nightfall, an unnerving sensation. However, you were safer in Germany – at least in the old days. There you could tell a witch straight off by seeing a red mouse hop out of her mouth.

These and ten thousand instances of comparable Christmastide traditions proliferate, some gone, others alive or revived, throughout the world. Mention can only be made of some of the most startling, like the Alaskan eskimo habit at the solstice of driving an imaginary evil spirit into a fire, over which there is then tossed, to the ritual sound of shooting, a pot of urine. And in the Basque Pyrenees one comes across the curious St Cat's Day at Candlemas, said to be a corruption of Saint Agatha into Spanish *gato* a cat; but possibly not, for there are very ancient traditions of cat-worship hereabouts. Later in January at Oyon in Alava a ceremony takes the mayor and his company to church along with an odd mediaevally dressed figure known as the *katxi* who carries a stuffed cat's skin and is ceremonially 'killed' outside the church: following which, there are rebirth fireworks involving the fertile bull symbol.

The Austrian mountains round Traunstein know a particularly effective bogey – a female called Berchte – who is supposed to look for naughty children on Epiphany Eve and cut their stomachs open. However, most

'The First Sight of the Christmas Tree',
by Josef Kelbner, 1800

ritual is prettier than this, largely a matter of libations of corn and wine and peas and oil, of decking and dancing to celebrate fertilities of the future. We shall examine more of these in detail in later chapters devoted to particulars like decoration, gifts and food; but in the meantime it would be well to take a general look at one selected country and summarise its whole Christmas procedure. Let the country be Germany, for among all nations Germany has fused a particular sanctity, or sentimental seriousness, or dedicated love or what you will into the great occasion. We know that various Christmas traditions have come from elsewhere, from the Norsemen, from the Jews and the Persians and the Phoenicians and even from the Aztecs ... but in Germany such customs seem to have gathered with particular strength – although it might also be that closer communications with Germany bring it all the more easily home; there may be similar claims from Poland, Russia or elsewhere.

The festival in Germany The German Christmas begins with Advent, when an Advent wreath of evergreen with four red candles fixed into it is hung or propped up in the home: on the first Sunday after the twenty-sixth of November the first candle is lit, and the second and third candles on the following Sundays. The last flowers into light on *Heiligabend*, Christmas Eve itself. Alongside this, Advent Calendars are distributed – silver-frosted winter landscapes with openings like windows or holes in trees numbered with the date of the day when they must be opened on the expectant journey towards Christmas; inside the little doors there is a secret picture or a message, or in the more elaborate cards, a small present.

During this time, priests change to a violet chasuble; the organ is silent in Catholic churches; an air of expectancy is fostered. It simulates the breath-held wonder of a family awaiting the time of an expectant mother; it also echoes a broader evocation of the deepest draw of Christmastide – the expectancy of a feast of light, of a great social commotion, to mark the close of the year. On the way through this remarkable, daily more excitant month, there are special prayers in the Catholic south for an inn to be opened, there are early morning 'angels'' masses, and in some homes a bed is prepared for Mary and Joseph to spend the night in.

A table is set, and food put out. But this custom, though now one of goodwill and generosity, is really a relic of the old propitiation of not the good but the evil spirits which were thought to be abroad at this time of year. At the same time, another old custom, without any such Christian disguise, may start up the rattling of cans and a yelling in the streets outside – the masked demon figures whose confused purpose is that of persons dressed as demons frightening demons away. Mightily mixed up, as all these traditions are: the cart and the horse seem intent over the centuries to put themselves before each other at one and the same time. Yet, in the simplest of terms, the action is an ordinary human one, and as obvious a function to stone and bronze age man, whose brain measured exactly the same as ours today, as would be our method of dealing with any materially evil visitor, like a savage dog: we would try either to soften its anger with food, or frighten it away with inimical sounds and gestures.

On St Andrew's Night, the thirtieth of November, young girls begin their divination of the future, using many old wives' devices to discern what is on their young minds, like the direction from which their future husbands will arrive – standing, for only one instance, barefoot beneath a plum tree and listening for a dog to bark. Later on, after Christmas, they will be dropping melted lead into cold water, or egg-white into hot water, to divine something of the shape and nature of their future *Mann*. Then, on St Barbara's Day, the fourth of December, early budding branches such as cherry will be cut and put into warm water by the stove to force a bloom by Christmas. St Thomas's Day, on the twenty-first of December, was, and somewhere still is, devoted to the making of a rich fruit cake, and St Thomas's Night, the longest night of the year, was devoted to making it shorter – St Thomas's became a dancing, games-playing, dicing night. In former days, girls would spin the harder and the longer to pass the hours of darkness away. When this was over, obsessed as always by their future and the man who should make it, the poor things had to spend the remainder of the night sleeping with their heads at the foot of the bed and their feet on the pillow to obtain a properly revelatory dream.

Does this occur in a modern apartment block in Düsseldorf? Likely not. But deep somewhere in the country such customs will still be observed; either in their ancient ways, or with some modern rationalisation, as, for instance, putting food out to placate demons now often becomes 'putting a few crusts or ears of wheat out for the birds'. The interpretation of customs changes all the time; traditions have a usage like language; today in Germany *Sünnerklas* or the *Klausemann* tends to leave his sixth of December date as St Nicholas and merges with the re-imported American Santa Claus, the old German *Weihnachtsmann* (Father Christmas), and the Protestant angel figure of the *Christkindl* as the gift-bringer on Christmas Eve. In passing, one may note a further significant difference between the American Santa Claus and the German *Weihnachtsmann*: Santa Claus, though partly of Bavarian and Norse origins, is a merry old soul; but the *Weihnachtsmann* is tired from toiling through the dark winter night with his heavy burden of toys, so that there is a German expression 'you weary old Father Christmas' for someone bowed and slow-moving.

A further difference between Santa Claus and his German version of the gift-bringer was the presence in Germany of that grotesque attendant whose duty was to mete out a traditional punishment to bad children. This carrier of the rod is variously named as Hans Muff, Knecht Rupprecht, Butz, Hans Tripp, Krampus, Klaubauf, Bartel – and he has his female equivalent in Berchtel, Buzebergt, Budelfrau and others. The creature is often shaggily dressed in fur, even with lighted eyes behind a mask; or blacked over, or given some other diabolic or animalistic attribute. Nowadays, even if anyone takes the trouble to manage this fearful impersonation, there is of course no punishment meted out. But long ago it was so; or at least the possibility of it was taken seriously by children being taught to distinguish between their own good and bad behaviour. Again over thousands of years the original intention of these rods or birches has been

Changing interpretations of the Father Christmas figure

The Schimmelreiter *performs in the*
Ruppin district of Germany, 1867

turned to suit new sophisticated conceptions of 'good' and 'bad'. Originally,
it is thought, there was no idea of punishment but exactly the opposite –
the rods were branches or twigs offered as a *good* wish, in fact as representa-
tives of the fertility of trees and of the vital vegetable world. Once again,
expedience has turned the whole thing upside down.

A further German version of the *Klausemann* is *Aschenklaus*. The old man
is pictured as carrying ashes from the yule-log: and this figure, directly
connected with ancient hearth-worship, seems to echo the exported Santa
Claus's predilection for chimneys.

One or other of the last Thursdays before Christmas is in some parts of
Germany held as a *Klöpfelnacht*, or Knocking Night. This is when the
mummers in fearful guise go from house to house rattling cans, ringing
cow-bells, cracking whips, throwing small stones against the windows and

knocking on the doors. Sometimes a pitchfork would be thrust through the open door for food to be put on it. 'Knockers' were asked to go and jump about the fields to work a magic of fertility. Today, as with so many of these old customs, the original intention of driving off evil is forgotten. Though some people now like to liken the door-knock to a knock announcing the coming of Christ, or of Joseph and Mary searching for accommodation, on the whole it has become simply an excuse for the more exuberant villagers to dress up and get a lot of fun and a little money out of it all. There was also the custom among friends of throwing an anonymous present in through the door and making off quickly – a *Klöpfelscheit* parallel with the Scandinavian *Julklapp*.

Cake and biscuit making rise to extremes of excitement and variety as the days mount near to Christmas itself. As usual, political conceptions like 'Germany' must here go by the board: like most other large countries it has a northern and southern climate; and it has mixed religions, and is in any case a fairly new confederation of a number of provincial courts jealous of regional accomplishment. Different centres feature large and splendid city fairs, as at Nuremberg, Munich, Hamburg, Bremen, Frankfurt and so on. Hundreds of lamplit stalls, garlanded with evergreen and often set up near the oldest church or cathedral, sizzle with cooked foods and the region's particular Christmas sweets and cakes for sale among the glitter of more durable presents. Thus Nuremberg offers its *Lebkuchen*, Aachen its *Printen;* the Rhineland offers *Speculatius*, Brunswick is known for fish-cakes, Lübeck for marzipans. There are the *Stolle* and the *Strietzel*, and *Liegnitzer Bomben* and *Thorner Kathrinchen* and gingerbreads called *Pfeffernüssen*. Many of them are moulded into seasonable shapes, both Christian and pagan; and their display in these markets, which are usually held away from motor traffic in a barred-off square, gives a convivial and magical feeling of the best of Christmas atmospheres. The world of machines has receded, the night becomes brilliant with colour – it is a scarf-wrapped, frost-breathed, exhilarating scene far removed from the tiring tread round the big department stores a street or two away.

The Christmas tree is recorded as having originated in Alsace and the Black Forest. But in passing it may be of interest to note that, though it is known throughout the world as originally a German export brought to America and England by immigrants, it also had to be imported into most of Germany. For instance, it took the Napoleonic Wars for Prussian officers to notice the tree on campaign and take the idea back as far as Pomerania – thus as late as the first decades of the 1800s; so that the tree's popularity must have grown at a surprising rate for it to be considered an all-German tradition by 1841, when Albert presented the famous royal tree to his Queen. It is said that Thérèse the wife of Ludwig I introduced the tree into Bavaria; so that the Bavarian industry of tree decorations must similarly have gone forward at a fast pace. The small spruce itself will have been used earlier as a sacred emblem, being so natural a part of the great German forests: it is the decorated fancy in the home which derives from Alsace – and even so, certain seventeenth-century engravings show it not

Origins of the Christmas tree

as a tree but as a gathered garland suspended from the ceiling, thus fortifying a relationship with the English kissing-bough.

The tree, of course, had been reported or brought back by travellers long before those Napoleonic Prussian officers; but one of the reasons for its late adoption generally throughout Germany was its legendary connection with Luther and Protestantism – in itself a bewildering instance of highly decorated Catholicism refusing a rogue gaudiness unusual in the white painted new purist church – and another reason was that certain German districts already had candle-lit tripods or pyramidal frames of wood decorated with local fruits or vegetation: the *Tunschere* of Friesland, the *Klausenbaum* of Bavaria, the *Pyramide* of the Saxon Ore Mountains, were themselves reflected in similar symbolic devices found in many other European countries and expressing ancient magics for the sun's rebirth and hopes for an abundant crop the following year.

German carols — Carols are sung in Germany by choir boys called *Kurrende* or *Quempas* (*Quem pastores laudavere*) or simply 'the Starlings'. Sometimes they sing high in the church tower itself, a mysteriously celestial sound on the still, star-lit frosty night; and sometimes, as we have seen, carols are trumpeted from such towers. The dominant German carol is nowadays '*Stille Nacht, Heilige Nacht*'. It was composed as late as 1818; and late in the day, too, if the story of its beginning can be believed. The tale goes that on Christmas Eve, 1818, the priest of the Austrian village of Arnsdorf, near Salzburg,

Above: *First full score of the carol 'Silent Night, Holy Night',
now in the Hallein museum, Austria*

Opposite: *A part of a painting by Jacob Jordaens of the Bean King's Feast. The crowned king and queen have been elected by finding the secret bean or pea hidden in food such as a Twelfth Day cake*

Overleaf: *The fourteen-pointed silver star, held to mark the birthplace of Jesus Christ in the underground chapel of the Church of the Nativity in Bethlehem*

found that mice had eaten away the cloth or skin of the organ bellows ... yet that night midnight mass was to be celebrated ... so that the appalled and organless Father Mohr took the words of a Christmas hymn he had written to the local schoolmaster, his friend Franz Gruber, and implored him to set this to guitar music so that they should be able to present something special at the mass. Gruber wrote '*Stille Nacht, Heilige Nacht*' in a few hours. It was sung that night of the church-mice to the sole and simple accompaniment of an Italian guitar. Its popularity spread – but slowly. Over a hundred years later the American singer Bing Crosby crooned it to its present world eminence.

Christmas Day itself is a day for the family, and is the quieter for it. But the next day, that of St Stephen, the patron saint of horses, sees a lot of visiting and in some parts parades on horseback. The character of Germany as a federation of many different regions again shows itself, for in fact the whole date position of the twelve days of Christmastide differs from province to province. Silesia, for instance, celebrates the twelve days before Christmas Day; Bavaria and Austria reckon them from Christmas Day to Epiphany; yet in Franconia they begin as late as New Year's Day. Old calendar customs and slower rates of change lie at the root of these differences. Bavaria follows general Catholic practice; Silesia seems to connect curiously with early Teuton yule dates, as in Sweden which stresses St Lucia's Day on the thirteenth of December; Franconia connects with the date of Old Christmas Day and the period of the Kalendae. Dates are dull things; but they well illustrate the strength of the long hangover from ancient times.

Altogether the mid-winter festival period, wherever it is, is dark with old magics and the dressing up and the clamour of devils driving out devils. England and America, apart from American similarities at Hallowe'en, have retained less of all this: the relic is often preserved in rather removed manners, one of which is a gentle passion for paper-hats. There is also a growing popularity of masks, which in the case of England are frequently manufactured in central Europe and imported. Though masks are nowadays among 'the most acceptable festive goods' at Christmas, there are nice lines in bloody faces with an eyeball falling out or the fanged face of the ever-popular Count Dracula. Pretty little animal masks come in handy for private pantomimes put on by dancing schools; and the false moustache and nose is a perennial pleasure whose success is only threatened by new niceties such as stick-on boils, pus-topped.

Sylvesterabend, or New Year's Eve, next comes to pep the German up – a scarcely needed injection – and again there are traditions of divining the future, and again a new child, the New Year, is born. After this, Epiphany – and the village boys are out again as star singers to honour the Magi and put in their pockets a further penny or two. Sometimes they carry a little house inside the star, and in the house their persecutor Herod: the Epiphany miracle plays have died long ago, but the figure of Kasperle in popular German puppet shows is said to descend from the putative Kaspar.

And after Epiphany everybody draws a breath, opens a further door in

Opposite above
Procession of a group of Austrian Glöckler, or bell-ringing-men, on the eve of Epiphany. Bells are worn attached to the costume or carried on sticks, candles are lit in the fantastic tall head-dresses; the ritual intention is to symbolise light and fruitfulness for the new farming year
Opposite below
The three kings singing carols on horseback at a farmhouse in Upper Austria. This is an annual event on the Eve and Day of Epiphany

89

the fancy-dress cupboard, and gets ready to embark on the biggest ball of all, night after night of carnival, when Munich (which has not in any case had much breathing space since the *Oktoberfest*) sings again with beer, and the Rhineland runs with wine and the streets parade with *Sekt*-filled girls in hussar jackets and bare, booted legs, a phenomenon which, like the Christmas tree and so much else, has crossed the Atlantic to reappear in America as that militant musical phenomenon, the drum-majorette.

Christmas in America The whole question of Christmas in America is, in all human terms, of remarkable interest. We have noted that in Germany, where Christmas traditions appear to be indigenous, many were in fact probably imported from elsewhere in early historic or prehistoric times. And now with America there comes a fascinating extension of this diffusion of traditions, the carrying across the seas of a hundred ancient customs, but this time well within historical times – all to a new land but not to a virgin one, for here again were found fairly primitive natives celebrating the seasons in much the same manner as primitive man everywhere.

Added to this one finds in America a very strong split between the usual human divisions of puritan and hedonist. It continues forcibly today, though it is probably more noticeable in America than elsewhere because of the nation's magnitude, because of its sense of public communication, because of an open democratic insistence on straight-speaking and on putting thought into action.

Apart from specific puritan sects and as well as the many quiet family Christmases, whose nature precludes their advertisement, but which are all a legacy of puritan ancestry, there are such solid factors as the day after Christmas not being a holiday – a direct inheritance of the days when observance of Christmas Day itself was forbidden. Against this the hedonist pits the usual proclivity for much eating and drinking, a hugely publicised worship of Santa Claus, and a love for large display as evinced by the size of many civic Christmas trees, each it seems trying to outdo the other, and such colourful set-pieces as the richly confected Californian parades both on water and in parks or the mumming procession in Philadelphia.

It would be superfluous here to reiterate the more usual American Christmas Day; the presents, the tree, the turkey, all diversified many times by imported European national customs where there is a strong enclave of, say, Swedes or Germans or Moravians and others. What is more fascinating is the retention in some places of customs long disappeared from their European parentland – like the highlanders of the Ozark Mountains clinging to the date of Old Christmas Day in January which disappeared in England in the eighteenth century; moreover these hillbillies, while spurning anything to do with such new-fangled conceptions as the twenty-fifth of December, mark their date as the fifth not the sixth of January, maintaining thus another old-fashioned custom of holding the Eve as the most sacred of days.

Then there is egg-nogg, more heard of formerly than now, which is said to be a descendant of the English syllabub, a spiced mixture of wine and creamed milk generally equated with the fifteenth and sixteenth centuries.

The American egg-nogg, which used to be served with free restaurant lunches in Christmas week in the last century, cuts the wine and substitutes hard liquor and with it beaten eggs. A recipe would say: beat up the yolks of a dozen eggs, beat in a pint of brandy (or rum and brandy), add a quart of cream and milk and sugar and spices, before adding the whipped-up whites of the eggs as a splendiferous crown. In a cut-glass goblet with a silver spoon, it is drunk cold and 'is to be commended'. All good hosts had their special ways of adding to this smooth nankeen-coloured drink which put such a glow upon the morning – particularly since, as on New Year's Day, any gentleman of standing, should he still be able to stand, was expected to make of the substantive a staggering fine verb and go 'egg-nogging' round a dozen different houses.

The Old South had its yule-log, called the Christmas log. Contracts between overseers and plantation owners often specified six to seven days' rest for the slaves – it was a time of high revelry and dancing in the quarters – and there was also the custom of allowing the holiday to last as long as the Christmas log burned. While the north had no holiday at all, down south there was no work till the log burned out – so the slaves sprinkled it with water to keep it going; any water-logged tree was, in consequence, known as 'having as much water as a Christmas log.' The southern Christmas is a scene of familiar amplitude and splendour, of old green sheen and brown-basted foods, of wild turkeys and sweet potatoes and sucking pigs and hams and all the gracious delights of a near-aristocratic table, in country of hickory and pine and holly, magnolia and mistletoe. Echoes of the pagan

Turkey-shooting match in the USA, Christmas 1852

sacrifice of the boar sound with hog-killing day before Christmas, and this was when children haunted the kitchen quarters in the hope of getting hogs' bladders, which made fine balloons for the festive time to come. Days too of the great deer hunts, and another form of hunting very peculiar indeed – the 'green hunt', when they *shot* down mistletoe off the trees.

The Christmas hunt Always a lot of shooting at Christmas – to men with firearms at hand, it is a pretty obvious and powerfully pleasing way of making a noise and adding to the excitement. Still – it is again an echo of old European beliefs that noise frightened away all those evil spirits which, like the winter darkness threatening the life-giving sun, were whipped up and flying abroad at this critical time of year. Jolly to use your gun, doubly satisfying when it can be done for good reasons of old custom whispering at the back of the mind. The same kind of double reason may have been behind the slaughter of pigs. A pig is not too big – it is a right-sized animal to feed a family or a small community, so that here is perhaps another case of an ancient and traditional custom being the more easily preserved because of its practicability. Man's complicated mind seldom conceives an action from one motive alone. It is also possible – though here one dives deeper into the misty waters of supposition and association – that originally the pig was chosen as a substitute for human child sacrifice because of some vague human similarities – size, smoothness of skin and lightness of colour, those eyes and eyelashes, and generally about the face an appearance more human than that of the long-haired animals. Calves, doves, and other animals like the ram substituted for Isaac by Abraham have all been sacrificial animals – yet it is only the pig which carries this strong traditional taboo. Possibly in the ancient East for hygienic reasons, probably not.

The making of noise by firing off guns is also explained by some as the means by which isolated people communicated, or in other words wished each other a merry Christmas. True, perhaps, of some parts. But it does not seem to be the first motive. There is an account of a traveller visiting an isolated Mormon settlement at Christmas-time, and being woken up on Christmas morning by the sound of gun-fire and shouting and general commotion. Thinking this to be an attack by the Utah Indians, he ran out into the adobe compound – only to be reassured by his host and that man's three wives that it was only the young men of the settlement ushering in the natal day. In this case, they would hardly have been sending a Christmas message to anyone else. Similarly, there was a tradition of noise-making in Kentucky which seems to be a direct descendant of all those European bands of semi-demons who went round making a devil's music before Christmas. There were, in Kentucky, young men who dubbed themselves the Callithumpians – assumably from Greek *kalli*, thus 'beautiful thump' – and went round banging anything from a stew-pan to a fire-shovel or a chamber pot to celebrate the bewitching and once witch-filled time of year.

Mormon communities had a rather special father's problem with the Christmas stocking – it is recorded that Brigham Young, in his residence of the Beehive House, had to spend some time before Christmas superintending the wrapping up of present bundles for his many children by different

'Red Man and Mountain Man
Keep Christmas', from Christmas
on the American Frontier
1800–1900, illustrated by Charles
McLaughlin

wives. The Mormons were no dour people – though they abstained from alcohol and stimulants like coffee, they celebrated Christmas with brass bands and balls. But everywhere Christmas was a good excuse for dancing, from the southern slaves' quarters to the cowboys' Christmas ball with its fiddles and polkas and scottisches, which is still held, for instance, at Anson in Texas. In early pioneer days, when Indian children were invited in to see the Christmas tree and were given extra food, they were found on one occasion – but one, obviously, of many – dancing round it, stamping and whooping in the familiar manner of ceremonially excited braves.

American Indians were accustomed to the idea of giving among themselves, though the habit was prompted less by ideas of charity than the more usual human one of raising prestige. They had, too, often a sacred tree upon which they hung gifts – though this was not a Christmas but a spring festival tree. A tribe in North Dakota would each year plant a young cedar near the big medicine lodge. Children brought gifts of moccasins, pelts, shawls and so forth to hang on the branches of what was called, simply, Grandmother. In the autumn, Grandmother was uprooted and set afloat on the Missouri river for her long journey into the Great Beyond.

It was recognised, of course, among the Indians that the pioneers' Christmas was a big occasion. It came to be called by tribes The Big Eating. By others, in districts frequented by French trappers, who kissed each other as they exchanged gifts, it was known as Kissing Day. The sense of occasion was also stimulated by the acts of missionaries: there is a record, among many occasions of multiple baptism, of a Belgian missionary in the Pacific northwest who on Christmas afternoon of 1844 united fifty or more couples in marriage. Some of these brides and grooms were over eighty years old – a Christian wedding thus becoming almost the concluding rite of a long life.

Much has already been said of the mimetic dressing up and ceremony of the horned gods and priests of early European religions, the pre-Druid antecedents of what were later considered to be witch-cultures. But among the American Indians, such disguising and ritual were found in full living swing. Among the Pueblo Indians a great 'buffalo' dance was recorded – at Christmas fifty Indians dressed as animals of the hunt, as bison and mountain sheep, deer and antelope, entered a mission and to the energetic beating of drums danced their mimetic ritual, their loving obeisance to the animal which they must kill to live, for fifteen minutes before going on to prayers in the Council Room. The dance is still performed at San Felipe Pueblo.

Night Fire in Isleta, near Albuquerque

These are the same people who, when introduced to church, either knelt down or stood by the wall, thinking it irreverent to sit in the presence of God, and thereby echoing unconsciously the early scene in all European mediaeval churches and cathedrals, which originally never had a chair. At Isleta, near Albuquerque, where Christmas is known as Night Fire, the Indians light bonfires in plaza and churchyard, and place on the flat roofs of their houses lanterns at night and paper bags filled with offerings to the Child Jesus on Christmas Day. A Christmas tree is placed on the altar in church. And here again primeval patterns recur, with a scene in church loosely reminiscent of the Provençal mass at Les Baux. There is no lamb, but there is the same kind of atmosphere when the Black Eyes, a group of Indian dancers, come to the crowded church at Isleta. First a space among the pressed, excited people is cleared by six red-blanketed men, white spots painted on their cheeks, who hold aloft candles of announcement. Then at the door a choir is seen, with drums: and there enter twelve dancers, men and women equally, who dance to and fro the altar. Rattle-shaking. Drumming. And then – just as at distant Les Baux – each one goes to kneel and pray separately to the figures of the Virgin and Child set up in readiness, and afterwards, one by one, ritually retire.

It was also in New Mexico, in a pueblo church, again near Albuquerque, that in 1851 an American surgeon, Ten Broeck, noticed small animal dolls like European yule doughs and heard an orchestra of a truly remarkable pantheist kind. First, he saw that the men and women in their buckskin clothes and red blankets each went up to the priest carrying some small something and stayed for a time in mysterious converse. It turned out that they carried little mud or dough images of their domestic animals or the beasts they hunted – images of the most successful of each during the past year, so that they should be blessed by the Great Spirit in the hope of a good and fertile year to come. Then, at a climactic moment in the service, Ten Broeck heard a marvellous sound of birdsong fill the church, echoing among the rafters, swelling round the walls – the warblings of a multitude of birds, among which he distinctly heard above the general orison the note of the wood-thrush and the trillings of the canary bird. It was as if all nature filled the little church, and glancing round for a reason behind this miracle, he noticed a small gallery at the back of the church. He went up.

I there found fifteen or twenty young boys lying down upon the floor, each with a small basin two thirds full of water in front of him, and one or more short reeds perforated and split in a peculiar manner. Placing one end in the water, and blowing through the other, they imitated the notes of different birds most wonderfully ... I believe I was more pleased with this simple natural music than I have ever been with the swelling organs and opera-singers who adorn the galleries of our churches at home.

Indians might have noticed a falling off of trade at Christmas-time, at least a temporary disappearance of the currency with which they were paid – coloured beads paid in Indian trade were used for decorating Christmas trees, along with such economical devices as gilt paper taken from cigar boxes and stars cut from yellow soap, a nicety noted in Minnesota in 1860. Of early Christmas trees, one of the most peculiar was that specified in an announcement in the York *Gazette* of December 1823. The text was headed *Society of Bachelors*, and this is what they had to say:

… the Old Maids have determined to present us with at least one cart load of Ginger-cakes the society in turn therefore intend fixing Krischkintle Bauhm for the amusement of such as may think proper to give them a call. Its decoration shall be superb, superfine, superfrostical, schnockagastical, double refined, mill' twill'd made of Dog's Wool, Swingling Tow and Posnum fur; which cannot fail to gratify taste.

This, and those later stars of yellow soap, suggest an earlier involvement with plastics and artificial Christmas trees than we usually assume.

Accounts of Christmases long ago always make fascinating reading, and in America, where climatically and historically there have been so many different kinds of celebration, from the palmy feasts of Florida to embattled times in the besieged stockade, from the frozen Alaskan north to the backward Appalachians where the old English Cherry Tree Carol was heard long after it was elsewhere half-forgotten – the whole terrain is naturally various, and so also, irrespective of climate, is the human incident. There are many famous episodes, such as General Sherman's telegram to President Lincoln on Christmas Day 1864 which contained the words: 'I beg to present to you as a Christmas gift the city of Savannah.' But life at a less heroic level went on everywhere, producing such professional dramatics as the Christmas appearance in Baltimore of a Mr Eggleston, the American Voltigeur, who ascended high on the 'Corde Volante' to suspend from a rope a pyramid of five men, and, not content with that, proceeded to swerve from rope to rope through five burning balloons, drawing from each such extraordinary *trouvés* as a flaming dragon, a live monkey, a live snake. A Happy Christmas to you, Mr Eggleston, you are remembered. As also may be the two gentlemen who chose the Christmas Eve of 1843 for a duel of honour. Of all the great accounts of duels, from Chekhov to Sacher-Masoch, none seems to comment on the pathetic human condition so poignantly as this long-ago American moment when, at eighty paces, the two men of honour raised their rifles. Two shots were fired. Only one bullet struck home. However, it neither killed nor wounded either adversary. Yet the two men stood transfixed by a more icy horror than either could have conceived. For from the face of one, a large part of his enormous whiskers had been shot away. … A flesh wound would have been acceptable – but not this offence to dignity. And one must remember that it was for dignity that duels were fought. At length both gentlemen, heartbroken, embraced; and parted 'not in anger but in tears'.

However, it is always to the picture of snow that the yearning Christmas-

*Anecodotes of
American
Christmases*

95

loving heart returns, snow is the sentimental necessity – and here again one finds a dream-picture from the always-so-good old days. In 1855 the scene is painted with pleasing simplicity, first day, then night:

If the weather should be fine, the principal streets are thronged with ladies shopping in sleighs; and hither and thither sleds shoot by, laden with parcels of painted toys, instruments of mock music and septuagenarian dread, from a penny trumpet to a sheepskin drum.

'Girls, get on your fur; wrap yourselves up warmly in the old bearskin; hunt up the old guitar; the sleigh is at the door, the moon is beaming. The bells tinkle and away we go!'

Pity then the poor muskrat trappers of the *prairie tremblante* area beyond New Orleans. They expect no snow, of course, but indeed still today they expect no Christmas at all until the spring. It is a time when the three-month hunting season is on, and they must be out with traps and lines, living in houseboats or huts on stilts, in the marshland of the Bayou du Large. Nevertheless, this small community still insists on having a Christmas at the end of February or the beginning of March, when in spring weather they bring mangroves, vines and palmettos into church and for their homes contrive a Christmas tree of a wax myrtle from the marsh, decorated with Spanish moss and the usual trinkets and sweets.

The Mummers' parade in Philadelphia

One factor has hitherto been left out – the ebullience of American enterprise and the national love of enlargement together often transform the traditional scene. For an immediate example, the parade in Philadelphia of New Year mummers (as opposed to 'bummers', which was an old derogative for children who only turned up once a year at Sunday School, at Christmas and for a gift). As we have seen, many of the older states continued the ancient Christmastide mumming and masquerading traditions, dressing up and going the rounds with fireworks or shooting or other noise. This grew so wild before the turn of the century, for instance in Baltimore, that the shops and stores, once delighted, were simply despoiled; police had to bring restraint and the whole custom declined. But its modern equivalent can be seen in Philadelphia in the enormous, organised, devised, staged procession called the Mummers which marches through Philadelphia on New Year's Day; it is so large that it takes all day to pass by the City Hall. Apart from the fancy dress and comic and heroic costume, there are well over a score of 'string bands', magniloquent affairs manned, for instance, by girls high with ostrich feathers and playing saxophones. It is a big show. It is a million miles away from the very personal, home-to-home junketings of the traditional American mummers, like the Fantastics of Savannah and those Callithumpians, straight descendants of other masquerades dating back to dateless times long before the oldest Saxon church was built, long before the Romans, long before to the days of the darkest old religion. But still – in Philadelphia it is a big show.

Similarly those giant municipal Christmas trees are big, at times well over two hundred feet all; and the thousands of lights which illuminate them and go stringing across great bridges – these are all on a big scale. The Rochester Twelfth Night bonfire is big, with the sanitation department

playing Santa Claus in reverse and collecting everybody's old Christmas trees put out on the kerb for the mass burning. The Californian conception of Forty Miles of Christmas Smiles, a competition for the best Christmas decorations and lighting, is big – with entries such as 'Santa's sleigh pulled by sea-horses'. In Newport Bay a lighted Christmas tree takes to the water on a barge; and, boasting of being the 'Lowest Down City of the Western Hemisphere', Calipatria in Imperial Valley strings Christmas lights up its 184 foot flagpole reaching to sea level. On the large side too, one may put the Cleveland boar's head ceremony held in Trinity Episcopal Cathedral, a procession after the Oxford boar's head ritual which in Cleveland involves five choirs and over a hundred performers dressed as shepherds, beefeaters, woodsmen, yule boys, Wise Men, heralds, knights and so on. Meanwhile Williamsburg fires off its doughty cannon the day after Christmas, a sound louder than any St Stephen's Day hunter's rifle but again a moment of revered tradition.

However, all the artificial enlargements of this large-minded large land pale beneath a natural gift – the winter migration of some four thousand Californian grey whales bent on celebrating their own Feast of Light and Fertility by choosing this time of year to swim from the Arctic to breeding waters in the Mexican sun. These giants pass monstrously close by the coast around Los Angeles at the rate of some thirty a day. Such a visitation could scarcely be ignored – in fact it is consciously used as a kind of prize of size by an official South Californian publication announcing December and Christmas attractions. Among all the other parades, parades of yachts and floats and film stars and stars of Bethlehem, it is known as The Parade of Whales.

The diversity of the American Christmas The American Christmas must not, though, be left on this note alone – the real note is one of great diversity, remembering how still today in North Carolina there is a steer's head and a sheet which goes flapping about with two men inside and known as Old Buck, again a millennial legacy of the horned religion; and remembering that in and around New Orleans there remain the French influences of serenading and *le grand boeuf*, a great ox paraded on the streets with holly on its beribboned horns, brief days of glory before the slaughterhouse; and that an echo of the old Scandinavian *Julklapp* story is found in the tale of Major Jones of Georgia, who wanted to present himself to his love as a Christmas surprise and spent the night in a meal-sack on her porch – anyone wishing to emulate the Major should remember to shave himself 'slick as a smoothin iron' to be at all presentable on Christmas morning, to take sea-sick pills against the sway of the wind, and to include some form of dog-repellent, for the house-dog hardly left the gallant man throughout the freezing night.

Remember, too, that parts of America were so immaculate in their retention of the old Celtic first-footing custom that to ensure the first entrance of a dark-haired man after midnight on New Year's Eve, some southern people employed a Negro; and in extension, if a young man saw a red-headed girl at this time of year, he should take to his heels – otherwise, said an ambiguous superstition, red-heads would be after him the long year through. While in the Spanish south plays of mediaeval origin are still enacted to depict the journey of the shepherds to the manger, battling on the way with all the devils in hell, including a once topical redskin in buckskin. And a most interesting moment of masquerading was known until the end of the century in Carolina, when Negroes dressed up in finery and masks and beards and horns and called it 'John Canoeing' or 'John Kunering'. Kuner-face was the word for a mask. Why such a word? It seems that the port of Wilmington was in frequent contact with Jamaica and the Bahamas, where there was a similar tradition based on the name of a man of gaiety called John Connu back on the African Guinea Coast. Could this, and not the more usually supposed racoon, be the origin of the derogatory term 'coon'?

So in endless diversity it goes on ... coffee and buns in church for the Moravian love-suppers ... in Virginia a yule-log and a libation of wine, and holly thrown on the log to sizzle up as departed troubles of the past year ... and odd extra demands on the turkey, like an old-fashioned calico-bagged wing for a hearth-brush ... all capped by the North Carolina people of Rodanthe, who insist on retaining Old Christmas Day as well as the 'new' date, and for whom thus Christmas comes *twice* a year, with Santa Claus, gifts and church services on the December date and January the fifth spent in an all-day serenade with Old Buck at night, a black stocking pulled over the face as a mask, and a Merry Christmas dance and roasted oyster feast among the driftwoods and winter winds from the wild wet wilderness of the Atlantic.

5

Giff-Gaff

Now, Dasher! now, Dancer! now, Prancer and Vixen!
On, Comet! on, Cupid! on Donder and Blitzen!
CLEMENT C. MOORE

In his *English Proverbs*, John Ray puts the question of gifts with a blithe Scottish sound. 'Giff-gaff makes gude friends,' he says. But later adds: 'Giff-gaff was a good man, but he is soon weary.' This is echoed down the centuries, and has a peculiar relevance to one kind of Christmastide gift. As that most fetchingly arch of columnists, Priscilla of Paris, wrote in 1922 in her letter for *The Tatler*: 'Well, I'm ... *bothered*, B'lov'dest! When there was a whole fortnight to run before Christmas, and yet the petit *télégraphist*, the *facteur*, the *"imprimés"*, the so-ons and so-forth were wearing out stair-carpets and 'lectric-bell-bat'ries in order to demand *étrennes* ...'

Thus France, and these worrisome seasonable tips deriving from the Latin *strenae*, originally gifts of branches from a sacred grove and of those dolls and candles exchanged during the Saturnalia and Kalends. England knows the same as Christmas 'boxes', a word said to be derived from a money-box once carried around by tradesmen and by collectors for charity. Until the latter part of the nineteenth century the adult exchange of gifts did not go beyond special foodstuffs, a Stilton cheese or a barrel of oysters, which was in line with a general opening of the purse-strings for festive and charitable purposes down the centuries. But this was very different from modern present-giving. The exception has always been for children alone. There is a nice feeling of a nineteenth-century boy's feelings about his presents in *The Real Diary of a Real Boy*, written reminiscently by 'Plupy' Shute, Henry A. Shute, and published in 1902. It tells in a boy's

own words of a Christmas shortly after the American Civil War. The diary first explains itself: 'Father thot i aught to keep a diry, but i sed i dident want to, because I coodent wright well enuf, but he sed he wood give $1000 dolars if he had kept a diry when he was a boy.' And the pertinent entries run: 'December 25. Crismas. got a new nife, a red and white scarf and a bag of Si Smiths goozeberries. pretty good for me. December 26. Crismas tree at the town hall. had supper and got a bag of candy and a long string of pop corn. Mr Lovel took off the presents and his whiskers caught fire, and he hollered o hell right out. that was pretty good for a sunday school teacher, wasent it. Jimmy Gad et too much and was sick.'

Santa Claus and the gift-bearers   The whole history of Santa Claus and the other magical gift-bringers is of weird and changing variety. In Europe the principal gift-bringers are St Nicholas on his saint's day of the sixth of December; his Anglo-American descendant Santa Claus; dwarfs and goats in parts of Scandinavia; the Christ Child of the Teuton Christmas Eve; the white-robed girl Kolyada who in pre-revolutionary Russia arrived by sleigh on Christmas Eve with attendant carol-singers; and the Epiphany gift-bearers associated with the Magi – like the Befana of Italy, old Babouschka again of old Russia, and the Tres Reyes Magos of Spain.

To begin with, Santa Claus. He is a fused creature, half St Nicholas and half an ancient yule god. St Nicholas himself was a bishop of Myra in Asia Minor in the fourth century. On Mediterranean voyages he miraculously stilled and created several storms, and so became the patron saint of sailors: his relic is housed in his church at Bari on the Italian Adriatic Coast, where his day is kept with much marine splendour. However, the good bishop has also become patron saint of maidens, since legend says that he saved the three daughters of an impoverished father from probable prostitution by giving each a quantity of gold for dowries with which to marry. He is supposed to have thrown the money in bags through the window – hence the stylised balls of gold he holds in his hand and hence also the three balls outside a pawnbroker's shop, for St Nicholas is honoured as

The landscape of winter. A seasonal detail from Pieter Bruegel's 'Hunters in the Snow'

patron of pawnbrokers and bankers too. Now this familiar sacred number of three also reverberates into a further legend told of the bishop, and introduces his immediate connection with children. Three boys were murdered by an innkeeper, cut up, and the pieces preserved in barrels of vinegar. St Nicholas found these soused truncations, fitted them together with a prayer, and brought the three results to life again. Hence the association with children. And, via the maidens, with the giving.

Now the good St Nicholas was not only well-wishing. He, and certain other versions of the Christmas gift-bringer, had, and sometimes still have, an accompanying servant with rods to punish naughty children. There is a relic of this figure in a few Germanic families in America, who keep up the figure of Pelznickel, or Fur Nicholas, a once terrifying figure dressed in furs, now become more jovial. And in Holland, say, where St Nicholas becomes Sante Klaas, children put out a pair of shoes or clogs filled with hay, water and carrots for the Saint's white horse: these are placed *before the fireplace*, and the next morning the shoes are found filled with either sweets and little presents – or birch-rods.

Holland, being a seafaring country, expects the Saint to come by ship. And by ship from Spain – an echo of the Spanish occupation of the Netherlands. In Amsterdam, for instance, he does indeed arrive from the sea fully accoutred in mitre and robes and accompanied by Black Peter in the puffed and plumed costume of Spanish Armada days. He lands to the music of brass bands, mounts his white horse and is welcomed by the Queen at her palace on Dam. In many households, parents and friends dress up as the saint and his retributionary servant. Then he makes a real and individual appearance; and he always impresses the younger children by already knowing all about their behaviour. Along with this, there is a giving of larger presents, often disguised by several wrappings each with a different name on it, or delivered by some strange servant or passer-by – any device to make the gifts the more surprising: though today this latter custom is often transferred to Christmas Eve.

Apart from the Christian benevolence of the saintly Nicholas figure, his arrival via the chimney seems of some antecedent significance. Who else ever went in and out by the chimney? Early hearth-gods and gods of the yule-log: and witches, devotees of the old and earliest religion of the horned god only much later made into a satanic or mephistophelian Christian devil-figure. These people used to absorb hallucinatory drugs when they greased themselves all over before a sabbat. Their ointments contained drugs like belladonna, for instance, which gave them the inward impression of flying, which they themselves recounted later to others (not under torture, which came a very long time later when witch-hunting became organised). Carrying broomsticks as props for the cloth of their Hodening horse or other animal costume, the conviction grew that they 'flew' on these broomsticks. And leaving the house by the chimney, as we have seen, was no more than climbing through a low hole in the roof. So Father Christmas or St Nicholas came flying too. It is notable too that he, or his equivalent gift-bringer at Christmastide, is the only *named* figure of a magical nature

St Nicholas and Black Peter

generally known to the children's and grown-ups' worlds; the others, fairies
and demons and ghosts of the risen dead, are less frequently given names, or
their names are either regional or have disappeared completely. Father
Christmas though, has remained solid in his invisible way: and this happened long before the expedience of commerce enthroned him.

Such, then, is the other facet of his character. He is partly benevolent
bogeyman. But benevolent? Possibly not always. New attitudes of kindness
to children have progressively dropped the dark companion and birch –
the American Santa Claus figure never had them at all except for the Germanic Pelznickel. But what further complicates the situation is that there
has always been a varying male yule-figure at Christmastide or mid-winter
festival – sometimes like a Silenus, sometimes a hoary old man, his head
often wreathed with mistletoe or holly, his gown varying in colour, white,
red, green or fustian brown. He may be a relic of the Saturnalian feast-king
or even of Druidical priest-kings. In a part of Switzerland we find a red-
robed Father Christmas in the company of, and sometimes said to be
married to, the female figure of St Lucy – a remarkable wedding of ancient
vegetation deities.

If, as some suggest, this old man of Christmas is a later impersonation of
Saturn – who ate his own children – then he is also allied to the Carthaginian Baal-Hammon, a ram-horned male god to whom children were
sacrificed. This is the same Baal which possibly gave rise to the horrid but
persistent myth, so much revived during pogroms, that Jews ate children.
The devil of course was also Beelzebub, Baal (Lord) of the flies. From this
branch of ancient history there may have developed the Saturnalian custom
of exchanging gifts of little dolls, possibly emblems of human sacrifice,

which in time became the little Christ Child dolls of later Christian ages. Nothing is clear – how should it be? But much can reasonably be suspected.

In Germany, the gift-bringer has become the Christ Child, a figure substituted during the Reformation for the goodly St Nicholas, who smelled too much of Roman incense. The Christ Child is supposed to be a messenger appearing on behalf of the newly-to-be-born Jesus, and is thought of as a girl. Still in some homes a female member of the family dresses up in white or grey, with golden wings and a pale veil over her face. She is supposed to enter the room containing tree and presents through the window: when the mysterious shut door is opened and the children are ushered into her presence, they feel the cold winter draught of the open window and see this pale faceless figure and the impact indeed is mysterious and memorable. Christmas-time in Germany is usually very cold, and houses often have double windows: nowadays, when the habit of dressing up is dying out, the window is still left open and the tale goes that the Christ Child has just left. The impact of *mitteleuropäischer* cold is quite enough.

In the USA the *Christkindl* became verbally slurred into *Kriss Kringle*, and also changed shape into a Father Christmas figure. In parts of Switzerland the Christ Child passes through the snowy streets on a sleigh drawn by small deer. It is very likely that this pretty conception, which cannot logically be the holy child born the next day but must be his representative on earth, was originally a wood spirit connected with the great German fir-forest atmospheres, a spirit represented nowadays by the fairy or angel on top of the Christmas tree. On early Christmas trees, there was a large picture of the Christ Child or a big dressed doll figure propped in the bottom branches of the tree. In passing, it is casually noteworthy that the frontispiece of the very first number of *The Strand Magazine* (January 1891) shows a white-nightied and wreathed Christ Child figure carrying a

The Christ Child, by Thomas Nast, 1889

'To "Absent Friends"', from Punch *during the Boer War, 1900*

Frontispiece of the very first Strand Magazine, *strangely captioned* 'Santa Claus'

Christmas tree through the woods. No explanation. Yet this was in England, which had never known the Christ Child.

In Spain, Christmas Eve is a day of devotion, with a long, late feast after the midnight mass. Christmas Day itself is spent in sleep or eating: the giving of presents must wait for the Three Kings who are supposed to pass by every house in Spain during the night of the fifth/sixth of January. Children again put out shoes, but now on the balcony or window-sill, and fill them with straw or barley – this time for the tired camels to the Three Kings: the Kings respond by leaving gifts. Together with many other Spanish influences, like bullfighting and various cuts of peasant dress, the Three Kings have established themselves in Languedoc and western Provence. Mistral and the Félibrige poets recall their presence in moving accounts of the Provençal little alpland of lavendered limestone.

Italy, too, waits for Epiphany before the giff-gaff begins. The bringer is traditionally the witchy woman figure called Befana, a corruption of Epiphania. Her legend is an unhappy one: at the birth of Christ she was told by the shepherds of the marvellous happening, and directed to the star of Bethlehem; but she delayed setting out, missed the star, and forever after wandered in search of the holy child, leaving gifts at each house in the hope that it contained the Christ. Part thus of the 'wanderer' myth, like the Jew and the Flying Dutchman, the Befana also joins the company of benevolent witches, using the traditional chimney as her point of entry. Italy also has big fairs for Christmas gifts, as in the Piazza Navona in Rome, whose beautiful fountains become a cynosure of Epiphanous wares and decorations; and one hears that the Roman traffic policeman mounts high on a deluge of present-day *strenae* donated by motorists with a local interest in his goodwill.

France is divisible, with Italian and Spanish influences in the south, with an importance of St Nicholas on the sixth of December in parts of eastern France, and with Paris, for instance, adopting the figure of Père Noël who arrives via the chimney, or at some nodal point such as the tree or the all-electric hearth.

In Sweden gifts are supposedly brought by a gnomish Father Christmas figure, *Jultomten:* but there erupt also a number of miniature elfin figures called *Julnissar.* Porridge must be put out to placate them. There used to be a spectacular and surprising manner in which gifts were delivered, the *Julklapp.* The gift is disguised in wrapping upon wrapping, and thrown into the house through an open window (unlikely at that season) or delivered at the door by a stranger. There is a record of one desirable lady who received, mysteriously, a very, very large *Julklapp:* when finally unwrapped, it contained her suitor. This tradition persists here and there in some country districts: but the urban Swede has substituted an even harder task – every present must be accompanied by personally written dedicatory verses, the longer the better. A few families in Sweden are now revolting against the plethora of present-giving, and in future are giving less, and then only things which they have made themselves, a return to nineteenth-century manners when people designed their own Christmas cards and genuinely and personally created the Christmas atmosphere.

The process of giving continues in much variation round the world. In Syria the camel of Jesus brings the gifts to the children; in Harlem, New York, a black Santa Claus has been seen distributing white golliwogs; in Finland the present-giver has been known as the great Ukko, an old man in a cap and furs but uniquely with no beard, only a long white moustache – possibly a Mongolian influence; in Poland a traditional mother star brings gifts, and in Hungary children look to the angels; in Mexico, and for instance, in parts of Arizona, where earthenware is cheap, a *piñata* or large decorated vessel is hung up and blindfold children beat it with sticks until it breaks, showering them with nuts and sweetmeats. Nevertheless in recent times the technical advance of image-communication and the international nature of commerce has seen the jovial, generous figure of Santa Claus appearing in many of these countries where he was never known before. Let us for a moment examine his own beginnings, how the nineteenth-century figure of this Santa Claus first evolved in America, before his export to England and variously to Europe, and gradually in these days to South and Central America and elsewhere.

He came first to New Amsterdam with the Dutch, as the old benevolent bishop Sante Klaas. The Dutch were a merrier lot than the puritan English, who retained their severity long after the Dutch had established their own tradition of the Catholic saint in his mitre. However, it was not until the early and middle nineteenth century that one poem and one artist popularised a new amalgam of the old saint and a more ancient elf-figure deriving from northern Europe. In 1822, on the twenty-third of December, a Dr Clement Clarke Moore, professor of divinity, recited to his children verses he had written for them as a Christmas treat. They made up a poem which he called *The Visit of St Nicholas* and which was published, anonymously, a year later in *The Troy Sentinel*. The public took it immediately to its heart.

'Twas the night before Christmas, when all through the house
Not a creature was stirring, not even a mouse;
The stockings were hung by the chimney with care,
In hopes that St Nicholas soon would be there;
The children were nestled all snug in their beds,
While visions of sugar-plums danced through their heads;
And mamma in her kerchief, and I in my cap,
Had just settled our brains for a long winter's nap, –
When out on the lawn there arose such a clatter,
I sprang from my bed to see what was the matter.
Away to the window I flew like a flash,
Tore open the shutters and threw up the sash.
The moon, on the breast of the new-fallen snow,
Gave a lustre of midday to objects below;
When what to my wondering eyes should appear,
But a miniature sleigh and eight tiny reindeer,
With a little old driver, so lively and quick
I knew in a moment it must be St Nick.
More rapid than eagles his coursers they came,
And he whistled and shouted and called them by name:
'Now, Dasher! now, Dancer! now, Prancer and Vixen!
On, Comet! on, Cupid! on, Donder and Blitzen!
To the top of the porch, to the top of the wall!
Now, dash away, dash away, dash away all!'
As dry leaves that before the wild hurricane fly,
When they meet with an obstacle, mount to the sky,
So, up to the house-top the coursers they flew,
With a sleigh full of toys, – and St Nicholas too.
And then in a twinkling I heard on the roof
The prancing and pawing of each little hoof,
As I drew in my head and was turning around,
Down the chimney St Nicholas came with a bound.
He was dressed all in fur from his head to his foot,
And his clothes were all tarnished with ashes and soot;
A bundle of toys he had flung on his back,
And he looked like a pedlar just opening his pack.
His eyes how they twinkled! his dimples how merry!
His cheeks were like roses, his nose like a cherry;
His droll little mouth was drawn up like a bow,
And the beard on his chin was as white as the snow.
The stump of a pipe he held tight in his teeth,
And the smoke it encircled his head like a wreath.
He had a broad face, and a little round belly
That shook, when he laughed, like a bowl full of jelly.
He was chubby and plump, – a right jolly old elf –
And I laughed when I saw him, in spite of myself.
A wink of his eye and a twist of his head
Soon gave me to know I had nothing to dread.

He spoke not a word, but went straight to his work,
And filled all the stockings; then turned with a jerk,
And laying his finger aside of his nose,
And giving a nod, up the chimney he rose.
He sprang to his sleigh, to his team gave a whistle,
And away they all flew like the down of a thistle;
But I heard him exclaim, ere he drove out of sight:
'Happy Christmas to all, and to all a good-night!'

Thereafter there was no stopping this 'St Nick'; and finally Thomas Nast, in *Harper's Illustrated Weekly* of 1863 and onwards, began to draw his conception of the figure invented by Dr Moore, and named it *Santa Claus*. Now observe this figure – it is very different from our present-day conception of Santa Claus. He is clad from neck to toe in what looks like a combination suit made of woolish fur. He had a short round hat possibly of mink fur. In the hat, a sprig of holly and mistletoe – remnant of the ancient wreath. Moreover, he is a smallish elfin or gnome figure, rotund, red-faced and grotesque. What he does bring to our present-day conception are the white whiskers and beard, and the sleigh and reindeer team. Previously the gift-bringer in Europe had come by horse or by various other means, from camel to goat-team. Washington Irving had put him up in the skies in a wagon in 1809, and there had also been one magazine article mentioning reindeer. But here is the first full popular reindeer team, apposite transport indeed for a figure coming from the North Pole via Canada. There is little doubt that this figure was the first real popularisation of Santa Claus, and owed by then only the name to St Nicholas himself. Nast was the son of a Bavarian, and Santa Claus's whiskers have a German upturn in Kaiserly fashion. But all in all, poem and drawings marked the beginning of today's Santa Claus as surely as the Christmas writings of Washington Irving and Charles Dickens established other atmospheres and traditions.

And the reason for the poem's popularity? First, as always, the time was ripe. A myth was needed, and the recreation of 'old Christmas' was well in

'*Santa Claus waiting for the children*
to go to sleep', *by Thomas Nast, 1889*

the wind. The poem itself is notably realistic, and this is probably its great success – the reindeer hooves scratch on the rooftop tiles, the winter moonlight and weather are well described, the atmosphere of the father up alone in the house and secretly watching is immediate. And the character of this twinkling fat gnome from the skies is sentimentally attractive.

Nevertheless the figure has changed through the years: for now the American conception of Santa Claus is red-suited and has a cap with a red point to it and a tassel like a snowball: while the English Father Christmas has a red hood trimmed with white fur. Whence, then, the English hood? We must go back to Germany and there it is in the early nineteenth-century engravings of Moritz von Schwind, who drew a hooded figure of Winter walking the streets as the Christmas Man. This snowy figure, his hood wreathed with leaves, is much nearer to the British Father Christmas than Nast's elf in fur combinations. The differentiation is still reflected in the present-day stock of a London theatrical costumier who hires out 'Father Christmas' outfits of hood and long robe and 'Santa Claus' outfits of suit and cap; they stock over forty of the first, only nine of the latter.

It has been a long and complex merger: one still finds as late as 1900 illustrations in *Punch* of the old holly-wreathed pagan figure of 'Father Christmas'. But the outcome has today become solidified by societies for the retention of Father Christmas, by organised charities and commercial interests, and by such a phenomenon as the town of Santa Claus, Indiana. How the town became so named is still disputed, but its industry is beyond all doubt. At Christmas-time hundreds of thousands of parcels pass through

'The Christmas Tree', from a painting by E. Osborn, 1864

its post office to be mailed with the local postmark. There is a college for department store Father Christmases run on psychological lines (candidates pass out with a BSC, Bachelor of Santa Clausing), and there is a Santa Claus park dominated by a giant brightly painted granite statue of the gift-bringer himself and furnished with all manner of other Christmas atmospheres, like a drive-way of firs called Christmas Tree Lane, candy and ice-cream castles, toy shops and a toyland and a deer park.

The Santa Claus college issues a pamphlet describing the correct dress and various niceties of deportment. One learns among much else that the good man's whiskers are often made of yak hair, and that one must always whiten the eyebrows to blend with this flowing shag. It is inadvisable to stuff a pillow down the front to give the proper portly appearance – a two-inch foam rubber layer is recommended as more convenient. A list of sensible do's and don'ts for the expectant Santa Claus suddenly pulls one up with: 'Don't fall asleep while on the job' and then follows the dark admonition: 'Don't accept money from a parent in front of a child.'

Rules for the perfect Father Christmas

It could have been no BSC from this college which produced a recent Santa Claus in a London store. When, after visiting this gentleman in red, a little girl asked her mother, 'And what did Santa Claus give *you*, Mummy dear?' mother said, 'Nothing, of course.' 'Then why did he put his hand in your pocket, Mummy dear?' '*Wha-a-t?*' And thus the mother found her purse was missing, and Santa Claus, on being searched, was found to have no less than fifteen purses distributed about his capacious and festive garment.

Today so many uncles and dads are shoved into red-and-white at Christmas-time, and so many others appear ringing bells and rattling boxes at street corners, particularly in America, that children have to be told they are really Santa Claus's *helpers*: the great man himself can only be admitted to in special isolated circumstances. And, of course, his empire of gifts has swollen to include everything under the winter sun, including such vital necessities as the gold-plated lavatory seat noted a year or two ago in a Dallas department store. The flood of gifts has become altogether so immense that a new tradition is now growing, particularly in the USA, of exchanging your Christmas gift at the store afterwards without shame: in fact, you are almost expected to do so. This indeed eliminates a sad and secret device known to many homes in the past, the 'present cupboard', where last year's unwanted gifts queue up for redistribution in the following December. But the new exchange tradition must naturally reveal the price: and this, of course, stimulates a dollar snobbery, or a dollar penance, in the giver. Nevertheless it is some improvement on a much earlier situation, where in the slave-owning countries Christmas could cause the appearance of such advertisements as: 'To be sold, a little mulatto, two years of age, very pretty, and well adapted for a festival present.'

Apart from Santa Claus and his character as the free giver, there remains another tradition of those who demand gifts, like the Christmas-boxers and demanders of *étrennes* we have already noted, and like several others, the star-singers and wassailers and devil-figures scattered across Europe. In

A silk-fringed Christmas card published by Louis Prang of Boston in 1888. Prang's company was the first large American supplier for the domestic market

Wales, children used to make a device called the *calennig* for New Year's Day. This consisted of a wooden framework topped by an apple or orange, and decorated with frost or floury snow. It was taken round from house to house, and pennies demanded – a straight descendant of pagan gifts given to ensure fruitfulness in the coming year. Carol-singers we well know: and we have seen how in many European countries the star-singers go round after Christmas and towards the date of the Three Kings; and others dressed as furred and grotesque demons make jovially hideous the nights of December, snapping their jaws and rattling money-boxes.

As to the original Three Kings or Wise Men – their legend follows in principle what would always happen if oriental magnates visited an important god; they would make propitiatory offerings. Gold, frankincense and myrrh are in nature magical gifts – gold the sun mystery, frankincense the smoke-maker with sacrificial associations, myrrh a substance of medical magic. It is necessary also to remember that no mention of 'three' visitors is made in the Testament, and that they are called not kings but Wise Men or Magi; the assumption of three seems merely to have followed the mention of three kinds of gift. One early oriental source numbers the Magi as twelve, a familiar magical figure again. The Magi came from Persia, where Mithra came from: and where priest-astrologers were men of great authority and would have travelled with the appurtenances of kings, or rulers of some of the many diverse territories of that time. From the word 'magi' we get our 'magic': but nobody exactly says where these particular magicians came from – one simply assumes some kind of Persian territory; and it is only a much later assumption that one of them was black, another young, another old – and that their names were Balthazar, Caspar and Melchior. Some sources say, for instance, that they were called Galgalath, Magalath and Tharath. What we know as a star in the east might have been for the travelling Magi a star in the west or north-west as seen from the east. Or it might have been a generalisation of Venus, the morning star, heralding a new day and thus new hope. The interest of the Magi in a star at all suggests their priestly rather than royal character. It was always customary for the birth of a god, or even of a hero, to be associated with a sign from the heavens and the seat of the mystical zodiac. The contrivances and fusions of legend are mixed: one can probe the mystery from innumerable angles – from a viewpoint of some modern scholars that the gospels were never written as 'truth' but as comforting statements of the fulfilment of Old Testament messianic prophecy; or one can take Michael Harrison's suggestion that the details of the nativity are intimately tied with the zodiac, with Taurus the Ox and a de-horned and thus de-devilled Capricorn as the ass in the manger; and Virgo as moon-goddess; and, since the solar and lunar haloes were known in Akkadian as 'sheep-folds' or shepherds of the stars, hence the presence of the earthly shepherds.

This is a far cry from the attitude of a convinced believer who once wrote to the Press dismissing all scientific investigation and curtly affirmed that of course the star was simply the light given off by a multitude of angels.

However, whatever the beginnings of the Magi, whatever the motives and ancient magics, we have a powerful legend and now a new priesthood of the Press careful to keep alive their tradition of giving. The following famous letter was once received by *The New York Sun*:

DEAR EDITOR: I am 8 years old. Some of my little friends say there is no Santa Claus. Papa says 'If you see it in *The Sun* it's so.' Please tell me the truth; is there a Santa Claus?
VIRGINIA O'HANLON.

In the editor's reply, he wrote:

... Not believe in Santa Claus! You might as well not believe in fairies! You might get your papa to hire men to watch in all the chimneys on Christmas Eve to catch Santa Claus, but even if they did not see Santa Claus coming down, what would that prove? Nobody sees Santa Claus, but that is no sign that there is no Santa Claus. The most real things in the world are those that neither children nor men can see. Did you ever see fairies dancing on the lawn? Of course not, but that's no proof that they are not there. Nobody can conceive or imagine all the wonders there are unseen and unseeable in the world. ... No Santa Claus! Thank God! he lives, and he lives forever. A thousand years from now, Virginia, nay ten times ten thousand years from now, he will continue to make glad the heart of childhood.

But not necessarily the hearts of older persons, if the pertinent parts of a letter from Anton Chekhov to his brother may be taken as any sort of guide:

December 30, 1894, Melikhovo
My Lord!
... I have not yet received the cigars and don't need your gifts. When I get them I'll throw them down the toilet ...
Three days ago I was at a Christmas party for the insane, held in a violent ward. Too bad you weren't there.
Since the New Year will soon be with us, may I wish your family a Happy New Year and all the best – as for you, may you see Beelzebub in your dreams.
The money has been given to the French girl, the one you liked so much, in payment for your immoral conduct with her ...
All the best, sir. Is everyone well, my good man?
Your, sir,
A. Chekhov.

'*The Coming of Santa Claus*', *by Thomas Nast, 1889*

6

The Decking and the Cards

Get ivy and hull, woman, deck up thine house.
THOMAS TUSSER

In a deciduous world, the evergreen tree demonstrates permanence. To a primitive mind its summer-looking leaf in winter would have suggested strange powers, as if it contained the sun within itself: and of all the evergreens, certain species, such as holly and ivy and mistletoe, bear recognisable fruit only in winter, a triumph of fertility over the elements. Small wonder that these should for as long as is known be brought into the winter house as symbolic magic of hope for a fruitful year to come. Small wonder that the fir-tree, whose cones do not look that succulent, should have been decorated with substitute fruit first in the form of paper flowers and gilded nuts and apples and nowadays with coloured balls of tinsel.

Today the Christmas tree in the home, originally, as far as we know, Alsatian, is the most universally popular of Christmas decorations – though it is well known that it was the last of the evergreens to be generally adopted as a tradition. It was not recorded in England, for instance, until the very end of the eighteenth century, and only popularised after the 1840s when the Prince Consort Albert introduced it into the Royal Family. It was essentially an import from Germany, first known among immigrants in the Manchester area. But America had it long before from German settlers in the mid-eighteenth century and from Hessian soldiers during the Revolution.

The story has it that Martin Luther was so moved by the brightness of the stars on a winter's night that, to simulate something of their effect, he set candles in a little tree of his own brought inside the house. A pleasing

Opposite: *Three crib figurines believed to be soldiers of a bodyguard. From the Cistercian Priory, Birnau, on the German side of Lake Constance*
Overleaf: *The front of the golden shrine (c. 1300) which encloses the bones of the Three Wise Men in Cologne Cathedral*

tale, and one which thereafter connected the idea of the tree with the Reformation. Nevertheless, it cannot be properly substantiated, and as far as the hard record goes, the first decorated trees in the home were noticed in Strasbourg in Alsace in 1605. That is, proper trees – in many European instances there were and still are pyramidal erections of wood, decorated like a tree with candles and fruit. In some cases these were carried from house to house with a request for money, much like the Welsh tripodal *calennig* at New Year. It is possible that these pyramids were an economical substitute for trees, since they could be used year after year, as in Saxony and Berlin; but possibly they were also of older origin, and simply missed the record. Large single decorated 'paradise' trees were sometimes carried round in Germany for display, or used in mystery plays, before the seventeenth century; but this does not necessarily suggest a home-decoration habit. It is also likely that north European tribes from the *Tannenbaum* forests will have held the tree sacred in earlier times – but again there is no exact record. Certainly there is a universal myth of a protagonist tree – Yggdrasil the ash in Norse mythology, Dodona's oak among the early Greeks, the Indian Bodhi tree, and Eden's tree of knowledge.

Before the arrival of the Christmas tree we know, it was a general custom to bring into the house small potted cherry or hawthorn trees, or branches water-potted, so that they might bud at New Year or Christmas. This echoes the legend of the Glastonbury Thorn, supposedly planted by Joseph of Arimathaea and supposed to flower or 'blow' on Christmas Day. It is a *biflora* which did and does in fact sometimes flower on Old Christmas Day – the sixth of January – the extra dozen days often reaping a climatic advantage at that time of year. And it is in line also with the wide lore that all nature is transformed on the eve of Christ's birth.

Precursors of the Christmas tree

Before this, one has the older Roman custom of decking the house with branches for the Kalendae of January; and in unromanised northern Europe with fir-branches, since these were both the reasonably available evergreen and also the emblem of the mystery of woods and their gods. In Greek Chios, an old and perhaps ancient custom was to take around a pole wreathed with myrtle and olive and orange leaves. Elsewhere the Circassians, for instance, carried a young pear-tree into their houses at autumn, topped by a cheese and covered with candles – and these autumnal traditions, as we have seen, were often moved forward to Christmastide. All in all there is much precedent for this Christmas tree which came to the Anglo-Saxon world so late, but whose popularity grows yearly and is reflected in the giant trees set up nowadays in civic centres, particularly in America, and even in the illuminations of oil-well machinery with coloured lights in the branched form of a tree.

One Victorian pleasure of the tree is quite lost to us: the sweetmeats and fruits with which it was hung remained there until the dismantling after Twelfth Night. Only then could they be eaten, so that once again the day of dismantling, so sad for present-day children, was the joyful climax of Christmastide and a moment to look forward to.

Children for a long time have thought of the Christmas tree and toys in

Above: *St Nicholas arrives in Amsterdam on the sixth of December. He comes by boat and transfers to a horse thought to be a legacy of the white horse of Odin*
Below: *Santa Claus in Harlem, New York*

Left: *Design framing the royal Christmas tree, 1848*
Right: '*The Mother on Christmas Eve*', *by Ludwig Richter*

one long and scarcely bated breath. In Germany, as Hoffmann of Struwwelpeter fame shows us, the toys beneath the tree lay under the charge of a slightly sinister wooden figure called King Nutcracker – Hoffmann, the director of a 'nerve-clinic' in Frankfurt, noticed that his rather frightening illustrations were greeted by children with 'squirms of half-fearful delight'. However, before the advent of toys the aforesaid gilded nuts and fruits and gingerbreads were the only decorations, together with a representation of the Christ Child angel; the fruits evolved only later into Victorian glass shapes to be used year after year, and the Christ Child into a fairy or star instead of the angel-figure. Today these have become our modern and frangible tinsels, while for the old angels' hair of gold and silver thread there is lametta representing the illuminated sparkle of ice.

Candles came to the tree later than the fruits, and since then have led a chequered history. In the very frozen north, when the first Christmas trees were presented by missionaries to eskimos, the candles thereon happened to be made of deer tallow and were accepted with some gusto as an edible windfall. In the torrid opposite of Australia, candles bent themselves double in the benign heat of the sun, and became a formidable fire risk. In Victorian times in Europe and America, muslin dresses and long hair made many a macabre blaze; and fire brigades knew the Christmas tree to be one

Illustration by Theodor Hosemann from E.T.A. Hoffmann's
Christmas story, Nutcracker and Mouse-King, *1844*

of the most dangerous fire risks at a time when candles were in any case the most prevalent cause of fires – particularly, official records show, the candle used to look under the bed for burglar or chamberpot. It was thus a triple busy time for the brigades: the Christmas burglar was a seasonable visitor; too much wassail sent the hand searching far more often for the other bowl; and there was the Christmas tree alive with the flaming tongues of dozens more dangerous candles.

Today's electrically lit tree is a safer matter. And the production of non-inflammable non-resinous plastic trees has exported the safely false fir or pine to climates where previously imports of the real thing were dry and doubly dangerous, and often a palm tree would be used instead; or where, as in Hawaii, the same substitute tree was painted white as snow. Brown bodies dancing round white trees, palms hung with fairies and northern ice – the disappearance of such delights is another loss to be laid at the door of the plastics industry. However, Hollywood still manages to mix matters, with houses in Beverley Hills gaily mounting giant illuminated fir-trees on roofs engardened by tall palms; and by spraying trees blue, red, gold and even black.

In the days before the Christmas tree, the kissing bunch was the nodal decorative point particularly in English and early Anglo-American households, and we see its relic in the bunch of mistletoe most people still put up at some point of passing advantage. The origin of the kissing is obscure – possibly a gesture of peace, possibly a sacrificial echo of some kind: but one certainty is that this is one Christmas custom nowadays peculiar to Britain and places influenced by the British, and not echoed in other European countries; with the exception of a Sylvester figure in Austria, the mistletoe-wreathed old man who lurks to pounce and kiss, though he indeed is more in line with the devil-figures who in many countries try to kiss any available maiden as part of their general licence.

The kissing bunch or bough was constructed of two hoops tied to make a global framework which was much decorated with holly and ribbons. Apples, oranges and other bright fruits were added: and in the centre, by candlelight, were placed the figures of the infant Christ, Mary and Joseph. In fact, a pendant and illuminated miniature crib scene. Beneath this was hung a sprig of the baleful mistletoe.

Mistletoe has the curious history of being both a killer and curer. The Druids used it as an all-heal: country tradition has since fed it to sick cattle and also used it as a human medicine. Yet in the old Baldr myth its wood was used to make the dart Loki threw to kill the beautiful god: a similar inheritance has passed into the Christian myth, many believing that the Cross was made from mistletoe wood, which thereafter as a plant shrank with shame to its present size. Because of this superstition, or some say because of more ancient Druidical connections, the plant is ordinarily banned from the Christmas decoration of churches; however its kissing myth has made it so popular in modern house decoration that in New York

Above: *An English kissing bough, engraving by Joan Hassall*
Right: *'Suggestions for a Christmas Day Costume', 1868*

green mink mistletoe has been on sale at the expected kind of price and advertised as 'For the man who has nothing – but money'.

Meanwhile the missel-thrush runs a mortal race with its favourite plant, feeding on berries which would otherwise be collected for staple use as a birdlime. And while old Culpepper recommends mistletoe in powder form as a cure for 'the falling sickness' (epilepsy), modern pharmacology warns that the berries are purgative, emetic and even ecbolic: while in larger doses the whole plant is a cardiac depressant – fickle end to a kissing-device.

Traditional Christmas plants

Rosemary was the most prized of Christmas decorations until the mid-nineteenth century. It is a casualty, one would guess, of the more brightly-coloured brilliance of the Christmas tree. Apart from its scent and its purple prettiness, rosemary was 'for remembrance'; it was also used to decorate and flavour the traditional boar's head. Now it has gone. As has gone the Rose of Jericho, whose dried leaves and flowers unfurl when moistened – once favoured as a monkish conceit to symbolise the opening and closing of the womb of Mary. Then there were the sumptuous, almost edible green and white flowers of the Christmas rose. This white felicity, known to botanists as the black hellebore, was again popular until the mid-nineteenth century, when Christmas rose farms supplied in bulk a first-flowering of winter flowers, 'star of fertility sprung from December soil'; its close follower, the snowdrop, though often too shy to bloom until February, used to be called 'Candlemas bells' and formed a bridge between Christmastide and early spring decoration.

Ivy and laurel, yew and bay are seldom seen nowadays, except to make the holly spin out in churches and large halls. Perhaps connotations of Bacchus, poison and death have put ivy and yew into disfavour, perhaps easier communications have made holly with its bright red berries more available – but however it is, holly, slow to grow but sturdy when it has taken, holly of the good shiny leaf, is the staple favourite today. Its thorn, together with the redness of its berries, has attracted to it associations with Christ's Passion; in Denmark, for instance, it is known as *Kristdorn* or Christ Thorn. It has, too, always been used as a protection against witches, who are held to hate it. Holly has always been known as the man's plant, ivy as the plant of woman the clinger: the two were represented in early carols in a kind of sex-battle for mastery of the house – 'Holver and Heivy make a grete party'. In these mounting matriarchal years one might have foreseen a return of ivy; but, of course, it has already crept in, potted, all the year round.

Red is cheerful, and that is the main thing. If the year is berryless, then plastic berries are available at the twist of a finger. In fact, the whole bough can be plastic, and since it is usually placed above eye-level, there seems little argument against this. Except pharmacologically: for only a century ago 'holly tea' was still recommended as a cure for such ills as measles and whooping-cough, and the berries were thought to alleviate rheumatism, gout and asthmatic complaints. Culpepper has the ripened red berries as a purge for gross and clammy phlegm. Before, however, the phlegm stage – if it be brought on by surfeit of wine – he recommends yellow ivy berries 'before one be set to drink hard'; and recognises an antipathy between ivy and the grape-vine which can be put to use as a pleasing hair of the dog with a handful of bruised and boiled ivy leaves in the recuperative wine-glass. Alternatively, ivy leaves boiled in vinegar can be applied locally, front and sides, for a headache. But that is Culpepper in stirring, hard-riding days: let us remember that holly berries are narcotic and make for vomiting, while ivy berries are gastro-irritant and the leaves poisonous. Meanwhile, a few million Argentinians tango along quite happily on the high caffeine content of maté tea, which is made from holly leaves. Better a cup of this on Boxing Day than the ivied risk of atropine poisoning.

Catholic countries have preserved and developed the most ingenious of all Christmas decorations, the crib. We have seen that the crib's antecedents may be looked for in Saturnalian doll-making, and that in Protestant England there was a minor survival in the three figures in the kissing-bunch: otherwise the only vestigial trace during the nineteenth century showed in the Advent box, glass covered and containing one or two holy dolls, carried from house to house in some parts towards Christmastide – though again these dolls might have been direct survivals of an earlier vegetation-spirit cult. Catholic churches, of course, continue the crib tradition as a direct inheritance, while many of the reformed churches have chosen to adopt what is both a pretty idea and also a pleasant preoccupation for human hands usually happy with the making of model scenes, hands nowadays too often starved of an excuse to do so.

Popularisation of the crib tradition

Giotto has painted a representation of St Francis and what is usually held to be the first popularisation of the crib at Gréccio in 1224. St Francis used a live ox and ass round a contrived manger, and a moving mass was celebrated with the night lit up as day, the woodland ringing with voices, while 'the rocks made answer to the jubilant throng'. St Francis is recorded as uttering the word 'Bethlehem' in the manner of a sheep bleating, and in naming the Child Jesus 'he would as it were lick his lips, relishing with happy palate and swallowing the sweetness of that word'. If this account of Thomas of Celano's is objectively true, it suggests much of the new humanity St Francis brought to his religion: of the same nature, though on a more glorious theme, as present-day instances of bringing what is now the human homely jazz idiom into church music.

Historically there are references to a *praesepe* long before the occasion of Gréccio: both in the eleventh century, and indeed earlier at the fourth-century church of Santa Maria Maggiore in Rome, a church especially devoted by Pope Liberius to the new festival of Christmas. However, it does seem that either St Francis did first popularise the *presèpio* or that his time was particularly suited to such a human conception. Thence the tradition grew hugely, in homes as well as churches, and even a few reformed German churches followed suit. The vast affairs to be seen in the major collections at Munich and Naples came into being. Members of the Neapolitan court of Charles III were ordered to busy themselves in creating what became more and more involved and rich Nativity scenes. Other Italians and southern Germans and the rest of the Catholics followed suit, and the ultimate result has been a diminution of the manger episode within a large display of life as lived at the time of modelling. Whole castles and villages and country-sides and towns were constructed, showing every variety of ordinary human pursuit – say, a baker at his oven, or ladies passing in powdered wigs; soldiers on guard, a peasant fishing in a river; anything that suggested the way of daily human living, for the underlying impulse was realism, so that the little Jesus of Bethlehem should be brought personally home to German frost and Italian arcades. Worship of a godhead became delight in a child. The custom long ago crossed the Atlantic to Latin America and, of course, to the United States, where it flourishes aptly and partic-ularly as the Putz among the Moravians at Bethlehem, Pennsylvania.

The attraction of the older cribs is often in their paradox: that Bethlehem should appear as a much detailed and a beautiful Italianate city, a dream of pediments and ionic capitals in classical grey; or as a mediaeval village of half-timbering with a castellated fortress aloft. While the best is good art, the main province of the crib is the lesser one of human ingenuity and pain-staking art-craft. The sacred message becomes largely lost in the love of model-making, so that today there are those cribs from Latin America and Africa showing tanks and dive-bombers, beloved evidence of the modern scene, with the Child of Peace still being born somewhere around in his rather minor manger. However perverse this may sound, it does imply – though without this intention – that Christianity lives on in the death-dealing world. But even more than that it shouts aloud that daddy is down on the nursery floor again, playing trains.

Page from a collection of folk-songs, by Emil Ludwig Grimm, 1806–08

One German custom allied to the crib tradition deserves remembering, the *Kindelwiege*. This was a cradle set up in church and containing an image of the infant Christ. One after another the congregation came up and rocked the cradle to the tune of a waltz-song, or rather a three-four beat round-song prior to our exact conception of the waltz, while the rest danced round. Such dancing was in no sense irreverent: the idea of God was a simple and glad one. One notices an echo of this ease of manner in the reasonable talk and laughter of Italians in church today, or of Jews in synagogues; and even, in muted form, among the very regular church-goers of Protestant churches.

Crib figurines were once for sale in the manner of toy soldiers: the home crib could be dismantled, and reconstructed the next year, and the figures used over and over again until they were broken. Not so the general Christmas greenery. Most of this should traditionally be burned. Exceptions were a branch or ember of the yule-log, always preserved to kindle next year's log: also the mistletoe should be preserved, and the rosemary, whose 'memory' association gave it the property of keeping young anyone who smelled it. Holly had to be burned, or fed to the cows. Yet ... what else would you do with it? In Sweden, where burning is difficult in the snow, there is no such tradition. As with most superstitions and traditions, one may look for a practical cause: and a bonfire is final, the imagination plays pleasantly with regret at the end of so much that was beautiful. Or, perhaps, in earlier heathen terms, wood-spirits brought into the house were liberated by such a fire.

In the eighteenth century and before, when there was much panelled wood, wooden furniture, wooden beams and bare floorboards, the effect of the living green against so much brown grained wood must have brought a formidable feeling of the outside tree-world inside the house. Today, and as from the late nineteenth century, the greenery has been overlaid with a papery impression – with streamers, paper chains, crackers, and large areas of propped up greeting cards. The growth of paper production techniques has coloured the scene with an air nearer to carnival – though one might search for an allusion between streamers and the coloured ribbons beloved of mummers and witches, and stretch the search improbably far. Similarly with crackers: certainly they go bang and could be associated with other fire traditions like the yule-log and the candle, but in fact they arrived because the French invented a *bon-bon* of sweets, with no banging device, which could be pulled apart. The bang came later, in England. Paper chains are nearer the traditional mark, in that they do represent garlands. But the adoption of most new decorative devices for Christmas will most likely have occured simply for a gay effect, with possibly only a contributory unconscious sense of their aptness.

It is the same with Christmas cards. Neighbours had always exchanged good wishes at Christmas and the New Year, but it took the development of a more efficient postal system to spread these wishes to friends and relatives in other towns and villages. Eventually this required too much letter-writing even for a good early Victorian; and so, in the 1840s, the Christmas

OVERLEAF
Left above
The first Christmas card of all, designed by John Calcott Horsley for Sir Henry Cole and dated 1843
Left below
The Presidential Christmas card for 1967 showing a Christmas tree and chimney-piece decorations in one of the rooms in the White House in Washington
Right: *A prize-winning Christmas card in a competition set in 1882 by the American lithographer and card-publisher, Louis Prang*

Opposite: *A painted roundel of the Adoration of the Shepherds from the Rosary Altar in the Cathedral at Überlingen, Lake Constance*

card came into being. Previously there had been sheets of writing paper decorated with Christmas themes – but these too necessitated a personally written message, as also did the specially engraved sheets of paper used for 'Christmas pieces', those laborious examples of handwriting required of children returning from school for the Christmas holidays. There were also all-purpose anniversary cards printed, into which the sender could write the word 'Christmas', and this was the nearest to a specific Christmas card before the generally accepted first card came to be designed by John Calcott Horsley in 1843.

The first Christmas card

The Horsley card was drawn at the request of Sir Henry Cole, an energetic reformer and a busy man, who had the card printed to save time on his own Christmas letters, but was prompted also by his interest in furthering the expansion of the postal system itself. George Buday, in his standard *The History of the Christmas Card*, records that not more than a thousand copies of this card were sold at one shilling a copy: but discusses in detail the runners-up for the honour of being first, such as W. M. Egley whose design is similar in many ways to Horsley's but whose own records finally state that his was the second card, designed in 1848. Both cards showed convivial scenes set in rusticated and ivy-leaved frames, with subsidiary vignettes of charitable gifts for the poor; only Egley introduces holly.

New Year cards had been printed for many years before this. Examples such as those by Johann Endletzberger in the City Museum of Vienna show austere classical motifs and no yulish greenery. The addition of Christmas coincides with its general early Victorian revival. Still today the written Christmas message includes the New Year, and of course the two occasions

The Piazza Navona in Rome at Christmas-time. The piazza is devoted to a notable Christmas market which culminates at Epiphany

were habitually thought of together. Historically Christmas Day officially began the New Year until as late as the thirteenth century: and today the twenty-fifth of December still marks in England the first day of the new legal quarter-year. Many Catholic countries still do not send cards with Christmas greetings, only formal good wishes for the New Year.

The Christmas card industry

The published Victorian Christmas cards did not achieve immediate popularity. People still went on decorating their own visiting cards, or appended 'scraps' of colour print in the approved manner of people accustomed to home accomplishments. The commercial production of cards did not begin to accelerate until the mid-Victorian 1860s. Thereafter, advances in the techniques of printing and of the postal service and the stimulation of commercial interests have seen the distribution mount to the tremendous total of today, which runs into thousands of millions. In the United States cards were not so very popular until the lithographer Louis Prang began producing them in 1875. Later, cheaper cards were imported from Germany and elsewhere in Europe. The first American Christmas card was produced much earlier, in the early 1850s, in the form of an advertisement for 'Pease's Great Varety [*sic*] Store in the Temple of Fancy'. The figure of Santa Claus and people pleased with their presents formed much of the illustration, with a Negro servant laying the Christmas dinner table. Horsley's first English card, though it was attacked for its depiction of drinking, nevertheless carried a strong pictorial message to stimulate charity for the poor: it has taken over a hundred years for Christmas cards to return to this first endeavour – but now in the more practical measure of manufacturing cards specifically for sale on behalf of charities.

Christmas cards have always had either a religious or a sentimental character. Often there have been mildly humorous cards, and cards introducing laughable new habits or machines – but never does this overstep an ordinarily convivial or genial mark. The 'sick' or ironically destructive Christmas card is exceptional, whereas other forms of 'sick' printed greeting, like birthday cards and Valentines, have in recent years proliferated. This is really remarkable. It shows indisputably the strength of the sanctity of Christmas – with a million tongues wagging against over-commercialisation, no one seems prepared to laugh at it all outright in terms of the printed card. Perhaps this year, the next? If it occurs, the change will be significant.

The variety of Victorian Christmas cards was enormous. Not only were they printed on paper, but dressed with satin, fringed silk and plush; they were gilded and frosted; they were made in the form of fans, stars, crescents and many other shapes; they were embossed and they were jewelled; they were made to stand up, they were made to squeak; and they illustrated anything seasonable from a fireside scene to a giant snowball, a skating session to a frosted church, from comic animals to the well-known stage-coach (it is said that the prevalence of the snow-bound stage-coach dates from hard winters in the 1830s and 1840s, which disrupted stage services in a manner unforgettable for many years to come). Holly and robins and snowflakes, mistletoe and trees and puddings, bicycles and balloons and

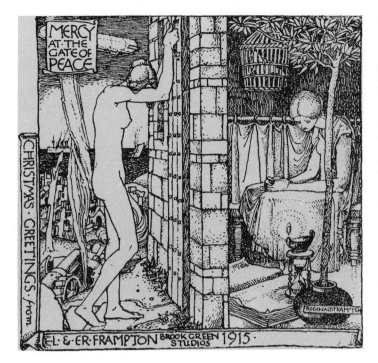

Left: *Christmas card produced at Brook Green Studios*
Right: *Christmas card designed by Aubrey Beardsley*

railway engines and pretty girls all got mixed up in every conceivable manner to celebrate the seasonable compliments. Birket Foster, who etched snow and the winter scene with such deep feeling, must have had a strong influence in preserving traditional winter atmospheres: but Art crept in on its own and with its capital A, and many cards later on had a summery or spring-time or simply floral look – a 'beautiful' picture became an ideal beyond any portrayal of Christmas flavours. Artists varied from Kate Greenaway to Aubrey Beardsley. All kinds of trick cards came in: personal silhouettes, cards you turned sideways or upside down to find a concealed meaning in the drawing, triptych cards opening on unexpected scenes, cards which could be set up as models; cards made of what looked like a treasury note, with apposite greetings, and cards like cheques – there is a beauty drawn on the Bank of Blessings, Unlimited, Blissville, in 1907. But they are beyond verbal description. With one exception – a series of late Victorian cards showing dead robins. The reason for this seems to be a mixture of the traditional slaying of a robin or wren over the Christmas period mixed with a new compassion for birds killed by sharp December weather. The series was very popular. Raphael Tuck's 'Silent Songster' of the 1880s was imitated by several other firms later. But as George Buday points out, the inscriptions accompanying the dead robin are indeed mysterious. 'Sweet messenger of calm decay and Peace Divine' and 'But peaceful was the night wherein the Prince of Light His reign of peace upon the earth began.' Possibly a card sponsored by a Nonconformist religious sect? Possibly some forgotten drive against the country killing of robin and wren?

'Sentiments' have always meant the making or breaking of a Christmas card's popularity. People choose cards as much for the words as the picture, and one may indeed watch today how in the shop a customer *reads* one card after another, very usually a customer who has never otherwise glanced at a line of verse the whole year round. What is appropriate becomes of some extraordinary vital importance. Could one imagine oneself saying these words? What would so-and-so think of me saying this? Even – will so-and-so *like* this? So that the difference between, say: 'Peace and love and joy abide/In your home this Christmastide' is very seriously weighed against: 'A happy, happy Christmas/A merry, bright New Year,/How sweet the kind old greeting,/To every heart and ear'. But reading through a pile of these, one begins to realise the real importance of what otherwise may seem absurd nuances and niceties.

The Christmas message

Many special cards appeared during wars and at other times of national stress. Humorous sentiments always had a side popularity: a good instance is an American card of the 1880s featuring an ebullient bewhiskered and angel-winged stockbroker whose verse reads 'I hope you will not think it strange,/If I fly from the Stock Exchange,/To bring to you the news surprising,/That all the New Year bonds are rising!' But sincerity and plain speaking, coupled with a certain euphony, usually win through. Buday quotes as perhaps 'the biggest selling sentiment ever made' an American prose text framed in holly which read: 'I am thinking of you today because it is Christmas, and I wish you Happiness. And tomorrow, because it will be the day after Christmas, I shall still wish you Happiness; and so on clear through the year.'

Nowadays verses and 'sentiments' are invited from the public, and also written by fairly full-time professionals who cover the whole year's varied greetings, Easter and birthday and Valentine cards and all the rest, and may write perhaps up to sixty or seventy trial verses a day, with a selected printed output of several hundreds a year. Christmas card verses have become more definitive, addressing 'Dear Husband' and 'Mum and Dad'. There are dog-to-dog cards and cat-to-cat cards – 'Hoping you have a purrfectly lovely Christmas'.

The upshot of so much industry has turned most sitting-rooms at Christmas into minor versions of the shops from which the cards came. Robins, coaches, churches, snowmen, Kings and Madonnas and many an abstraction of non-figurative art or what you will – not only is the traditional chimney-piece covered but people have had to begin pinning them to ribbons and running them up the wall. The whole thing has spread outrageously, the business world has added to it all with the good wishes of firm to firm and management to employee.

Appalled by the cost, trouble and apparent superfluity of the Christmas card agglomeration, more and more people have begun to insert newspaper messages that no longer will they send out cards but instead give the money

St Francis is held to have first popularised the presèpio *or crib. Here he is seen officiating at the initial Nativity performance at Gréccio, near Assisi, in the painting by Giotto*

to charity. Social changes produce small side difficulties: with a greater frequency of divorce, cards signed by simply 'John and Joan' present a new problem – which John, which Joan, and are they still together?

Meanwhile new social awareness has brought the great charity organisations for the relief of sickness and want into the card business; and many smaller individual charities are following suit. Naturally enough the printing trade and the Christmas card shops are not too pleased about this; but they do pretty well all the same, and hopefully few subscribe to the sentiments of a shopkeeper, interviewed on television, who was asked whether his complaint against charity cards was not mitigated by feelings of peace and goodwill at this time of year. 'Peace and goodwill?' he said with a jolly laugh. 'Those are things of the past. Business is business.' That may not look so earth-shaking in print but it was indeed shocking to see a human being saying it and believing it; not only cruel but also stupid, in that his very business was based on dispensing these sentiments.

So boards of card and papery things drown the old greenery: and new materials, gilt paint, coloured waxes, bright viscose ribbons flash a further new character into a scene which can now indeed be sprayed all over with plastic snow. Altogether the ingenuity of Christmas decoration increases each year with the greater general public interest in all decoration and home display. Now people want to improvise – and elements like pineapples, autumn colourings and spring flowers are vitiating the traditional scene in just the same way as they entered into the Christmas card illustration lists long before the turn of the century. 'Cut feet from old nylon stockings!' an editorial says, 'and stuff with tissue paper to make continuous cascades of swags ...' There will be no end to it.

Crackers have never ceased their appeal: only their insides are changing. The objects contained in nineteenth-century crackers or 'cosaques' included such felicities as a bottle of hair dye, a flexible face, a fountain of scent, a harp and a night-cap. Today, smaller objects of plastic drop out – but still the paper hat, relic of old misrule, retains its popularity particularly in England and America. A lugubrious face under a many-splendoured cap is a familiar national joke. It never fails to look extraordinary; but the Christmas tradition accepts it as ordinary and few refuse

Above: *The parcel department of a cracker factory, 1891*
Opposite: *A tinsel angel made about 1900 in Thuringia. Now in the German Toy Museum at Sonneberg*

it. When one remembers that moment after the Christmas dinner when such hats are put aloft, and the eyes are down with Japanese flowers expanding in a glass, and the nose smells the pungent smoke of those little pyramids you light to make brown wormy snakes, and all around is the close world of crackers and their paper messages – 'Have you ever heard the story of the two wells? Well, well.' 'Why is the word kiss spelt with two s's? Because it takes two to complete the spell.' 'Where were the first doughnuts fried? In Greece' – and everywhere there is the glint and feeling of crackling coloured paper, the floor still strewn with gift wrappings from the morning … then this high peak of the papery moment is really more reminiscent of the turkey-fed fullness of the Christmas feast than any holly and mistletoe of old.

It is outside in the streets that lights and greenery predominate. Holly wreaths on front doors, Christmas trees in front windows like a series of lighted little theatres, large lighted Christmas trees in front of churches and in squares and in America in suburban front gardens. And the main shopping streets strung with fabulous garlands of golden stars and angels, with illuminated papier-mâché reindeer and Santa Claus knows what else. Sometimes it is all done beautifully – as in New York and the ranks of lighted firs along Park Avenue, as in Altadena in California with its unique avenue of giant blue deodars, and as in Washington with the national Christmas tree near the White House, lit personally by the President's hand – though if he is elsewhere, then via the mysteries of remote control. But often the matter descends to a fearsome low level of vulgarity. Nevertheless, it brings to large towns each year larger traffic blocks of families 'in to see the decorations'. And where, after Twelfth Night, do these costly baubles go to? One reads of at least one case when the Oxford Street decorations in London turned up much later in Kuala Lumpur to decorate Mountbatten Road for an Independence anniversary.

The selling orgy The ever-increasingly arrant display of gifts and foods at Christmas-time has come in for much criticism; 'unbridled' becomes the popular epithet of horror, and people who normally seldom give a thought to the Christian story suddenly shake their heads at such a selling orgy at so solemn a time of year. But of course the orgy would not exist without their initial demand. Yet in spite of these strictures there are treasurable moments – on the whole, shops do look brighter and gayer and exciting, and at certain hours like four o'clock on a dull winter's afternoon the yellow lights and the glittering colours merge with a damp brownish smell of winter pavements to remind many of their childhood, of the particular excitement of parcels and home-for-tea by a warm fire and preparation for all the great things to come. And one may ride home through streets of Christmas trees glowing with yellow and red and green lights, and find urban nature imitating art in the same two or three colours of the traffic light standard. A glance at the heavens shows an airliner passing with the colours again aglow, red, green, and yellow-lit windows – at such a time dazzled by it all, such a reflection high in the dark sky seems grotesquely comforting and right.

The Christmas shop-display exhibition in such a centre as London takes place in early May. There, with the chestnuts blooming in the parks –

other candles ghostly on other trees – a sweating Santa Claus presides over stalls marketing prototypes of decorations to come, plastic holly, witch-balls, electrified stained glass windows, golden reindeer and snow, snow everywhere. Snow will be manufactured throughout the hot summer months, and in the list of goods suggested one finds 'icicle curtains in Gold Silver [*sic*]', 'Polystyrene cut-out 3-D "Three Kings" unit', and among trees a 'Pure White Chevron-cut Tinsel. An unusual tree'; also a sad little note, worthy of Hans Andersen, 'A discontinued tree at give-away prices'. The poinsettia, Christmas flower of the tropics, is found in red velvet or satin; and there are 'Glass Fibre Bambis'. It is all a highly organised business; as efficiently conceived as our modern version of the Christmas candle, that traditionally large affair supposed to burn throughout Christmas Day – now it is sold with stained glass windows let into the sides, and known as Instant Church. Meanwhile early in the summer months advertising agencies begin considering their Christmas press campaigns, and magazines start to confer on the make-up of Christmas numbers. In America, in the very first days of January, the spirit of next Christmas arrives with a kind of super-phoenix of a Santa Claus effigy and the message 'Join Our Christmas Club NOW'.

The growing of Christmas trees has become an industry in itself. In America the balsam and Douglas fir, the hemlock and the Scots pine are most popular, while the British favourite is the Norwegian spruce. Spruce is a corruption of the word Prussia, where these trees were first named, but now plantations in such an area as Scotland alone contain well over 100,000,000 spruce trees: many are sold rooted, but there is also a big market for the tops of plantation thinnings which at other times of the year are simply left to rot for humus. As with turkey farms, there is some attempt at organised theft each year: but the police are organised too, and include tree plantations in their 'turkey runs', while forestry keepers keep a night and day watch with dogs and radio.

The Christmas tree industry

And all this great greenery, all this effort must come down after Twelfth Night. Once, unforgettably, I saw this happen after a Twelfth Night dance held in a Women's Royal Navy station. The station was a building on the dry land of a north London suburb. At some appropriate and grimly early hour a middle-aged lady officer strode up to some eminence, a rostrum or dais or something, stood there magnificent on this poop in her three-cornered hat like a well-shaved Captain Bligh of the Bounty, and then, as the music stopped, rapped out a command to the dancing landlocked sailor-girls. Two words only: 'UNGREEN SHIP!'

7

The Groaning Board

Next day Pete was so ill that I had to feed him with chips of ice and egg flips.
ELIZABETH O'CONNOR

In the villages of valleys like the Gurk in Carinthia it is still the custom to slaughter a pig on Christmas Eve. This is not eaten whole but made into special fresh sausages which are eaten at convivial suppers after the midnight mass. It is only one instance of the continuance in many parts of Europe and their American counterparts of what is thought to have been an ancient sacrificial ritual; though now, of course, simpler and tastier thoughts occupy the minds of villagers returning from church to home across the blue-lit snows.

In the larger community of London, *The Royal Magazine* estimated that in the year 1900 'the turkeys and geese cooked for Christmas would form an army, marching ten abreast, which would reach from London to Brighton'. Where would this gobbling army get to now? Paris? Nice? Would it occupy Berlin? In 1900, the champagne alone drunk alongside this enormity of bird would 'keep the Trafalgar Square fountains working incessantly for five days'. It is all a long cry from little Gurk; but the same symptoms are involved.

One must take the sacrificial story with its usual pinch of practical salt – in this case the scarcity of fodder in winter and thus the necessity of slaughtering beasts for salting down or for drying. This usually took place in northerly parallels at the beginning of November when pastures were dead or snow-covered. It was an economic necessity: but took to itself the sacrament of earlier days – Bede uses the Anglo-Saxon word *Blot-monath*, or

The traditional English boar's head

slaughter or sacrifice month, for November. Lord Mayor's Day in London on the ninth of November still seems to be fixed at this time of the old Teutonic New Year; Christianity has renamed it Martinmas, the British still celebrate it on the fifth of November with the fires of Guy Fawkes, the Americans still make much of Hallowe'en at about the same time.

Martinmas traditions

Martinmas had once all the customary accompaniments of Christmas, bogeys and angels and gift-bringers and the rest: but gradually, from the time of the Roman occupation of Europe and its later solstitial New Year, the majority of those celebrations were moved forward to the later December date. All Souls' Day and Hallowe'en – a time of falling leaves and fire festivals to help the sun's struggle with darkness – have in most countries similarly moved forward much of their old ritual to the Christmas period. All in all, though, the English seem to have taken to this feasting with the greatest enthusiasm – if an old Italian saying can be believed: 'He has more to do than the ovens in England at Christmas', of a person who is very busy.

The head of the wild boar, a beast extinct in England by the sixteenth century, was the great historical dish for the nobleman's table. His pallid cousin, the pig, was a near substitute. Perhaps the two were concomitant, the boar a legendary triumph, the pig a customary sacrifice. However it was, the boar's head decked with rosemary and with a round solar fruit like an apple or an orange placed in its mouth was the main decoration of early mediaeval Christmas feasting. The boar, too, was the enemy of crops, trampling them, as is echoed in the boar's head carol sung at St John's College, Oxford: 'He livinge spoyled/Where good man toyled,/Which makes kinde Ceres sorrye.' Yet there is also a legend that man learnt to plough by watching the boar root with his tusks in the ground, and by noticing the fertility of such a patch of earth afterwards. And one may go back earlier to the Adonis myth, and the origins of the totem tabu of the pig. In Scandinavia corn-cakes made in the shape of a boar or pig were eaten at yuletide; and these also are thought to have been again a propitiation of the vegetable spirit of corn.

Later on, the peacock became a specially prized head dish, and was brought into the eating hall with much ceremony. It was gilded – the skin was first stripped off with feathers still stuck to it, the bird then roasted and, half-cooled, sewn up again in the feathered skin, when the beak was gilded. Sometimes the whole bird was covered with leaf-gold. It was stuffed with spices and herbs, and a cotton-wick saturated in spirits placed in its beak and lighted.

In Germany and elsewhere the goose was the recognised Martinmas dish. And in England, as a large and succulent bird, it took its place for a long time as the most popular Christmas dish. The sausages that go with it were once served in string form, and represented the boar's old garland. The turkey was a gift from the New World. Spanish ships first brought it back from the Aztecs of Mexico to Spain: thence it would have arrived in the Spanish Netherlands and finally it came to prosper in England's Holland of East Anglia where the great turkey farms were started. It arrived in Spain in 1519; and it is said to have been eaten in England in the third decade of that century, though possibly the bird was then confused with the guinea-fowl.

When the guinea-fowl, well-known to the ancient Romans and Greeks, was rediscovered by the Portuguese in Africa at the beginning of the sixteenth century, it came to England dubbed as the 'Turkie-Henne'. Why? Because the Greeks had got what we now call guinea-fowl from Asia Minor? Or because political pressure at that time made anything exotic 'Turkish'? Or, since there is some affinity with the bustard, because travellers knew of the Turkish bustard? It is difficult to tell. One may be pretty sure that its growing popularity as a Christmas or feast dish came from its size and succulence, with the added circumstance of a pompous fine appearance in feather. But here we do come across a most extraordinary coincidence. For the legendary sacrificial boar was killed by the Greek Meleager of Calydon who gave the head to Atalanta. And when Meleager died, the women who mourned him were turned into guinea-fowl – *meleagrides*. There is a reference to the boar's head as 'Meleager like' – again in the boar's head carol; and the established genus of the turkey from its guinea-fowl confusion is *Meleagris*. And both these creatures form our best-known Christmas dishes....

In America the turkeys ran in wild flocks and there was much wild turkey shooting: in a controlled degree, there still is. In England George II kept some thousands in Richmond Park for what must have been rather a slow sport – the wild birds attaining sometimes a weight of fifty to sixty pounds – though accounts of American shoots describe the necessity of stalking these huge, grotesque birds well-hidden up in the trees. The eighteenth century saw great droves of turkeys proceeding on foot all the way from Norfolk to London – just as one may see them today, bald-headed and worried-looking as a crowd of gobbling old gentlemen, driven through the streets of Portugal. On Christmas Day 1815 Charles Lamb wrote of 'the savoury grand Norfolcian holocaust'; but it was not until late

'Who said anything about Christmas dinner?', by Thomas Nast, 1889

Victorian times that the turkey properly superseded the goose, or in the north roast beef, as the leading Christmas fare in England. In America, of course, the indigenous turkey was a general festive dish, according to pocket, much earlier.

The usual harem of the male turkey in captivity numbers about a dozen hens. To concentrate on these womenfolk during the mating season, he has developed a special heavy pad of fat to sustain him and so avoid wasting critical and valuable time looking for food. But the time of the natural mating season of the turkey is one of the saddest facts ever – it begins, O Sisyphus, in January. This is almost as macabre as the time-table of a bird some years ago which was bred for the feast by a family who, as the months and the flesh mounted, grew so much attached to it that they even gave it a name, Lesley. But when Christmas came they could not find it in their hearts to kill Lesley. Instead, they dressed him up with ribbons and sat him with them at the Christmas table. So there he was, sitting regal in full plumage and ribbons, to watch some naked relative of his, though possibly only by marriage, carved up and consumed in the curious beakless mouths of his loving masters.

The Christmas pudding, though legless, is as prize a plump course as any boar, goose or turkey, and must as importantly be discussed. But first a word about the many pies and cakes which have traditionally proliferated everywhere at Christmas-time. Nowadays, the ordinary English home is satisfied with mince-pies and perhaps a Christmas cake, that heavy fruity affair marzipanned and iced and probably the old Twelfth Night cake moved back to an overloaded Christmas Day position. The mince-pie had earlier a meaty content, was called a 'shrid pye' (shredded) and contained mutton and ox-tongue; before Cromwell outlawed the observance of Christmas it was baked in an oblong form with a top crust which sank into a concave manger-shape, wherein a doll or Christ figure of dough was laid. The custom never returned. With the royal return the pies were baked in a round shape, and as time went on and preserved fruits became cheaper, they grew sweeter.

Cakes, pastries and gingerbread biscuits In Europe, cakes and biscuits were baked in the shape of oxen or pigs, or in the shape of the horns of oxen, or of the Christ figure, or as wheels into which a candle was placed – a complete hotch-potch of the usual sacrificial, Christian and sun symbols, and all based on reverence for the wheat grain or oat retained from the harvest of the year gone and baked in hope of a good year to come. The different kinds of cakes and pastries and gingerbread biscuits were specialities of different districts, and very many are still made in usually a somewhat simpler form; according to family tradition this or that has been lost, or today in many cases rediscovered. The list is enormous, particularly in Germany with its *Lebkuchen*, *Pfeffernüsse*, *Printen* and others, and today in the great German Christmas fairs one still sees a variety of spiced cakes and gingerbreads and marzipans decorated with such figures as the old German version of the *Weihnachtsmann*. Spain and Italy, nut countries, go in also for *turrones* or *torroni*, nutty nougats. France has *pain d'épice*, sometimes gilded, and a cake in the form of a yule-

Title page of Der Struwwelpeter *by the Frankfurt doctor Heinrich Hoffmann, showing the* Christkind (Christ Child) *angel figure flanked by two Christmas trees whose candlelights merge with the stars according to the Lutheran legend*

Der Struwwelpeter

oder
lustige Geschichten
und
drollige Bilder.

Wenn die Kinder artig sind,
Kommt zu ihnen das Christkind;
Wenn sie ihre Suppe essen
Und das Brod auch nicht vergessen,
Wenn sie ohne Lärm zu machen
Still sind bei den Siebensachen,
Beim Spaziergehn auf den Gassen
Von Mama sich führen lassen,
Bringt es ihnen Gut's genug
Und ein schönes Bilderbuch.

Literarische Anstalt.

Frankfurt a. M.

Ere doth the floral pageant close
With one last flower –
a Christmas Rose.

∞ The End. ∞

log or *bûche de Noël;* and a large Twelfth Night cake, and the doll-cakes called *naulets.* Sweden had its loaf in the shape of a boar, Poland specialised in holy wafers which are broken by the family in a ritual fashion. And so the thousandfold toll goes on; sweet delight for children, but long ago a sweet propitiation for the gods – just as today the harvest sheaf of corn is put out in Scandinavian houses to favour the birds, but formerly to feed darker spirits winging through the ancient air.

Ingredients of the Christmas pudding

Christmas pudding had its origins also in a cereal of sacred purpose – it began as frumenty (Lat. *Frumentum* = corn), or hulled wheat spiced and boiled in milk. It was sometimes used as a fasting dish on Christmas Eve, and sometimes as an accompaniment to a meat course. Gradually more was added to it, in the form of eggs or mace, dried prunes, and later lumps of meat. It was then served in a tureen as plumb porridge and only later stiffened into the meatless plum pudding we know today. At some point this seems to have either merged or competed with the hackin, or great boiled sausage, a once popular dish possibly surviving in Scotland as the haggis. This hackin ('hacked meat' or mince) had traditionally to be boiled by daybreak, or otherwise the girls of the house were heavily penalised, run round the market-place and ostracised for the rest of the day: the hackin itself seems to have suffered a similar fate, it becomes most elusive in records of Christmas eating after the eighteenth century – either disappearing or becoming one with the pudding, which as it became more solid had of course to be boiled in a sausage-skin-like cloth.

Thus at Christmas today we attack a kind of skinless ex-haggis or ex-gruel soused with fire, sprigged with evergreen, and secretive with sixpences symbolic of the Saturnalian drawing of lots. It should be a dark fruit-rich monster intended to go down a treat, which it really is: and it is still a ritual affair in that it must be stirred from East to West in honour of the Three Kings, and by every one of the family, or, on board ship in the navy, given a first stir by a senior officer. Its present-day vegetarian constituents (except suet) should make it a happy climax for a vegetarian Christmas meal headed by mock turkey made largely of nuts: and Mrs Beeton in her famous Victorian cookery book even excludes the suet with a recipe for 'Fruitarian' pudding.

Recipes for making the real thing, of course, vary. There is a good and possibly true story told of a group of English students puddingless in Paris at the beginning of the nineteenth century and their means of procuring an orthodox British pudding. Unable to get one from a grocer, they decided it might, of course, be made up by a chemist, for the pharmacies of those days normally stocked the necessary raw ingredients, such as eggs and almonds for emulsions, suet for ointments, raisins for boluses, laxative prunes and so forth. So a prescription of the order of Ova viii, Fruct. parv. Corynthii, zinziber pulv., etc., etc., was despatched. The result? A fine pudding elegantly wrapped in parchment and labelled in medical Latin: Apply the hot poultice to the affected part. F. A. Allen, in the M & B *Pharmaceutical Bulletin* of December 1960, discusses the pharmacology of plum pudding, and provides much food for thought – quoting, for instance, that it is the

The Christmas Rose, a white flower known to botanists as the black hellebore from the colour of its roots, as illustrated in Flora's Feast *(1890) by Walter Crane*

149

suet with a solidifying point of 38°c which secures the succulent viscosity –
'on the dynamic boundary between solid and liquid states in the buccal
cavity' – much as the demon barber Sweeney Todd's pies of human meat
were found to be so suety succulent at 37°c. The mixed spices, he empha-
sizes, have their necessary good effects, expelling wind and staying vomiting, while the turmeric stimulates the gall bladder; moreover, the absence
of flour is important, for 'its stretched molecular threads of gluten would
bring heaviness and give to the cut surface a glairy smoothness'. No, the
pudding should crumble slightly: but not to a powder, as with a reported consignment of overmatured pudding attacked by the *Carpoglyphus
lactis*, a mite which is also a dab at corking your wine.

A well-kept pudding should be pretty proof against most things. Augustus
Sala tells of a Christmas in Constantinople, in 1876, when his hostess, wife
of a Pera consular official, apologised for the pudding before it arrived.
She explained that she had just had a row with the cook and had dismissed
her. Then the cook came in, cursed her and everyone else in the house, and
left. But ten minutes later she returned to curse the plum pudding, which
she did solemnly, three times. Sala adds that the pudding survived.

And do we survive the rich, rotund ex-haggis? One always marvels at the
enormous meals eaten years ago – capons followed by a haunch of venison,
a second remove of ducks and so on – but then one sagely nods that those
were horse-riding days, unlike these ulcerous times spent crouched over
desk and steering wheel. Yet there is before me an up-to-date Christmas
dinner menu served at an English holiday camp. Remember – in most
homes the Christmas dinner is the one real meal of the day, and ordinarily
consists of two main courses, a bird and the pudding. But at this camp one
was invited to a full breakfast, a three course lunch, and then a dinner

Twelfth Night, 1794

150

of smoked salmon, vermicelli soup, fillets of sole, roast turkey, chestnut stuffing, cranberry sauce, roast potatoes, Brussels sprouts, creamed celery hearts, Christmas pudding, brandy butter, mince-pies, followed by iced pudding, cheeses, and dessert. Presumably there was a donkey-ride put on in the afternoon. But it is a pointer to a season still of fair plenty, a fact which has also been epitomised by the outstanding warmth and generous abandon of a notice seen in a London café – decorated with yuletide holly, it carolled tidings of infinite gladness and joy in the proud and simple statement, *Fully Filled* Sandwiches.

To wash all this down, the centuries have prescribed mead, wine, ale as at any feast. The two Christmas specialities were church ale and the wassail drink of lambswool. We have seen that lambswool was a hot concoction of beer mulled with apples bobbing on the foaming surface: church ale was a strong brew broached at Christmastide and sold in the churchyard, even in the church itself, which resulted again in that conviviality and dancing on sacred ground which the austere condemned but which confirmed the church as a live institution and part of everyman's mortal day. There are records of dancing after prayers in church, to the cry of 'Yole, yole, yole ...'. Once again, as with the German *Kindelwiege*, and the ceremony of the bambino at Aracoeli, we see how easy the manners in church once were: as with even a Swiss church which permitted firecrackers to be exploded throughout the Christmas service, and as with an old custom in the Doubs of France where Christmas food and wine were brought into church: and when a point in the vespers service, '*De fructu ventris tui ponem super seden tuam*', was reached, the good things were attacked by the congregation and carried off with much singing and shouting.

The wassail bowl was served in households either as a convivial drink, or,

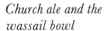

Church ale and the wassail bowl

'*Jolly old Christmas*'

according to very old tradition, passed from lip to lip in the ancient manner of communion with the vegetable spirit of its content. Originally, pieces of toast floated in it – hence our phrase 'to toast' someone. More simply the wassail was a formal affirmation of non-enmity or friendship, as its meaning 'good health' or 'be whole' (Anglo-Saxon *wes hal*) implies, and as in the same manner any company today enforces the laying down of aggressive attitudes by the taking up of a glass.

An empty wassail bowl or beaker was also carried round by carol-singers, and a drink extorted from door to door. This was again part of the approved begging at Christmas, which we have noted of star-singers and mummers of various kinds, and which, based on mixed traditions of sacred feasting and Christian charity, was more necessary than we can now know. Mid-winter was always a poor time of year for the poor. There was the cold to contend with, and the higher value of stored and salted food, and lack of work in the fields; and for the beggar, doors are more easily closed during winter, summer is an easier time for giving. So any contrivance was welcome; and today there are many customs such as the November Guy and Christmas carolling which might have fallen into disuse were it not for the collection box. In Cromwell's time, part of the Puritan propaganda for the abolition of Christmas closing appealed to the shopkeeper who could keep open his shop or the craftsman who could continue his piecework. One may wonder, too, whether the effect of Dickens's *Christmas Carol* on the closing of Victorian sweatshops and factories for Christmas was quite as popular as at first glance it seems, with so much work paid for by the piece. It is doubtful that factories would have paid for the holiday.

However, those who could get the food ate well: though the kind of food chosen varied from country to country and district to district. In Roman Catholic countries, fish naturally takes its part in the traditional eating, particularly on the holy fasting day of the Eve. On Christmas Day stuffed baked carp in a rich sauce was the head dish in Czechoslovakia and in other mid-European districts where this lake-fish was specially available: in northern Europe, one finds in Poland pickled fish, and in Scandinavia and Finland dried or lye-treated cods. Fresh eels are traditional in parts of Italy, and octopus and squid by the sea. Availability seems to dictate the tradition. As they say in Spain, the rich man sits down to his turkey, the shopkeeper to his chicken, and the working man to a stew.

Nevertheless, the pig, either roasted or in ham form, revives its ancient sacrificial role on many European and American tables as a main Christmas Day dish. In Finland and Sweden as ham, in Yugoslavia on the spit, in Austria as fresh sausage, in the deep American South as black-eyed peas and hog jowls, or symbolically in France as the *boudin aux marrons*, and so on. One may pick up old accounts and find a long assorted catalogue of foods customary once – but much has changed, new communications and changes of income have made other foods possible, and on the whole it is in the cake and biscuit department that old traditions have best been retained, for these confectioneries are in part decoration. In the New World one may find many of these old traditions well preserved. As with the preservation of

Figurine of a butcher in his shop, from a Neapolitan crib constructed about 1750

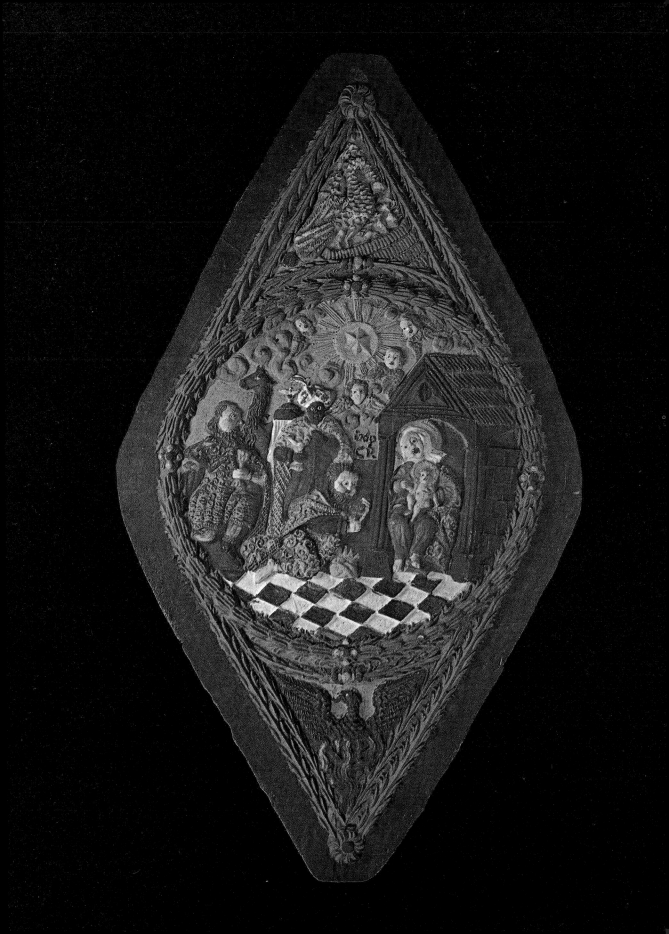

CHRISTMAS SEASON.
PEEK, FREAN & CO.
Biscuit Manufacturers, London,
DRAW SPECIAL ATTENTION TO THEIR
PLUM PUDDINGS
Ready Made, and Partially Cooked, supplied either in Basins or Tins. The QUALITY of these
Puddings is regarded as UNSURPASSED.
TEETOTAL PLUM PUDDINGS are a Speciality that can be Highly Recommended.
MINCEMEAT Carefully Prepared, and sent out in Glass Jars.
EMPRESS CAKE, NEW THIS SEASON. Fruit Cake covered with Almond Paste and Fondant Icing.
HEARTSEASE CAKE. Fruit Cake, with PANSY in Fondant Icing on Top.
WINDSOR CAKE. Fruit Cake, with Fondant Icing.
FLORENCE WAFERS. Oblong, Sandwiched with Cream Coffee, Lemon, or Raspberry.
VENICE WAFERS. Finger Shape, Sandwiched with Cream, Coffee—Lemon, or Raspberry.
AND WAFERS IN VARIOUS STYLES FOR TAKING WITH ICES, ETC.
May be Ordered through any Grocer.

sixteenth-century language, the Spanish of Peru and the vocabulary of English in North America, so Moravian cakes and Lithuanian poppy-seed loaves may be nearer to their originals in America than in the mother-countries of those immigrants.

Apart from traditional food, everybody at Christmas seems to eat more of everything. For instance, the snail is not a particularly Christmassy beast; but the books of one French wholesaler report that whereas he usually sells about two tons of snails a week, he sells four tons in each of the weeks of Christmas and New Year. And a ton of snails splits up into an average of ten thousand servings.

However, this has no bearing on tradition. And whether the Argentinian still eats as many *niños envueltos* ('wrapped children' in the form of stuffed steaks) as before, or the northern Italian bakes in the home his own raisin-filled *panettone* cake, is a matter for the particular family: habits are changing faster than ever before, and this can be epitomised in not a Christmas but a Harvest Festival offering noticed in an English chapel recently. Among the traditional fruits and corn sheaves and vegetables of the harvest offerings there stood, in a Victorian Gothic niche, in the light of stained glass windows, a tin of sardines. Should one shudder? At first glance, it seemed a sad little solecism; but on second thoughts, it became rather touching – after all, it was an offering, and in the hard good terms of common sense. Moreover, if we wish to pray for a fertile future, then the little fish of the Atlantic and their Portuguese fishers are nowadays as close to our stomachs as the next mangel-wurzel.

With its echo of canned Christmas pudding, the sardine tin says something of the future: but of the submerged past there are certain famous feasts which cannot be forgotten. We have already reviewed some of the banqueting in royal English halls, something of subtleties and the heads of boars. Such feasts were held on a huge scale: but then the mouths of retainers were many too. Henry III ordered festivities in York in 1252 which included the slaughter of six hundred fat oxen; at other times, county sheriffs were ordered to supply such immediacies as ten peacocks, twenty salmon made into pies, and ten brawns with their heads, and much else. A brawn was flesh of the boar, which was not wild but fattened up before Christmas and strapped round the belly to keep the flesh dense. It was usual to send brawn to market in rolls two feet long and ten inches in diameter. It was always eaten with mustard. King Henry also remembered the poor – it is recorded that in 1248 he had them fill Westminster Hall and there feasted for a week. Certain foods were specially kept for nobles – 'for a great lord take squirrels, for they are better than conies' and 'seven mackerel in a dish, with a dragge of fine sugar', while the gilded peacock was the dish for a king. All this was accompanied by great finery and richness of cup. A poet wrote of pheasants drenched with ambergris, and of three fat wethers bruised for gravy to make sauce for a single peacock. One single course served at a banquet given by Henry V contained 'dates in composite, cream mottled, carp, turbot, tench, perch, fresh sturgeon with whelks, porpoise roasted, memis fried, crayfish, prawns, eels roasted with lamprey, a leche called the white leche flourished with hawthorn leaves and red haws, and a march pane ...' followed by an enormous subtlety. This was one of three equally sufficient courses.

Historic Christmas menus

There have been many other specialities – for instance, the huge pie ordered by Sir Henry Grey which was nine feet in circumference, weighed 165 pounds and was carried on a four-wheeled ox-cart built for the purpose. And in America there was the celebrated great cake made by Martha Washington, with a resounding recipe which begins: 'Take forty eggs & divide the whites from the youlks & beat them to a froth ...' and ends convivially with a touch of 'frensh brandy'.

Much later we find the large ship made of frosted sugar in Edwardian days for Lord Londesborough, as Vice-Admiral of the Coast of Yorkshire. But no Christmas menu could be more provoking than that of the notorious Christmas dinner at Voisin's in Paris during the Prussian siege of 1870: the zoo and the sewers combined to produce a consommé of elephant, braised kangaroo, truffled antelope pâté and a decorative climax in *le Chat flanqué de Rats*, a whole roast cat garnished with rats. Perhaps it was Voisin's chef whom Labouchère met earlier, and who described how he was fattening up a huge cat to be served at Christmas surrounded with mice 'like sausages'. Goncourt records on New Year's Eve how he saw in Roos's, the English butcher's, the skinned trunk of young Pollux, an elephant late of the zoo; and that among 'nameless meats and unusual horns', camels' kidneys were for sale. It must have been a memorable Christmastide. 'I had a slice of spaniel the other day,' Labouchère records, and Hoffman of the American Legation preferred the taste of light greys to blacks in terms of horsemeat. Many a Londoner will remember, at a much later date during some of the Christmases of the Second World War, how curious was the bone formation of a leg of goose served in certain Soho restaurants; hardly to be mentioned, but *very* like a cat's.

Elephant has been served at other Christmas dinners, including one given to hunters at Koba on the White Nile. John Boyes records a menu headed by *points d'éléphant* and completed by *plum pudding sans reproche*. But the mixture of elephant trunk and feet was hardly without reproach, it was like eating cooked rubber. All the guests were in any case suffering from fever, and the temperature was 102°F.

That, though, is far from the winter wonderland of British wassail, and to remember the mood, one can do no better than quote Whistlecraft's Victorian rhyme of the good old days:

> They served up salmon, venison, and wild boars,
> By hundreds, and by dozens, and by scores,
> Hogsheads of honey, kilderkins of mustard,
> Muttons, and fatted beeves, and bacon swine,
> Herons and bitterns, peacocks, swan and bustard,
> Teal, mallard, pigeons, widgeons, and, in fine,
> Plum puddings, pancakes, apple-pies, and custard,
> And therewithal they drank good Gascon wine,
> With mead, and ale, and cider of our own,
> For porter, punch, and negus were not known.

And one must recapitulate once more the sacrificial nature of the pig, father of brawn and Christmas sausages everywhere, in a possibly common instance of a Christmas custom recorded from Gotland, the Swedish island in the middle of the Baltic where much that is ancient is preserved, the Gotlanders even today speaking with an Old Norse or Icelandic kind of accent. This record tells of a game where the 'victim' is slaughtered with a knife by a woman dressed in terrifying attire: afterwards, the victim rises and dances with his slayer – just as, in Christmas mumming-plays, the slain Turk or central sacrificial figure is brought to life again, symbolising the year's rebirth. But in this Gotland case, the dress of the victim is of particular interest: he is clad in a skin, and holds in his mouth a wisp of straw frayed at the ends – and this represents a swine's bristles, and the victim a hog sacrificed to Frey.

The boar is everywhere; and at its nicest in a story attached to the famous carol sung as the boar's head is brought into the dining hall of Queen's College, Oxford. It is said that long ago a young student was studying in the quiet of Shotover Forest when suddenly that quiet was broken, and he lowered his Aristotle to see charging him at full tilt a mighty wild boar. Whereat the student raised his Aristotle again, but this time to ram it sharply into the boar's jaws with the cry: '*Graecum est!*' Thus, as the saying went, he choked the savage with the sage.

He brought the head back to be able to retrieve his good copy of Aristotle, and ever since then a boar's head has been borne to table to the words:

> The boar's head in hand bear I,
> Bedeck'd with bays and rosemary;
> And I pray you, my masters, be merry,
>   *Quot estis in convivio.*
>   *Caput apri defero*
>   *Reddens laudes Domino.*

'*Christmas lunch in the tropics*', by Daphne Jerrold, 1932

8

The Feast Far-Flung

Or Southern Christmas, dark and dank with mist,
And heavy with the scent of steaming leaves,
And rosebuds mouldering on the dripping porch.
CHARLES KINGSLEY

Always an intemperate feast, Christmas has wandered far distant to excessive temperatures indeed, to tropical summers on the other side of the world and to wastes frozen deeper than any white wonderland dreamed up at home. The Christmas pudding knows piping hot jungles, Santa Claus arrives on tropical surfs, carols are sung in the wide open air of a candle-lit night beneath the southern stars. Wherever Christian armies or traders or missionaries have gone, the story of Christ's birth has been taken, and along with it those many mixed-up pagan elements which now fuse further with whatever pagan elements existed in each land before ... bringing extra complications to the gunpowdery Chinese solstice, bringing to the eskimo's furry dancing a new dimension on ice.

Of all these opposites to the traditional scene, perhaps the antipodal Australian Christmas comes most dramatically to mind. December the twenty-fifth can be a blazer, and the bikini-ed feast of pudding on the beach is a familiar paradox. It is too often, though, forgotten that Australia extends beyond Bondi Beach, and that Christmas Day falls at a time of year when large tracts of the country look forward either to the danger of vast bush fires or to the Big Wet, whose sudden torrential rains defeat the burning but also isolate whole towns for days or weeks by flood. Many are the stories and poems of the smouldering fires thrashed by sixty-mile-an-hour winds into walls of flame travelling faster than a man can run, and of

Abandoned 'Christmas trees' found on a coral islet off Costa Rica: in fact, ordinary tropical shrubs hung with bright things by children belonging to a fisherman in seasonal residence during winter months

the farms and stock swallowed, of gullies filling with blazing grease from the burned bodies of sheep, and of the black land left. Homes vanishing in one lick of flame, stockmen and squatters out day and night beating and thrashing – and the pause as the clouds mass and the first lightning flashes and then the downpour ... and if it is Christmas Day, it is easily seen as coincidence mounting to miracle.

There are prettier aspects in milder parts of the continent, even though the thermometer can still touch a hundred degrees during that Australian particular, the Christmas Day picnic. Victorian engravings show parasolled women in long white skirts, and men in straw hats bound with veils lounging on the grass by a cloth laid with the ubiquitous plum pudding and bottles of indigenous wine; and of the crowds milling on Brighton Beach, kite-flying and bathing and playing cricket on the sands – while beside the genuflection to the pudding, with a sprig of green wattle stuck on top of it, there would be eaten braised kangaroo and parrot pie. It was always a popular outing, and, since Christmas falls in the prime dog-days of mid-December, today it invites people to make of it the beginning of their summer holiday, not only a feast but a real relaxer, and for those far distant the long return home. One hears of iced plum pudding, and one vision is of naked flesh broiling on the sand and great stretches of beach serving bronzed ball-players fed on turkey legs glacés; elsewhere there sweats the image of man in his broad-brimmed, greasy hat mulling the wassail beer and munching a sizzling bird with all the sogged suet of pud to come, a tin roof making an oven of the shack and the sole cool relief a spine-chilling ghost story. But more sensibly, as in most hot countires, the more fortunate and judicious hold off Christmas dinner until the debatable cool of the evening, hoses playing on the lawn, candles fluttering to catch a breeze, langour in the cane chairs and music of snow and rimy wonderlands coming canned through the loudspeaker. People of other warm climates like the American South will recognise this atmosphere.

The Christmas Day picnic

A great Australian tradition is the open-air community singing of carols by large crowds assembled by night in the light of torches and candles. Melbourne is said to have begun it on a large organised scale in 1937, followed soon by Sydney. Special candles are sold in the shops, all profits go to charity – Melbourne's 'Carols by Candlelight' gets a crowd of 150,000 and about as many Australian dollars go each year to sick children. As darkness falls, the candles are lit and a procession of white-clad choristers moves to the big floodlit stage by the Yarra River. The whole park is filled with people holding candles, whose lights shine magically through the trees, and the carols continue until a climax at midnight when 'Auld Lang Syne' is sung, and broadcast far round the world.

Though its organisation thus is of fairly recent origin, the real beginning of this choral carolling in Australia is found with the Cornish miners of the last century out in Moonta in South Australia. On Christmas Eve the men left the coal-face and gathered at the loading platform to sing Wesleyan carols by the light of fatjacks, tallow candles stuck with clay to the brims of their safety hats. Later the custom spread to the air above, editions of the

'A Christmas Dinner on the Heights before Sebastopol', a chromolithograph from the Crimean War period, and *'Christmas in India'*, from The Graphic *of 1881*

163

'Christmas in Australia: pudding time', from a drawing by W. Ralston

carols were printed, and concerts by Chinese lantern-light were held in the nineties in Victoria Park. An account by Oswald Pryor, in *Australia's Little Cornwall*, tells of one carol depending on successive part-singing which led the conductor to address his choir with the command: 'Now, boays, all together – one after t'other.' These old Cornish carols have florid airs and a rolling base; and it is related of one sung in the eighteenth century to an accompaniment of seven bassoons: 'When they all closed down on low F, 'twas like 'eaven.' There are now, of course, many locally inspired Australian carols, with lines such as: 'Bell-birds shall ring their silver peal/From gullies green and deep', and: 'Our wattle trees shall shower their gold/ In tribute to our King.'

Where there was no plastic Christmas tree, local flora was collected to decorate the home, Christmas Bell and Christmas Bush. Anything green would do to tie to the doorposts, and holly became mauve wistaria or the ardent flame of the flowering gum-tree. There was also 'the fanlike orange brush of Christmas Tree from bright Westralian plains'. Nasturtiums, wistaria, and honeysuckle always made a traditional festooning of the goods in Sydney shops and once, in 1900, an undertaker thus improved his window for the festive season, prompting from Creeve Roe celebratory verses ending:

Then let us all, dear Brethren,
    Go gaily to the tomb,
In the merry Christmas season,
    When coffins are in bloom.

During the gold rush, there are records of nuggets being hidden in the plum pudding instead of sixpences; the gold 'beans' were afterwards kept for brooches or tie-pins – preserved, in fact, with some vague apprehension of their ancient magical significance. Mutton comes in for one of its few appearances as a Christmas dish in a shearing shed – but only because there was no other meat; and in that intriguing compendium *The Australian Christmas*, to which we are indebted for much of this antipodal information, Henry Lawson records a gold-fields Christmas with a Chinese Santa Claus (of Sun Tong Lee & Co., Storekeepers) with exotic sweetmeats and Chinese dolls for the children; and at one out-station spending Christmas on potatoes and honey, for there were no other stores; and at another stuck with a large surplus of plum pudding and so picking out the raisins to boil the remainder down with salt kangaroo; and on New Year's Eve lighting fires not of joy but of camel dung against the mosquitoes.

Back in civilised parts, the day after Christmas brought its immediate call to hunting and racing – the horse of St Stephen come far across the world, and always most energetically anticipated, as is well described in John O'Brien's poem giving the country boy's answer to the bishop's question: 'What is Christmas?'

The ready answer bared a fact no bishop ever knew
'It's the day before the races out at Tangmalangaloo.'

So we read of Christmas dinners of suet pudding and stewed cockatoo, of camel-riding opal prospectors in the old days eating cow-heel and pledging their wives in Christmas cocoa; and nowadays of Thursday Islanders sitting down to a dinner of turtle roasted in an oven of stones; and of Christmas at Lockhart where Father Christmas sweats away in his nylon beard while the gleaming brown bodies dance in their lava-lavas before a feast of dugong. On the Nerang River, Father Christmas comes roaring down on water-skis, white-bearded and wearing red bathing trunks. Over flooded farmland, across seas to outer islands, and down to the frozen polar south the Christmas meal is got by plane, by hook and by crook: and a further Australian particular being the inter-farm radio network centred on the flying doctor, this is given over for a time on Christmas afternoon to greetings from station to station. Aboriginal girl children look forward to little black dolls to carry in wooden carrier-cradles, and tribes like the Warrabri look forward to a dinner of roast kangaroo. And it all goes on alongside modern Sydney and its iced plum duff, under a Southern Cross where more shepherds watch their flocks than anywhere else on the upside down world.

Christmas has not always been a severe festival for British pioneers in what was the far-flung empire. Chambers's *Journal* of 1869 gives an extraordinary account of a white man's Christmas spent in darkest Africa – the

Christmas in a hot climate

ambience of Gambia is suggested. First he sentimentalises upon memories of nights of clear, frosty air while the crocodiles are 'moaning in the river beyond'; and listening to carols; but then comes down to earth with a meal of oysters torn from trees, gazelle steaks, stewed iguana, smoked elephant, fried locusts, manati breasts, hippopotamus steaks, boiled alligator, roasted crocodile eggs, monkeys on toast, land-crabs ... plantains, paw-paws, palm cabbage ... after which, and assumably some time later, evening fell and the author and a friend went down to the river:

... the rosy wine had rouged our yellow cheeks, and we lay back in the cushions, and watched the setting sun with languid half-closed eyes ... Two beautiful girls, who sat before us in the bow, raised their rounded arms and tinkled their bracelets in the air. Then, gliding into the water, they brought us flowers from beneath the dark bushes, and kissed the hands which took them, with wet and laughing lips. Like a dark curtain, the warm night fell upon us; strange cries roused from the forest; beasts of the waters plunged around us, and my honest friend's hand pressed mine. And Christmas Day was over ...

Forward to the 1920s, and we read of an East African Christmas among the great brass doors and fretted lanterns of Zanzibar, where an exotic feast of boned duck and coconut-palm heart and spiced guavas is served by loin-clothed slaves in the court of a Sheikh Hassan, son of a slave-trader and an Oxford graduate, who finally calls for silver flagons of sherbert, one scarlet, one green, and speaks for the first time that evening in English: 'Gentlemen, Wassail! I wish you a merry Christmas!'

In the 1950s Christmas was still held in some style in Kenya, with a formal turkey dinner in the cool of the evening on a candle-lit verandah. Africans had several days' holiday to visit their families, and for the English there was a drag-hunt on Christmas day itself. At the Nairobi country club, Hogmanay was celebrated with a haggis borne in by a long-robed African, but preceded by a kilted piper; later in the evening the company would dance 'slow and very solemn eightsome reels'. In South Africa, families kept up a traditional Dutch or English Christmas; and there were surreal effects at some of these formal, richly dressed dinners served out in the warm night air – one hears of African servants tending the plates with white-gloved hands, headless phantoms as their dark faces merged with the night above. And at a children's party, how African children were given little masks to wear – a generosity of little imagination, for they were dark masks the colour of the children's own skin, so that with the high white of eyeballs, and by torchlight, no difference could be seen.

A snow cathedral in the Arctic At the other end of the thermometer's scale, one finds eskimo families gathering as in pre-Christian times for a solstitial festival, and building a special communal igloo for the purpose. This takes the form of five separate domed ice-houses set in a thirty foot circle, with one in the middle – and then one large igloo is built above these as supports. Finally, the central igloo is removed and the inner sides of the five others cut away so that there is left a 'snow cathedral' with a roof fifteen feet high, and five alcoves in the walls. Such an edifice is large by eskimo standards, and, with stocks of caribou meat and fish and black tea and candy, accommodates a whole

Christmas in the jungle, 1878

community over the Christmas period. A service is held by a missionary, and there are drum dances, story-telling and games and matches of skill among the furs, stocks and equipments of this strange iced marabout of the Arctic wastes.

Japan provides a tripartite conflict of three Christmas-time forces – the Christian Christmas for the relatively few Christians, the traditional Japanese New Year festivities, and the Christian-commercial overlay of western Christmas trees, paper holly and red and green festoons, which have been adopted for display purposes and a conveniently imported sales stimulation. In Christian communities, nativity plays are acted by children in Japanese dress, when Bethlehem must look fused with *The Mikado*; but the indigenous New Year festival is a time for pine tree garlands, kite-flying, lanterns, and one particularly unusual character among decorations – a small lobster. This merry crustacean, among ferns and pine-branches, is supposed to represent great old age – and symbolically wishes everyone a very long life until their backs are bent like the bent back of the lobster.

Chinese New Year celebrations

Kung Hsi Hsin Nien bing Chu Shen Tan is the Chinese Christmas greeting. But again, of course, the non-Christian New Year is the great celebration when one may shorten one's breath to *Kung Hei Fat Choy*. The New Year has no definite date to match our calendar, since it is celebrated on the first day of the lunar month: but when that time comes, the inventors of gunpowder declare total festival with fireworks and crackers, lanterns and dragons and the honourable custom of settling all debts before the great event, the renewal of the new borrowing year. Among Chinese in Hong Kong, for instance, Santa Claus is known as Nice Old Father or Christmas Old Man. The scarlet poinsettia, as throughout much of the world of warmer countries, is the brilliant Christmas flower. Echoes of China, of course, redound in San Francisco: but in London's old 'Chinatown' the dragon in the streets seems no longer to survive. And in thinking today of all these far eastern Christmases, one must see them not against a background of junks and josses but instead against the painted steel of ordinary traffic, the neon, the plate glass. Nevertheless, as in the West, the idea proliferates and wherever it is allowed, there is more Clissmus than ever before.

Santa Claus covers the Cingalese lagoon in a catamaran, and in California he comes sweeping in like a hairy sea-born god on a Pacific surfboard. In India, during the last days of the British Raj, the Christmas Day doorstep of a colonel might glitter blue with the piled corpses of slaughtered peacocks, a gift from his native staff; and one hears of servants decorating the house with marigolds and roses, and even lacquering with gold the nails and claws of pet dogs and birds. In Siberia in Czarist days peasants put a portion of the Christmas dinner just inside a darkened window for 'those whom nobody must see', escaped prisoners who travelled only by night. In the Peruvian capital there is a bullfight on Christmas Day – shades of Mithra intervening once more – and in Mexico and nearby we find the complicated ritual of the *posadas*.

The *posadas* is a party centering on a long ritual procession and play which together dramatise the search of Mary and Joseph for room at the inn (*posada*). Families play the parts, dividing themselves between ignorant inn-keepers and holy family, and from the sixteenth of December onwards visit each others' houses to enact and re-enact the play, and to admire each others' cribs or *nacimientos* and Christmas decorations of Spanish moss and Canadian pine. Mexico, we have seen, is also the home of the *piñata*, the highly decorated sweet-filled earthenware pot which children break with a stick, and Mexico still honours Epiphany with a proper Twelfth Day cake, the *Rosca de Reyes*, with instead of a bean a small plastic doll hidden inside for the ancient drawing of the royal lot.

Latin American countries all tend to persevere with the legend of the Three Kings as gift-bringers, though in more Americanised cities Santa Claus is creeping in. Generally, too, the Iberian Catholic background of these countries ensures an enthusiasm for the crib; and in the case of Brazil, where carnival is rehearsed from as early on as November, the Christmas moments become twice as colourful in the streets, for the fancy-dress and the dancing are already there, and very easily the conception of the birth of Christ gets mixed with spontaneous, sporadic revelry of other kinds. Up in Central America there is one extra hot point to a hot feast, the food takes a turn towards the *tamale*, corn and meat stuffing flavoured with peppers and wrapped in a big leaf, such as that of the banana: turkeys and hens, though, as usual, for those who can afford them.

In Chile an outstanding pilgrimage is made to the Virgin del Rosario, a miraculously discovered wooden image at Andacollo; and in Colombia we

Chinese New Year Feast at Canton, 1861

find a special masking on Christmas Eve, a time of fancy-dress and unusual gaiety. But on the whole these countries of Spanish and Portuguese influence generally preserve their Catholic ritual in the old manner of the mother countries – with a devout Christmas Eve and feast but a louder Epiphany, with a *nacimiento* or *pesebre* and with various indigenous Indian or Negro particularities added. Thus, a Peruvian peasant party will find women in those bowler-hats worn over head-scarves; and in Brazil the full colour of a freed Negro imagination runs as riot as it may. It is a long, long way from the words of a nineteenth-century journalist on a plantation in the south of the United States: 'Slavery ... had at least some genial features; and the latitude which the masters gave to the slaves at Christmas-time, the freedom with which the blacks were *wont to concentrate a year's enjoyment into the Christmas week*, was one of these.' (Italics added.)

Stag-hunts and superstition in the USA

The United States as we have seen, is large enough to be far-flung within itself. Warm Christmases again – invigorated by old accounts of the stag-hunts of the South, through forests of live oaks pendulous with streamers of moss; and one notes unusual superstitions, such as the old Negro belief that Christmas *falls* – that there would be some mighty and material movement of nature on that day – derived from half-understood sentences such as 'Christmas falls on a Monday' etc. But old records from anywhere carry a peculiar magic: one would not easily believe that the Christmas dinner of trappers in early Canadian forts was boiled buffalo hump and moose's nose. And if they had gone further north, as did the sailors of the *Germania* in 1870, they would have eaten roast seal among 'fir-tree' decorations made of Greenland andromeda and hung with gilded walnuts which had already seen Christmas service in far-off Germany. Afterwards there was a polar ball on the ice, the men dancing together to a hand-organ played by the boatswain seated on the antlers of a reindeer.

During the Indian Mutiny, Lord Clyde's army at Intha interrupted their campaign against the Sepoys to hold a Christmas banquet at which officers enjoyed old port 'rather bothered by travelling twenty miles a day on a camel back'. Another military Christmas, with Sir Sam Browne under a flag-staff bedecked with holly, provided an *haute cuisine* of *Côtelettes aux Champignons*, *Poulets à la Mayonnaise* before the roasts: and this in the thick of a hard campaign in the Khyber Pass.

Christmas on board the *Sunbeam* in 1876, as recorded by Lady Brassey, gives a beautiful picture of the yacht at rest in the Hawaiian harbour of Hilo – her masts tipped with sugar-canes in bloom, flowers massing her stern, and a big bouquet clasped in the arms of her figurehead ... a fragrant and musical relief after Christmas Eve spent on the edge of a live volcano in what were then the Sandwich Isles.

Against such exotic moments it must always be remembered that across the world simple services of more ordinary Christian drama were and are still being held in missions and in minority Christian chapels everywhere. Bare huts are decorated with whatever green there is to be found, the corrugated iron roof echoes the singing of carols and nativity hymns, and with humble resources some sort of Christmas party is put on. It may be in the

Santa Claus arriving in a surf-boat on the white waves of Christmas at Bondi Beach, Sydney

Liberian jungle, where children were given as a particular treat 'a new pan to eat out of' and sat in a circle with their new pans eating 'a generous portion of rice, a good piece of beef, and two cookies' before the candy and the fireworks; it may be in an African leper hospital, with gifts of corn, rice and cassava to the patients; it may be in New Guinea, with a nativity play put on by the doctors of a hospital and their wives; everywhere something is done, everywhere accounts marry phrases like 'Hark! the Herald Angels sing' with 'the palm-trees swaying, the drums beating'. That is today: in the past we find harsher memories, as in a distant part of nineteenth-century China, with a Christmas Day service held in 'a cold, cheerless room in a clay-built cabin down in the corner of a bare valley in a trap and basalt district with sparse vegetation and a bare aspect. A cold spot with a handful of Christians ...' Not all missionary Christmases are a smiling paradox of sun and cotton-wool snow, a tale of carols sung to the warm frosty breath of steaming rice.

Carols, of course, have gone into many languages, and one of the most charming is what is known as the Huron Carol, composed by an early Jesuit missionary in Canada: when this was performed, the Three Wise Men from the East were portrayed as three Indian Chiefs, and the gifts were of fox and beaver pelts. The least charming of carols comes in a horrifying report, in December 1964, from the war in the Congo – after rebels had massacred white missionaries and priests, they sang carols in Swahili in front of the survivors.

But elsewhere, as across the world in Melanesia, the following words are spoken amongst once warring people now at peace: *The Nativity in Neo-Melanesian*

... na Maria i gat bel. Tupela i stap long dispela ples, na taim bilong Maria i karim pikinini i kamap pinis. Em i karim namba wan pikinini man bilong em, na i karamapim em long laplap na i putim em i slip long bokis kaikai bilong ol bulmakau. Haus pasendia i pulap pinis, na olsem.

This is Luke II 5-7, and the language is Neo-Melanesian or otherwise Pidgin English. It has a new literation, and forms a lingua franca spoken by many hundreds of thousands in islands north of Australia like New Guinea, and is the only means of common communication between people of many diverse native tongues. If we substitute spelling familiar from tales of the South Seas, then 'bilong' is soon recognisable as 'belong' and 'dispela' becomes 'this feller' and 'namba wan' becomes 'number one'. It is a language of touching simplicity: and the familiar story comes freshly to life with so strange a syntax, such humbly moving word formations. Mary's pregnancy is as direct as the stroke of Piero della Francesca's brush – again using the old literation, 'Maria 'e got belly'. Then: 'Two feller (Mary and Joseph) stop along this feller place, in the time belong Maria 'e carry 'im pickaninny 'e come up finish. And 'e carry 'im number one pickaninny man belong 'em and carry 'im up along laplap (cloth) and 'e put 'im 'e sleep along bokis (box) kaikai (food, cake) belong all bull and cow. House passenger (the inn) 'e full up finish, and all same.'

The New Testament is known as *Gutnius bilong Jisas Kraist* or 'Good News belong Jesus Christ': and in it we find the Lord is *Bikpela* (Big Feller) and the shepherds are *wasman bilong sipsip* (watchman belong sheep-sheep); and in *Matiu I Raitim* ('Matthew 'e write 'im', or the Gospel according to St Matthew) we find the Wise Men are *sampela saveman* (some feller savvy man) and the East is *san i kamap* (sun 'e come up); and gold is *golmoni* (gold money) and frankincense is *samting bilong makim smoksmel* (something belong make 'im smoke smell). One may first smile at these simplicities, but on deeper consideration wonder at such extraordinary evidence of a birth of communication and the poetry of it, the spellings and the sounds of the story of Herot and Jisas and Sisa Ogastas.

The original Biblical land of which the story tells has appropriately a more complicated Christmas season than anywhere else. There is a well-known story of the party of travellers en route for Bethlehem who were much delayed; and when one of them expressed the fear that they would now probably miss Christmas Eve there, the answer came from a wise old man: 'It is always Christmas Eve in Bethlehem.' Nearly true, at least at this time of year – for there are certainly three Christmas Eves observed. That of the Roman and Protestant Churches on the twenty-fourth of December; of the Greek Orthodox, Syrian and Coptic churches on the fifth of January; and of the Armenians on the seventeenth of January. These adherences to various dates from new and old calendars make worship at the Church of the Nativity less complicated than it looks – for in the cave of the Nativity beneath the church six Orthodox lamps burn, five Armenian and four Roman Catholic, and the nave above is owned jointly by these three Churches.

Television and Santa Claus in Manger Square

The crowds from Jerusalem flow in, but the church is too small to accommodate them; so closed-circuit television broadcasts the service to a screen outside in what is called 'Manger Square', and which also has temporary broadcasting studios and Press telephone booths. It would be naïve to expect much different. A Santa Claus has also appeared in Manger Square. The area is particularly policed for fear of religious antagonisms roused by irregularity at such a time. Inside the church, the story goes that the different priests have to police each other: a Greek monk shifts his carpet a little further over the floor each day, thus taking a mite more of the holy ground – and the eagle-eyed Catholic responds by taking a pair of scissors to the encroaching carpet. And, they say, vice versa. Below, in the ancient rock-shelter for animals, the inscription *Hic de Virgine Maria Jesus Christus natus est* on a silver star inlaid into the now marble floor records the supposed place of the momentous birth. The present silver star, donated in 1852 by the Ottoman Sultan, replaces a similar one stolen in 1847, a theft contributing to the causes of the Crimean War.

In Persia a small Christian community observes Christmas as the Little Feast, but fasts for the first twenty-five days of December. In Syria the celebration begins on St Barbara's day, the fourth of December, and continues until Epiphany; St Nicholas Thaumaturgus, or the wonder worker, a local version of Nicholas of Myra, is revered on the sixth of December, and on Christmas Eve bonfires of vine branches are lit in

Dream and reality in British Columbia, 1879

churches and in the courts of houses, 'to warm the Magi on their way'. There are magical stories of trees bowing to the Wise Men, and of a wonderful mule who brings gifts; in the south, the mule becomes the gentle camel of Jesus: it is odd here that there is no human gift-bringer – though in all European cases a most important part of the ritual was also attached to the animal, in that children were expected to provide fodder for the horse or whatever animal bore the bringer of gifts. There is also a notable echo of the flowering Glastonbury Thorn in this activity of the trees. In Israel and among Jewish people across the world, Hanukkah the Feast of Lights is the 'fire' festival at this time of year: its occurrence varies with the Jewish calendar, but, although it celebrates the cleansing of the temple after the Maccabean victory in 161 BC, it is probably an earlier solstitial fire festival connected with December. The general Moslem attitude to the Christian festival is ambivalent, for though the Christian is an infidel nevertheless Jesus Christ is recognised as a major prophet. Far across Moslem lands, far to the south of this ancient area of Christian beginnings, Christianity flowers strong again in the Abyssinian enclave of the Coptic Church, with an unbroken continuance since AD 330.

That the Abyssinian may still feast on raw meat, that the Armenians may tie up money or raisins in their handkerchiefs, that the Navajo Indians leave their hogans for a feast at the 'Trading Post', that there is still some yulish egg-nogg drunk in America and that in England old Catholic families may still light the big candle – the enormous catalogue of all such detailed observances of the wide world's Christmas varies from decade to decade, from year to year: they are matters that come and go, fall away and are revived. One village cut off by mountains retains the old rituals, another on a new motor highway exchanges them for modern devices: we see Santa Claus taking over from the Three Kings where the influence of the United States is strong in Latin America, we see in Soviet Russia the old Babouschka and the Christian liturgy fall away, but in compensation the emergence of a popular Father Frost and a shifting of exuberance to New Year's Eve.

Returning from the East to the nearest point in Christian Europe, Greece, we may be sure that somewhere the children still knock on people's doors and sing the old Christmas songs (*Kalanda*), some of which are touchingly practical, telling how 'Good Mary – lying in labour – begged her woman: Help me, I pray ... and go fetch the midwife'. The singing, of course, is as usual rewarded with food or some small gift. Once again, too, we find a pig is slaughtered at this time of year; and special breads are baked, with designs in dough symbolising farming implements or farm animals, and these may be nailed to the wall for a year. Wine and oil are poured near the hearth – it is the same story reverberating everywhere, the story of fire as a symbol of the sun to come. Echo after echo persists – in Epirus the village girls mix flour with water drawn at the dawn of Christmas Day, then light a candle and repeat three times: 'Christ is born – the Light is rising – so that my yeast may be good'. In Macedonia they carry embers from the hearth to the stable and sheepfold, swing them in a censer over cattle and tools. In thousandfold variation these same beliefs echo through the villages not only of Greece but the world. The catalogue is again endless. The Greeks have their goblins called the *Kallikantzaroi* – again the souls of the dead abroad, the spirits of more ancient times – and a yule-log is burned to frighten them away. Occasionally one finds odd exceptions to the broad general rule, for instance the belief that a child born on Christmas Day will become one of the *Kallikantzaroi*, so that its toe-nails must be singed, since – and one can just hear grandmother boom this resounding piece of etiquette – *no one can become a goblin without toenails.*

Christmas at the front during the Afghan campaign, 1879

Opposite above: *American Pueblo Indians dancing the deer and buffalo dance at Tesuque at Christmas-time*
Opposite below: *Children in Tucsan, Arizona, taking part in the traditional Mexican ritual Las Posadas representing the search of Mary and Joseph for room at the inn*
Overleaf: *The winter atmosphere and the sense of sleigh at its most ideal as conveyed in the nocturnal promenade of a king, Ludwig II of Bavaria. A painting by R. Wenig*

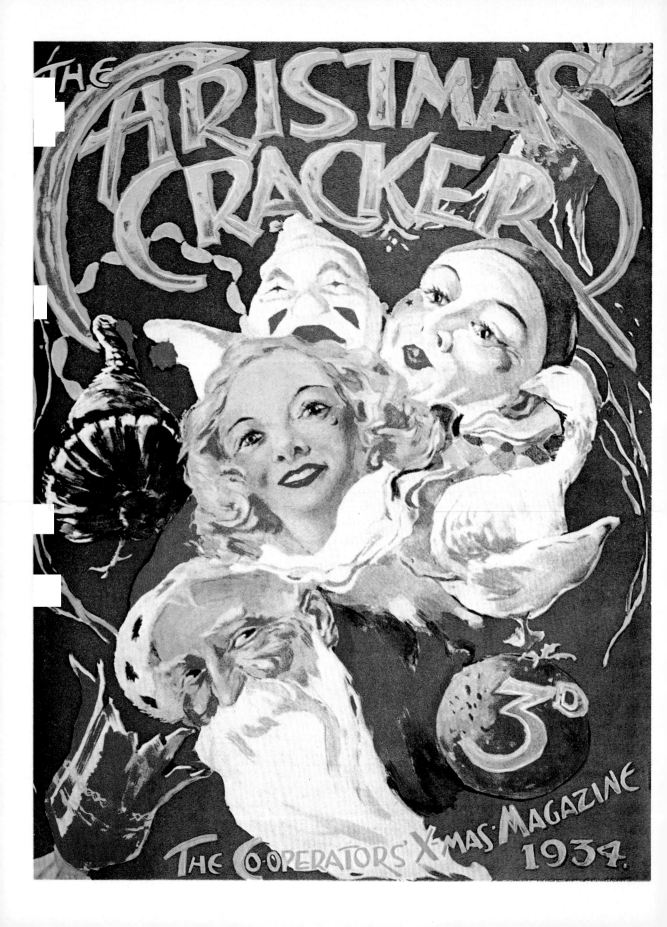

THE CHRISTMAS CRACKER

3D

THE CO-OPERATORS' X-MAS-MAGAZINE 1937.

9

Selective Pens

They talk of Christmas so long that it comes.
GEORGE HERBERT

The literature of Christmas abounds not only with those broad veins of traditional atmosphere noted earlier, but also with many a sharp selected nugget – close looks from a poet's eye, slanted salients from pens held at acute and at times aggressive angles. Once again the album is enormous; and again one may only hope to glance at a few pertinent examples, glance with the eye, say, of D. H. Lawrence noting the calligraphy of small animals on new-fallen snow – 'beautiful ropes of rabbit prints,' 'odd little filigree of field-mice' and 'the leaping marks of weasels' ... all in a winter landscape set hard by a single sentence: '... a tiny clump of trees bare on the hill-top – small beeches – writhing like iron in the blue sky.'

Lawrence presents an icy house instantaneously with his apparently simple: 'But it is immensely cold – everything frozen solid – milk, mustard, everything.' It is the mustard that does it. Just as a seldom noted but immediately recognisable kind of Christmas chill entered the nose and the journal of Arnold Bennett in 1903: '... the orange-apple *cold* Christmas smell of the greengrocers' shops.' A detail, but sterling stuff for the starched shirt-cuff, writer's lifeblood.

One may cut Longfellow short by simply quoting what must be the snowiest lines in the language:

Silent, and soft, and slow
Descends the snow.

and one may immediately again recognise the gifted, nail-on-the-head chat of Dickens in *The Holly Tree* with: 'The old lady up in the sky is picking

A magazine cover from the mid-thirties designed in period style and still showing the old ball-shaped plum pudding and the faces of Columbine and Pierrot once so popular as fancy-dress figures

her geese pretty hard today.' These are more than felicities, they are strong sensuous effects, different in quality from the nice and amiable 'household bird with the red stomacher', as John Donne has the robin.

Great feeling for the hard cold of winter and the tree's mystique drums with gentle awe through C. Day-Lewis's 'The Christmas Tree':

> Put out the lights now!
> Look at the Tree, the rough tree dazzled
> In oriole plumes of flame,
> Tinselled with twinkling frost fire, tasselled
> With stars and moons – the same
> That yesterday hid in the spinney and had no fame
> Till we put out the lights now.
>
> Hard are the nights now:
> The fields at moonrise turn to agate,
> Shadows are cold as jet;
> In dyke and furrow, in copse and faggot
> The frost's tooth is set;
> And stars are the sparks whirled out by the north wind's fret
> On the flinty nights now.
>
> So feast your eyes now
> On mimic star and moon-cold bauble:

Worlds may wither unseen,
But the Christmas Tree is a tree of fable,
A phoenix in evergreen,
And the world cannot change or chill what its mysteries mean
To your hearts and eyes now.

The vision dies now
Candle by candle: the tree that embraced it
Returns to its own kind,
To be earthed again and weather as best it
May the frost and the wind.
Children, it too had its hour – you will not mind
If it lives or dies now.

A winter's night several centuries earlier brought a vision of a very The Burning Babe different kind to Robert Southwell. 'The Burning Babe' is a poem of colossal theme, odd simplicity, and the intense thereness of good story-telling. It must be quoted in full here not only for all these qualities but also for the impact of its final lines:

As I in hoary winter's night
Stood shivering in the snow,
Surprised I was with sudden heat
Which made my heart to glow;
And lifting up a fearful eye
To view what fire was near,
A pretty babe all burning bright
Did in the air appear;
Who, scorchèd with excessive heat,
Such floods of tears did shed,
As though His floods should quench His flames,
Which with His tears were bred:
'Alas!' quoth He, 'but newly born
In fiery heats I fry,
Yet none approach to warm their hearts
Or feel my fire but I!

'My faultless breast the furnace is;
The fuel, wounding thorns;
Love is the fire, and sighs the smoke;
The ashes, shames and scorns;
The fuel Justice layeth on,
And Mercy blows the coals,
The metal in this furnace wrought
Are men's defilèd souls:
For which, as now on fire I am
To work them to their good,
So will I melt into a bath,
To wash them in my blood.'
With this He vanish'd out of sight
And swiftly shrunk away,
And straight I callèd unto mind
That it was Christmas Day.

Terror and tenderness in strange quantities, a hell-fire sermon from a Child very different from the innocence of so many early lullabies and carols. But this awful knowledge and severity is also found in other poets, as if Christ were born with the full authority later registered in paintings and mosaics of the Byzantine Pantocrator. Take Milton's huge and blasting poem on the Nativity – part of a single verse shows the feeling as he writes of the fate of the old gods and of Osiris:

> He feels from Judah's land
> The dreaded infant's hand,
> The rays of Bethlehem blind his dusky eyne...
> Our babe, to show his Godhead true,
> Can in his swaddling bands control the damnèd crew.

And in his poem 'The Nativity of Our Lord', Christopher Smart begins, at least, on a menacing note:

> Where is this stupendous stranger...

while W. B. Yeats, when he wrote of the Magi, has one most un-nerving and comprehensive line for the Saviour they were seeking:

> The uncontrollable mystery on the bestial floor.

The literature of the Nativity is immense and the above lines are, of course, singled out simply for their particular attitudes. No place here for a general Christmas anthology – but rather for an opportunity to illustrate a few evocative moods and salients, as, for instance, the sense of elation *before*

Left: *Cover of* Christmas Carrolles newely imprinted, *W. Copland, 1550*

Above: *Christmas display shop window at Lord & Taylor, of New York. The scene is an exact replica of an eighteenth-century ballroom at the imperial palace of Schönbrunn, near Vienna; with its aristocratic dancers circling a Christmas tree, this window was one of four illustrating Austrian Christmases of the past*
Below: *The old Italian Epiphanous witch Befana and the more modern mystery of Mary Poppins assist a nordic Santa Claus as their roads cross in Rome at Christmas-time*

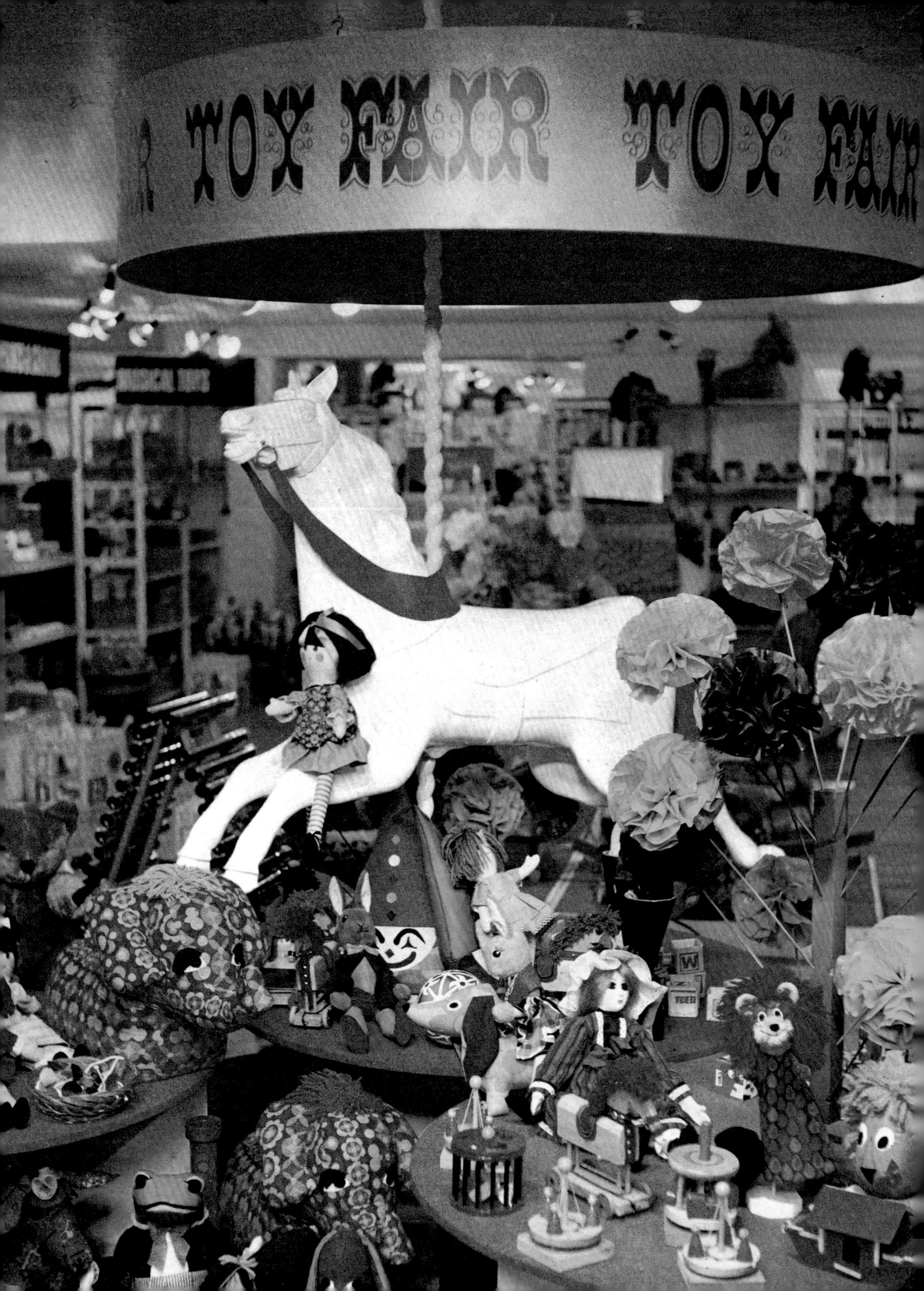
TOY FAIR TOY FAIR

Christmas, the mounting days of excitement and preparatory ritual, as so exactly evoked by D. H. Lawrence again, this time in *The Rainbow*:

Gradually there gathered the feeling of expectation. Christmas was coming. In the shed, at nights, a secret candle was burning, a sound of veiled voices was heard. The boys were learning the old mystery play of St George and Beelzebub. Twice a week, by lamplight, there was choir practice in the church, for the learning of old carols Brangwen wanted to hear. The girls went to these practices. Everywhere was a sense of mystery and rousedness. Everybody was preparing for something.

The time came near, the girls were decorating the church, with cold finger binding holly and fir and yew about the pillars, till a new spirit was in the church, the stone broke out into dark, rich leaf, the arches put forth their buds, and cold flowers rose to blossom in the dim, mystic atmosphere. Ursula must weave mistletoe over the door, and over the screen, and hang a silver dove from a sprig of yew, till dusk came down, and the church was like a grove.

But this is soon followed by a well-known sense of satiety:

It was bitter, though, that Christmas Day, as it drew on to evening, and night became a sort of bank holiday, flat and stale. The morning was so wonderful, but in the afternoon and evening the ecstasy perished like a nipped thing, like a bud in a false spring. Alas, that Christmas was only a domestic feast, a feast of sweet-meats and toys! Why did not the grown-ups also change their everyday hearts, and give way to ecstasy? Where was the ecstasy?

Depressive? But it is as familiar as the knowledge that alcohol will be followed by a hangover. We pay for everything, depression is the cell-mate of mania. Louis MacNeice in 'Twelfth Night' puts it more sweetly:

… For now the time of gifts is gone –
O boys that grow, O snows that melt,
O bathos that the years must fill –
Here is dull earth to build upon
Undecorated; we have reached
Twelfth Night or what you will … you will.

And W. H. Auden embraces the matter in one of his huge and masterly nutshells:

Well, so that is that. Now we must dismantle the tree,
Putting the decorations back into their cardboard boxes –
Some have got broken – and carrying them up to the attic.
The holly and the mistletoe must be taken down and burnt,
And the children got ready for school. There are enough
Left-overs to do, warmed up, for the rest of the week —
Not that we have much appetite, having drunk such a lot,
Stayed up so late, attempted – quite unsuccessfully –
To love all our relatives, and in general
Grossly overestimated our powers. Once again
As in previous years we have seen the actual Vision and failed
To do more than entertain it as an agreeable
Possibility, once again we have sent Him away
Begging though to remain His disobedient servant,
The promising child who cannot keep His word for long.

In *The Fir Tree*, Hans Andersen echoes the whole life and coming and going of Christmas through the thoughts of a little fir cut down for a Christmas tree and eventually banished to an attic, until much later it is brought out and burned – a tender and beautiful story, however hackneyed its reputation may seem to be. Similarly, Andersen's *The Little Match Girl* well bears re-reading: it is not as tritely sentimental as one somehow believes; it is based on the terrible snow-cold barefoot truth of the children of the poor of those days – yet at the same time it is a fair exposition of the fundamental and necessary illusion and illumination which Christmastide is and probably always will be. To think that Andersen who wrote this very tender story is said to have hated children ... no, he was simply scared of them in the raw and in the rough and *en masse*. He liked to stand away, and love them at their best – as many others do without admitting it.

But let us look at someone who would have none of this illusion business, at Edmund Gosse's father, and the episode of the plum pudding in the middle of the last century as recounted in *Father and Son*. Old man Gosse fulminated against the popish idolatry of 'Christ's Mass!' and 'the horrible heathen rites' until he almost made his son 'blush to look at a holly-berry'.

On Christmas Day of this year 1857 our villa saw a very unusual sight. My Father had given strictest charge that no difference whatever was to be made in our meals on that day; the dinner was to be neither more copious than usual nor less so. He was obeyed, but the servants, secretly rebellious, made a small plum-pudding for themselves. (I discovered afterwards, with pain, that Miss Marks received a slice of it in her boudoir.) Early in the afternoon, the maids – of whom we were now

From Hans Andersen's The Fir Tree, *1850*

advanced to keeping two – kindly remarked that 'the poor dear child ought to have a bit, anyhow,' and wheedled me into the kitchen, where I ate a slice of plum-pudding. Shortly I began to feel that pain inside which in my frail state was inevitable, and my conscience smote me violently. At length I could bear my spiritual anguish no longer, and bursting into the study I called out: 'Oh! Papa, Papa, I have eaten of flesh offered to idols!' It took some time, between my sobs, to explain what had happened. Then my Father sternly said: 'Where is the accursed thing?' I explained that as much as was left of it was still on the kitchen table. He took me by the hand, and ran with me into the midst of the startled servants, seized what remained of the pudding, and with the plate in one hand and me still tight in the other, ran till we reached the dust-heap, when he flung the idolatrous confectionery on to the middle of the ashes, and then raked it deep down into the mass. The suddenness, the violence, the velocity of this extraordinary act made an impression on my memory which nothing will ever efface.

And among many great diatribes against the whole immovable feast, there is George Bernard Shaw at his bitterest and most biased. From *Our Theatres in the Nineties*, the pertinent part of a biting paragraph:

I am sorry to have to introduce the subject of Christmas in these articles. It is an indecent subject; a cruel, gluttonous subject; a drunken, disorderly subject; a wasteful, disastrous subject; a wicked, cadging, lying, filthy, blasphemous, and demoralising subject. Christmas is forced on a reluctant and disgusted nation by the shopkeepers and the press: in its own merits it would wither and shrivel in the fiery breath of universal hatred; and anyone who looked back to it would be turned into a pillar of greasy sausages.

Dr Samuel Johnson made a rare reference to Christmas in a letter to Frances Reynolds on the twenty-third of December 1783:

Dearest Madam, You shall doubtless be very welcome to Me on Christmas day. I shall not dine alone, but the company will all be people whom we can stay with or leave ...

Evelyn Waugh has a few saddening words to say on a visiting uncle's Christmas in *Sword of Honour*, summed up in the phrase:

A forlorn relation was part of the furniture of Christmas in most English homes.

This commiserative sentence reflects a situation of our island culture rather better than that of the French. The de Goncourt brothers record New Year's Day (a rough social equivalent to our Christmas) of the year 1862:

New Year's Day, for us, is All Souls' Day. Our hearts grow chill and count those who are gone.

We climbed five flights of stairs to call on our cousin Cornélie in her poor little

room. She was soon obliged to send us away, so many ladies, schoolboys, and relatives came to see her. She had not enough chairs to seat us nor enough space to accommodate us. It is one of the admirable things about the aristocracy that it does not shun poverty. It closes its ranks against it. In middle-class families there are no relatives below a certain degree of wealth or above the fourth floor of a house.

Ten years later, and after his brother's death, Edmond wrote sourly indeed of the New Year:

> Monday, 1 January
>
> Last night I sought in vain in the brutality of animal pleasure forgetfulness of the first hour of a new year.

Tch! Away from such Parisian devices to the Anglo-Saxon heritage and a refreshing cold bath with Kilvert. In the diary for Sunday, Christmas Day 1870, the Rev. Francis records:

> As I lay awake praying in the early morning I thought I heard a sound of distant bells. It was an intense frost. I sat down in my bath upon a sheet of thick ice which broke in the middle into large pieces whilst sharp points and jagged edges stuck all round the sides of the tub like *chevaux de frise*, not particularly comforting to the naked thighs and loins, for the keen ice cut like broken glass. The ice water stung and scorched like fire. I had to collect the floating pieces of ice and pile them on a chair before I could use the sponge and then I had to thaw the sponge in my hands for it was a mass of ice.

Better? But it goes on better still:

> The morning was most brilliant. Walked to the Sunday School with Gibbins and the road sparkled with millions of rainbows, the seven colours gleaming in every glittering point of hoar frost. The church was very cold in spite of two roaring stove fires...

Kilvert was obviously conscious of the cold till the last, but would never give in. We can be proud of our parsons.

And, in other spheres, would Jane Carlyle give in? For we read in her letter (23 December 1843) to Jeannie Welsh:

> ... I have just had to swallow a bumper of my uncle's Madeira (which *is* capital drink!) to nerve me for writing at all! A huge boxful of dead animals from the Welshman arriving late on Saturday night, together with the visions of *Scrooge*, had so worked on Carlyle's nervous organisation that he has been seized with a perfect *convulsion* of hospitality, and has actually insisted on *improvising two* dinner parties with only a day between. Now, the *improvisation* of dinner parties is all very well for the parties who have to *eat* them simply, but for those who have to *organise* them and *help to cook them c'est autre chose ma chère!*

This kind of browsing on such a wide subject as Christmas can go on somewhere near to ever. There are Trollope, Pepys, Mayhew, Shakespeare, Clare ... O'Henry, Ring Lardner, E.E. Cummings ... the list goes on and on. Sherlock Holmes provides a Christmas Goose in which to hide his *Blue Carbuncle*, Bret Harte writes a rattling Western story in his *Santa Claus at Simpson's Bar*. There is the Countess von Arnim giving us a *gemütlich* scene in *Elizabeth and Her German Garden*, for the time an interior garden furnished

Christmas street-sellers in Berlin, 1869

with a lighted Christmas tree on Christmas Eve, when the *Christkind* brings presents:

My three babies sang lustily too, whether they happened to know what was being sung or not. They had on white dresses in honour of the occasion, and the June baby was even arrayed in a low-necked and short-sleeved garment, after the manner of Teutonic infants, whatever the state of the thermometer. Her arms are like miniature prize-fighter's arms – I never saw such things; they are the pride and joy of her little nurse, who had tied them up with blue ribbons, and kept on kissing them. I shall certainly not be able to take her to balls when she grows up, if she goes on having arms like that.

The Countess adds, a page later:

I cannot see that there was anything gross about our Christmas, and we were perfectly merry without any need to pretend, and for at least two days it brought us a little nearer together, and made us kind.

Guy de Maupassant takes a rather harder view in three separate stories of Christmas Eve in Normandy and Paris. The cold of a white Normandy is bitter: in one story his narrator finds himself visiting very poor peasants who are taking a meagre meal off the top of a large country breadbin containing the newly dead corpse of the grandfather – they had been sleeping on the cold floor while he was ill, and had only now removed the body from the one bed in the cottage. The second Norman story tells of a country-woman who is given a mysterious egg found, inconceivably, out in the numb miles of dead hard frost; she goes mad; the madness is amazingly exorcised by the priest during mass on Christmas Eve. The third story is told by a Parisian bachelor who is fond of fattish women, who goes out to find one to share his rich but lonely Christmas Eve dinner, and who dines her and finally gets her to bed, where she begins to groan and is delivered of a child. The bachelor, kindly, allows them to stay until the child can be sent away to foster parents. Meanwhile the young woman has fallen in love with him – but she has also resumed her normal shape, and he only likes fattish women. She haunts him on the streets, begging to kiss his hand.

All these three themes are brutal, beautifully told, poetic and horrifying: yet they are tender, Maupassant is subtly on the side of the victim although he never states it so, he leaves the reader to judge these cuts of life; a warmth has crept in from nowhere, and – as I think – that nowhere is largely the sacred state of its being Christmas Eve. Ultimately, the judgment is the same as the Countess von Arnim's.

Mürger's original story, and the libretto of Puccini's *La Bohème*, begin on 'a cold Christmas Eve' in Paris. But here we have, in most productions, a moment of absurdity which neither the great good music nor the spirit of Christmas Eve can sober – when in the cold artist's garret, full of bric-à-brac to burn, an author wildly consigns his manuscripts to the stove in the fraternal cause of heat; whatever excuse is momentarily made not to burn a chair, you can *see* that the studio is stuffed with odd burnabilities. A Gordon Craig is needed to straighten the moment out; though the opera is so good that soon all bathos is forgotten and Christmas Eve continues its un-Christmassy way through the Bohemian supper-streets of the luminant town.

But let us forget this excursion, only excusable here because Christmas Eve gives the opera an added strength of occasion, and return to the true pathos of Anne Frank. This heartening girl, her name by now almost a synonym of hope, wrote, from the room in which she spent the years of hiding from the Nazis, a letter describing her Christmas to the imaginary pen-friend Kitty: from the secret room in Amsterdam, with the dentist's footdrill in it, and Deanna Durbin on the wall, and the rules of quiet and the blind year-in-year-out listening, and outside the occasional thump of a jackboot, or worse, the silence of a possible spy:

Monday. Dec. 27. 1943.
Dear Kitty,

On Friday evening for the first time in my life I received something for Christmas. Koophuis and the Kraler girls had prepared a lovely surprise again. Miep had made a lovely Christmas cake, on which was written 'Peace 1944'. Elli had provided a pound of sweet biscuits of pre-war quality. For Peter, Margot, and me a bottle of Yoghourt, and a bottle of beer for each of the grown-ups. Everything was so nicely done up, and there were pictures stuck on the different parcels. Otherwise Christmas passed by quickly for us.

Yours,
Anne.

Of the many Christmas folk-tales, one especially deserves to be recorded here. It is for those who love, and perhaps also for those who hate, spiders. It is a story told in parts of Germany, and is quoted here from an account written down by Robert Haven Schauffler. First, the situation – the Christmas tree at which all the house animals, cat, dog, canary, even the shy little mice always took a happy peep each year. Except for one kind of house animal – the little grey spiders. Why? Because before every Christmas the 'house-mother' went round with a big broom everywhere sweeping things up, so the spiders had to run off double quick. Impasse. So eventually they went to the Christ Child, complained, and the Christ Child was sorry for them so he let them in when no one was looking. And here is the big passage:

They came creepy, creepy, down the attic stairs, creepy, creepy, up the cellar stairs, creepy, creepy, along the halls – and into the beautiful room. The fat mother spiders and the old papa spiders were there, and all the little teenty, tonty, curly spiders, the baby ones. And then they looked! Round and round the Tree they crawled, and looked and looked and looked. Oh, what a good time they had! They thought it was perfectly beautiful. And when they looked at everything they could see from the floor, they started up the tree to see some more. All over the tree they ran, creepy, crawly, looking at every single thing. Up and down, in and out, over every branch and twig the little spiders ran, and saw every one of the pretty things right up close.

The result? They left their webs everywhere they went. So the Christ Child, knowing that house-mothers do not like cobwebs, touched them and turned them all to gold; hence the golden 'angels' hair' on the Christmas tree.

Another animal story, a true one as remembered of his youth by Claud Cockburn, seems also particularly trenchant. Writing of a time long ago alone in Berlin with an Airedale dog, and flat broke, he says:

This episode occurred in Berlin, and who wants a big Airedale dog in Berlin in the middle of winter? The reason I had this sad, savage brute was, to make things entirely simple, that he belonged to the ex-husband of the wife to be of the American novelist and Nobel prize-winner Sinclair Lewis. By biting, he was breaking up the romance. So I tended him, for I liked Sinclair Lewis very much and was opposed to seeing him bitten and having his romance broken up.

When I bought food, the butcher gave me free food for the dog: offal. Came this penniless Christmas Eve and I said to the butcher that personally I was dining with some millionaires but that maybe given the Festive Season we could get a free double portion for the dog. The stench when I cooked it next day was awful. My hunger was worse. But worst of all was the expression on the face of that poor dog which had never thought to see a human being take the other half-portion of the Christmas dinner.

Man's Best Friend   Truman Capote, in *A Christmas Memory*, obliges with somewhat greater goodwill towards Man's Best Friend:

Christmas Eve afternoon we scrape together a nickel and go to the butcher's to buy Queenie's traditional gift, a good gnawable beef bone. The bone, wrapped in funny paper, is placed high in the tree near the silver star. Queenie knows it's there. She squats at the foot of the tree staring up in a trance of greed: when bedtime arrives she refuses to budge.

This story, set in old-fashioned country surroundings, gives a sensuous picture of silvered winter woods where 'A wild turkey calls. A renegade hog grunts in the undergrowth' – thus doubling up in the open air on two established Christmas dishes – and gives a fine picture of holly and tree-gathering and a particular trick with regard to the choosing of the tree. As the boy and the old woman cross the morning country:

'We're almost there; can you smell it, Buddy?' she says, as though we were approaching an ocean.

And, indeed, it is a kind of ocean. Scented acres of holiday trees, prickly-leafed holly. Red berries shiny as Chinese bells: black crows swoop upon them screaming. Having stuffed our burlap sacks with enough greenery and crimson to garland a dozen windows, we set about choosing a tree. 'It should be,' muses my friend, 'twice as tall as a boy. So a boy can't steal the star.' The one we pick is twice as tall as me.

And who perhaps best of all retrieves the sentiment of Christmas fairly up-to-date, the childhood Christmas as many would wish it? Dylan Thomas.

... I can never remember whether it snowed for six days and six nights when I was twelve or whether it snowed for twelve days and twelve nights when I was six; or whether the ice broke and the skating grocer vanished like a snow man through a white trap-door on that same Christmas Day that the mince-pies finished Uncle Arnold and we tobogganed down the seaward hill, all the afternoon, on the best tea-tray, and Mrs Griffiths complained, and we threw a snowball at her niece, and my hands burned so, with the heat and the cold, when I held them in front of the fire, that I cried for twenty minutes and then had some jelly.

All the Christmases roll down the hill towards the Welsh-speaking sea, like a snowball growing whiter and bigger and rounder, like a cold and headlong moon

Christmas decorations in Carnaby Street, London

bundling down the sky that was our street; and they stop at the rim of the ice-edged, fish-freezing waves, and I plunge my hands in the snow and bring out whatever I can find; holly or robins or pudding, squabbles and carols and oranges and tin whistles, and the fire in the front room, and bang go the crackers, and holy, holy, holy, ring the bells, and the glass bells shaking on the tree, and Mother Goose, and Struwelpeter – oh! the baby-burning flames and the clacking scissor-man! – Billy Bunter and Black Beauty, Little Women and boys who have three helpings, Alice and Mrs Potter's badgers, penknives, teddy-bears – named after a Mr Theodore Bear, their inventor, or father, who died recently in the United States – mouth-organs, tin-soldiers, and blancmange, and Auntie Bessie playing 'Pop Goes the Weasel' and 'Nuts in May' and 'Oranges and Lemons' on the un-tuned piano in the parlour all through the thimble-hiding musical-chairing blind-man's-buffing party at the end of the never-to-be-forgotten day at the end of the unremembered year.

And later he writes:

Now out of that bright white snowball of Christmas gone comes the stocking, the stocking of stockings, that hung at the foot of the bed with the arm of a golliwog dangling over the top and small bells ringing in the toes. There was a company, gallant and scarlet but never nice to taste though I always tried when very young, of belted and busbied and musketed lead soldiers so soon to lose their heads and legs in the wars on the kitchen table after the tea-things, the mince-pies, and the cakes that I helped to make by stoning the raisins and eating them, had been cleared away; and a bag of moist and many-coloured jelly-babies and a folded flag and a false nose and a tram-conductor's cap and a machine that punched tickets and rang a bell; never a catapult; once, by a mistake that no one could explain, a little hatchet...

Dylan Thomas's Christmas in Wales

And again later:

Christmas morning was always over before you could say Jack Frost. And look! suddenly the pudding was burning! Bang the gong and call the fire-brigade and the book-loving firemen! Someone found the silver three-penny-bit with a currant on it; and the someone was always Uncle Arnold. The motto in my cracker read:

Let's all have fun this Christmas Day,
Let's play and sing and shout hooray!

and the grown-ups turned their eyes towards the ceiling, and Auntie Bessie, who had already been frightened, twice, by a clockwork mouse, whimpered at the side-board and had some elderberry wine. And someone put a glass bowl full of nuts on the littered table, and my uncle said, as he said once every year: 'I've got a shoe-nut here. Fetch me a shoe-horn to open it, boy.'

And dinner was ended.

And I remember that on the afternoon of Christmas Day, when the others sat around the fire and told each other that this was nothing, no, nothing, to the great snowbound and turkey-proud yule-log-crackling holly-berry-bedizined and kissing-under-the-mistletoe Christmas when *they* were children, I would go out, school-capped and gloved and mufflered, with my bright new boots squeaking, into the white world on to the seaward hill, to call on Jim and Dan and Jack and to walk with them through the silent snowscape of our town.

We went padding through the street, leaving huge deep footprints in the snow, on the hidden pavements.

'I bet people'll think there's been hippoes.'

Coloured metal Christmas decorations, a speciality of Mexico

Eno's Fruit Salt advertisement, 1882

10

The Love-Hate Luxus

... to keep wold Chris'mas up.
WILLIAM BARNES

The mid-Victorian who wrote the above line may rest assured that in these mid-to-late twentieth-century years wold Chris'mas is indeed kept up. Advertisements to do so by buying, and warnings about local travel, begin to appear in October, and by mid-November the shops are already showing a tentative tinsel. No sooner, in fact, has modern man recuperated from the ravages of his August holiday than he must go into training for the hard run up to December the twenty-fifth.

The big buying spree is on, and there is little doubt of the love-hate with which it is generally greeted. Perhaps this suits a civilisation devoted to its dichotomies; certainly, as we have seen, a sunburst in darkest winter seems necessary, but today it is of a luxuriance never before conceived, and, as with anything from politics to poodles, when too much is said or seen of it, the result is likely to be a soulful nausea.

It is too facile to blame commerce, the agent of so great a proliferation, for all this. A study of Christmas advertisements shows that few complex appeals are made, there is little recourse to fear, sex, health or vanity campaigns: no, this is largely a laying out of goods for display, and who can be blamed for that but the buyer? Commerce knows that the things are wanted, and simply – though on a scale not so simple – sets out to provide them. The fact that plastic snow is manufactured in July, and that someone has thought up a do-it-yourself Christmas tree of three thousand different component parts, is part of a drive to satisfy – no one is forced to buy them. Nor are you forced into a restaurant to pay double prices for a

Christmas dinner. You are only tempted. It is really no more sinister than the arrival of a particularly succulent basket of crabs at the fishmonger. It is more a matter of generosity or an anxiety to impress which forces you to accede to the Big Buy. There is also a school of thought which welcomes the afflatus of Christmas advertising as a diversion for the lonely or needy; something to read about, dream about, vicariously to live.

The cost of Christmas goes up every year. The demand for bank withdrawals increases, in Britain for example, by well over one hundred million pounds each year and still rises faster. The figure of national savings withdrawn grows equally enormously. In the United States over half the entire toy sales for the year are attributed to the Christmas turnover. And – perhaps the most telling figure of all – it is noticeable that in certain published family budget statistics the word 'Christmas' has suddenly crept in among the usual items of 'food' or 'car' or 'insurance' as a vital expenditure. No more significant acceptance of Christmas the succubus is needed.

So – a Merry Commerce to you, whether your gifts are a simple packet of white chocolate snowballs, or, as suggested by a New York jeweller, a diamond ring as 'a last minute gift suggestion guaranteed to surprise her'. That ring cost $176,000. 'Mink covers for his golf-clubs' is also on the American agenda, and there is marketed as a Christmas novelty a pair of gold thermometrical cuff-links with Fahrenheit on one side and Centigrade on the other.

However, apart from such ambivalent pressures, the modern approach to Christmas has its reliefs and conveniences. No more the curse of sticky white berries on the mistletoe – like much else they can be plastic. And the plastic Christmas tree is non-inflammable. 'Original Finland Christmas snow from the land of Santa Claus' comes out of a jolly red and white aerosol spray. And for those who like something different, perhaps a green seven foot tall man-made tree complete with rotating music-box base which plays 'Silent Night' and 'O Come, All Ye Faithful' as it turns? Decorated with sixty 'classic Bavarian' ornaments in silver and gold? Or, for those who prefer real candles, there is a little 'hand-beaten one-dimensional metal tree' twenty inches high, and made in Mexico for the American market, which comes complete with six candles for the small candleholders that tip each branch plus one indeed for the top of the tiny wee tree. Meanwhile ordinary household goods come in holly-enriched wrappers. White, white detergents become even whiter with gifts of plastic snowflakes. Tree decorations given away 'absolutely free' bind a breakfast food to the festive season.

Thus, as Aldous Huxley said, 'the deep festal impulse of man was harnessed and made to turn a very respectable little wheel in the mills of industry' and we find shops stocking and selling tree ornaments and crackers and artificial snow for the long-sighted all the year round: and in America there is an establishment called Santa's Workshop, North Pole, in New York State, where Santa Claus is on duty most of the year round. With his large and jolly staff of helpers he is ready to welcome young visitors to his zoo and workshop and even give them a ride in his reindeer-drawn

sleigh. One may tarry for a chat with Tannenbaum the Talking Christmas Tree: or with Elmer the Elf. On the way out, the young visitor can scrape a little souvenir ice off the pole called North which is kept frozen even in mid-summer.

Post Offices jump on the profitable bandwagon with special Christmas stamp issues – but they most of all deserve it, for of course the whole organisation of Christmas posts is a technological nightmare of its own. Apart from parcel, card and letter trouble, the telephone has an appalling weight to bear, so that Christmas Day calls overseas have to be booked good and early indeed. Meanwhile the transport industries are in for their own particular seasonal joys. Every year more and more people celebrate Christmas by avoiding it, and leave for the ski-slopes; and the colder-blooded take to the boats and a subtropical cruise. Christmas cruise advertisements start appearing in the press in April; package winter sport holidays are heavily booked even before the brochures appear, and these are also published in April. But wherever these people go, they will still meet up with Christmas in one or other of its national forms – a turkey off the Canaries, a darkly devil-horned Krampus in white Austria, a shower of sweetmeats in Mexico.

And there are the multitudes of those who work away and come home for Christmas. Railways and roads and airlines are wildly overworked, the roads are a metal bedlam of convivial anxiety. Plainly such conditions, together with possibilities of bad weather, lead to a formidable number of accidents. A time of joy, a time of national disaster – if all the accidents happened in one place, a relief fund would be started. But by Christmas Day itself, when most travellers have arrived, life and limb are relatively safer: indeed, an extraordinary quiet settles on large airports and on stations, on empty buses and trains continuing a reduced service – so that from the streets it must seem that everybody has retired to the quiet 'family' Christmas Day of most European nations. Not so, of course. It is simply that the feasting is localised, and largely within doors. Only the longer distance travelling has stopped – to recommence with the day after Christmas and the opening of theatres and the doors of further friends and relations.

In the most dangerous days mounting towards Christmas Eve, alcohol and the steering-wheel have been obvious incompatibles; and add the rolling, carefree pedestrian. New laws are now after the drunken driver. What marked decades like the fifties and early sixties, when many more millions became motorised, was a new affluence of 'little parties' and 'office parties' in mid-December. Irrespective of any particular saint's day or traditional occasion, people got the habit of simply meeting for 'a Christmas drink' weeks before the occasion; and numberless office parties, with people unused to alcohol suddenly taking far too much of it, were a particular menace in congested city areas; so much so that they have tended to become voluntarily unpopular and often stopped among the more responsible in the most troublesome centres of Britain, America and Germany.

In its heyday, the office party was indeed an extraordinary phenomenon in that here there thrived again the true atmosphere of Saturnalia, the overturning of authority – yet by people who knew nothing of such ancient traditions, though they very naturally took to their intention. Office boys slapping the boss on the back, typists trilling the year's suppressed emotions, a playful waste-paper basket crowning the assistant cashier, an awful lot of liquor gaudying the grey filing cabinets ... all of which, of course, seldom occurred in the larger and naturally careful financial offices, but in those of smaller companies everywhere. The far-seeing executive would canalise the affair away from the office into a dance or party held elsewhere: but even so, there has always been a danger in the last day of work,

Cartoon by Pete from The Argosy *Christmas number, 1967*

the moment of the early laying down of pens and tools. At mid-day in office centres the bars are full to bursting point. Possibly most of these earlier revellers rely on public transport home: but it all still makes for much staggering of pedestrians. But then – what bean-feast, wayzgoose or *Kermesse* was ever safe?

Superstitions and resolutions

The idea of Christmas is indivisible from the mathematical superstition of the End of the Year. 'It'll all be over by Christmas' is a notorious phrase remembered from the first months of the 1914–18 war: the same concept recurs in everyone's minds about almost everything, and deeply celebrates the common human wish to wrap up matters, to end and start again. Hence the tradition of New Year's resolutions, quite a strong force with some people. It needs to be. Questions of rent and income tax arise. There has been the cost of a golden sunburst, now the New Year gnashes at the silver lining of your pockets. It is altogether a time for emptying those pockets and gritting the teeth to fill them again; for filling the stomach and then mending it with indigestion and headache remedies whose sales, according to a central London chemist, rise by *five hundred per cent* over the holiday. Doctors recognise that there is a pronounced psychosomatic factor abroad – a decline in illness before the great occasion and, quite apart from any digestive troubles, a strong propensity for any old illness afterwards. Thus we see a further bewildering paradox – a wish to wrap up the old year and start afresh with the best foot forward, but also a strong desire to put that foot to bed.

While we finger our New Year's diaries and look with mixed feelings at the blind roster of new blank days, and read in those bewildering texts at the beginning that the Missouri River is 2,945 miles long or that Ulm Cathedral spire is 528 feet high, we may pause to remember that the New Year has always shared with Christmas the symbol of a newborn child. There is a Greek sarcophagus which records a babe cradled in a winnowing basket at the January Dionysian festival, and again cradled among farm animals, among oxen and sheep: and everyone knows the cartoonists' angelic New Year Child, and the bearded Old Year declining. Death and birth again, it is rightly part of the time of year. Only a week after the holy moment of midnight mass, everybody is out again to celebrate an outwardly different but essentially similar midnight. In Paris every car hoots, in harbour cities like Oslo the sirens of hundreds of ships wail and shriek as the Norwegians plunge their noses into the blue flames of a lighted brandy glass. Crowds everywhere in most of the world are out dancing and throwing streamers and kissing and singing – the same who celebrated so gravely a week before the birth of Christ, the coming of another form of hope for the future.

It is largely accepted today that Christ is too much forgotten at Christmas. There is the old American joke of the woman who saw a crib outside a church and whose immediate thought was: 'What? Even the Church horning in on it all?' A possibly true story. But it is certainly true that the quieter character of the religious scene is simply overwhelmed by an acceleration of the kinds of noise and colour which so easily distract a

materialist world; ironically that world itself is exactly like a child in a cradle responding, innocently enough, to the glittering necklace or watch-chain held before it.

However, it is also true that the Church itself is projecting much more at Christmas than in previous years. There are many more carol services, many more masses, and more of all the colour which catches a colour-conditioned people's eyes – simple matters such as a lighted Christmas tree on church precincts, or newer initiatives such as a pop group playing for charity on St Paul's Cathedral steps. The press devotes space to Christian messages from prominent clerics, and radio and television play a part in diffusing elements of the Christian story further than ever before. And there is a new vigour with which the Church attacks the practical necessities of charity and serving the poor. Dwarfed by the great gorging buy-sell spree, but alongside it, there is room for an accelerated projection of the Christian image, both visually and in its message – which anyway thousands have learned without ever knowing it to be Christian. The quick nervous responses of today's world make it possible for many different influences to be absorbed at the same time. There is room, in fact, for everything – except for the nausea of too much of one thing. Thus, against the reitera-tion of a million Santa Claus images, it is a relief to see the great and simple Cross formed by lights left on in the rooms of a façade of a New York sky-scraper; it is a relief to see the calm of Madonna and Child on a postage stamp; and human delights like crib-making, and those speckled silver advent cards where you open a little door each day up to Christmas – these are increasing and absolutely acceptable.

Nevertheless, the preponderance and ubiquity of gift displays in shop windows and in advertisements are the real disservices of commerce to the Christian image. Innocent enough in motive, the sum total of glare and weight overpowers. Christian imagery cannot be used in this direct context of selling – although it would be almost reasonable to suppose so today, since advertising techniques are so much part of life. Attempts of bad Good Taste, such as in America a full-page prayer in gothic lettering ending up with words of 'confidence for the future' and the name (in dramatically deliberate small type) of an insurance company – these cannot pass with a sensitive public. But a shop window can be devoted entirely to a crib, with no mention of gifts, much as it might be devoted to a national flag in time of emergency, with ambivalent good effect. And the Three Kings (but not as Wise Men) with their direct story of gift-bringing, may just legitimately be used though with much, much care.

The spirit of goodwill itself persists in ways beyond the commercially stimulated conception of giving. The use of Christmas as a reason for amnesty – historically a particularly strong tradition in Spain – still occurs sporadically all over the world: even if political expedience may partly underlie such a move, its driving force and occasion are very much the Christian idea. All over the world, too, there is obviously a special spirit of generosity about – it is almost as if people feared to be generous ordinarily and longed for an excuse. One reads, for instance, of strange sudden gifts –

'Christmas comes but once a year' – a scene at the Evelina Hospital, London, from The Graphic of Christmas, 1882

like the mid-upper gun turret of a Lancastrian bomber, an esoteric rarity, presented to New Zealand's Auckland Transport Museum by the Argentine Air Force. While at a London hospital for ophthalmic diseases a particular effort is made, involving accelerated hours of surgery and nursing beyond the normal schedule, to give to a number of children the gift of their eyesight on Christmas Day itself. The organisation of charitable gifts to the poor, and of Christmas dinners for the old and lonely is, of course, a long established Christian tradition. The most modern note in this context is the new sense of global rather than local poverty – so that a definitive note of guilt now coats the gingerbread, as the turkey-laden open their papers to see more and more photographs of the emaciated and starving in less fortunate countries.

Meanwhile the great golden bandwagon rolls along and many are the *Commercialisation* ingenious jumps for it. The sentiment of the Germans has now to allow for *of Christmas* share certificates to be hung on the traditional tree; in America you are advised to purchase stock certificates for your son 'to teach the young mind about capitalism'. American enterprise tempts with ever more varied confections such as a solid gold half-opened sardine tin to be used as an ashtray, or those mink covers for golf-clubs; British initiative sends a Father Christmas parachuting down over London with gifts for a children's home; while Paris has its telephonic service *Allô Cadeaux* which you can ring up for an immediate list of available new gift suggestions. In Britain one comes across a heady news item in the July press: 'Christmas cards are selling well in Yarmouth'; and friends from Africa will perhaps oblige with an atmospheric greetings card showing neither holly nor Kings nor robins, but simply a dark grey mass of hippopotamuses photographed in a wallow of lighter grey mud. Similar to the personal thought and sometimes the appearance of these fat river-horses are the family group photographs which some choose as their rigidly smiling Christmas beneficence.

Few enterprises resist the bandwagon. Stripteasers fling off veils of mistletoe, the sex-stimulant 'girlie' magazines photograph their nude girls arriving in a reindeer-driven sleigh or lying warm as toast in the snow by a Christmas tree. Magazines of all kinds have their go – an accoucheurs' journal suggests the 'very acceptable gift' of a key fob in real leather bearing the arms of the Royal College of Midwives; eminent art quarterlies cannot resist the reproduction of a Nativity masterpiece or two; a gardening paper will send you out whittling or potting something or other 'to while away an idle Christmas hour after the pudding'; and so on ad infinitum, together with thousand upon thousand of party hints in more general magazines and papers – 'if you lack cheerful red holly berries, gather some green fir-tree fronds, arrange these nicely and place a red candle in the midst' (and watch your party go up in flames) and ideas for new foods and drinks like 'to make a good Ale Punch, take a quart of old ale, a quarter pint each of gin, rum and whisky, cinnamon, cloves, nutmeg' (and go off your head). But stay ... if one considers again this welter of new niceties, and the subtler ways of wrapping presents and prettier forms of decoration, they are all probably beneficial in that they stimulate the expertise of *doing* rather than turning a

Design from the top of a box of crackers, c. 1910

switch; and the result is always possibly happier on eye and stomach. That is, if there is time. But time at Christmas-time is a rare commodity. At best, it all looks exciting on the glossy coloured magazine page, accelerates the general festive mood, and can be vicariously enjoyed.

Christmas advertisements German magazines seem to be more reticent in these matters than English and American ones: on the whole they become more excited about *Sylvesterabend* or New Year's Eve than about Christmas itself, much of whose traditional apparel they exported to the world from its exceptional blossoming in the native forests. French and Scandinavian journals are equally undedicated; and even in America specifically Christmas advertising and feature matter is not so mightily whole-hearted as in Britain, which seems indeed to hold on to its tradition of making the merriest yule of all. Britain and America are the only countries which go on feasting and merry-making at the highest pitch through the holy Christmas Day itself; but America has no Boxing Day and resumes business immediately on the twenty-sixth; and though all European countries have their extra traditional days before and after Christmas Day, most usually reserve Christmas Day itself for a quiet though well-fed day within the family.

During the last decade or two, since there has been a general rise in wages, and the custom of tipping has in many sectors fallen away, the habit of so very many people demanding Christmas boxes or *étrennes* has declined; though a number of fairly well-paid service bodies, such as dustmen and lift-operators and others, still demand with the authority of a possible backlash their ancient rights. One of the newest and neatest of contemporary attitudes is that of the smiling and open-handed visit of a delivery boy to say that this year his employer has asked him not to call for a Christmas box.

As interesting as all those who jump on the great bandwagon are those who jump off at the height of its speed. Great new Winter Sales advertisements appear on the last days before Christmas, and at least one forward-looking London dress shop divests itself in mid-Christmas week of frost, holly and snowballs to blaze against its neighbour's tinsel with a wildly incandescent glare of yellow daffodils, lime-green saplings, white sports clothes and all other things of spring. It is a vernal thunderbolt of no mean impact.

Beyond the plastic decorations and the tremendous influx of 'novelty' gifts which everyone sees, new industrial inventions of an arcane nature owe their being to Christmas. A fair example, which one may vary and multiply in the imagination with scarcely any rein on fantasy, is the American development of a petrol-driven shear with a cutter at the end of a long shaft for trimming fir-trees to the desirably symmetrical conical shape; the cutter head is balanced by the weight of the tiny petrol engine, and everybody is the happier. One hears, too, of the production of lighter, nylon beards for centrally heated Santa Clauses, and of a certain seasonable production of red tropical Santa-wear.

The general impetus to action stimulates all sorts of energy. On the Serpentine lake in London there is held an annual Christmas Day swimming race. Very English? But they are popping in and out of holes in the ice all over Finland, and one of the thirty Serpentine contestants in a recent year was a seventy-nine-year-old Frenchman. Outdoor games of all kinds erupt, and horse racing, hunting, and, if the weather is reasonably clement, even alfresco band concerts by the grey winter seaside and a Christmas Day cricket match. Nearer to the tradition of Christmas, choirs and solo singers go down coalmines to sing carols – 'Blonde Linda joins in coalface carols' runs a typical headline – and a helicopter is got ready to hover Christmas fare to an oil-rig far out to sea. The spirit of giving extends towards animals – as it always did in the ancient tradition of sympathetic magic, though now in the simpler form of an impulse to give – and one reads of a group of warehousemen sending cards and giving fruit, nuts and even a plastic rattle to a runaway monkey found sheltering deep among the crates.

Weather, of course, affects many things. In London you may have a red-hot robin stomping round in the shirt-sleeve sunshine, yet the next year an east wind freeze-up. But elsewhere expectations are different, for instance Stockholm and Oslo expect snow to have fallen by then, and in Finland father entering dressed in his shaggy fur coat as the goat gift-bringer expects to knock real snow off his boots. Nowadays in Scandinavia the groan of the snowplough and the special susurrus of chains on motor-wheels provide a strange percussive background to the quiet of the country snow, or the metropolitan air tinkling with canned carillon music; and if there is snow in New York the giant plastic figures of reindeer and choirboys, angels and Santa Clauses form a weird background of waxwork stillness against the sanitation department's great chimneyed vehicle sucking up the guttered snow and spewing out its merry grey-white fountain. Rockefeller Plaza gives an extra icy dimension with its ice rink and coloured skating figures,

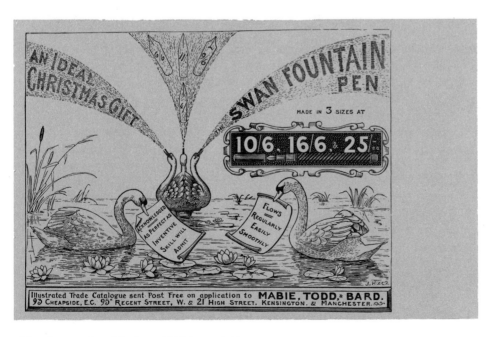

Advertisement from Black and White, *1896*

and the city is brilliant with Christmas trees on a grand scale. The American habit of a holly wreath on the door can be varied with wreaths of silver and coloured gourds made in such places as the Nebraska centre for homeless children at Boys' Town; and with wreaths of red chili peppers from Mexico complete with a free cookery book and the assurance that thus at last you can both have your wreath and eat it.

To collect street money for Christmas dinners for the poor, American city streets see thigh-high red-brick cardboard chimney-boxes attended by bell-ringing Santas. But in these so centrally-heated cities Santa Claus finds few real chimneys nowadays: it is thus sometimes the custom to leave one window uncurtained for the guidance of Santa Claus or Kriss Kingle, as some families have always done for the *Christkindl* in Germany. Otherwise Santa Claus is ready for children in many a big store, seated very often in an old-fashioned sitting-room or other romantic circumstance, taking the believers one after another on his lap and whispering sweet somethings into their hands. A further pleasure for young and old New Yorkers is the annual presentation of Tchaikovsky's Christmas ballet *The Nutcracker*, by now an established tradition. Occasionally also there is, as in London, *Peter Pan*, and the exhilarating panorama of a largely adult audience clapping their hands and calling for 'Tinker Bell, Tinker Bell!'

Christmas songs old and new

Both America and England have long ago entered the lay Christmas song market. As we have noted, many early carols were non-Christian folk-songs; so there is nothing very new in the impulse to write a song called, say, 'Im gonna spend my Christmas with a Dalek', except for the updated content. But the most popular atmosphere of all still reflects the traditional longing for snow (unlikely in England, but expected in much of the north United States), a longing coupled always with a yearning for the Victorian scene. Thus the largest sales success of all has been that of 'I'm Dreaming of a White Christmas', and others of very great popularity are 'Winter Wonderland' and 'Sleigh Bells Ring'. Hardy perennials these, as now for a long time 'Jingle Bells' has been: this latter one may have heard sung in French with a typically Gallic transference from all things white and wonderful to 'Je t'adore, Je t'adore'. With musical fashions among jazz and pop groups changing today with such rapidity, new songs attached to those fashions do not seem to have the same chance of becoming traditional – 'Rocking around the Christmas Tree' or 'Blue Christmas'. In Victorian times, contrived Christmas songs were of the ballad type and kept to the parlour piano, with little chance beyond the music-hall of becoming generally broadcast. A gem among these, including a rhyme which one was sure some day to find, is called 'A Song of the Wassail Bowl' with words by Beyley (1842), in which, to an atmosphere of 'There's no old boy/brings so much joy/As jolly, holly Christmas!' there occurs the splendid line: 'Ho, ho! for Christmas!/on island, sea or isthmus!'

Modern songs have a new sly precocity, with for instance 'I saw mummy kissing Santa Claus': which a new liberality has even heard parodied with 'mummy' changed with the times to an epicene 'daddy'. There is a reindeer department apart from the red-nosed Rudolph's, which obliges with

'Thirty-Two Feet and Eight Little Tails' and an appropriate and down-right demand to Father Christmas is made in: 'All I want for Christmas' (is my two front teeth). Meanwhile, a very popular parody going round the school playgrounds and asking for traditional status, pipes high that:

Good King Wenceslas looked out
In his mini minor,
Ran into an atom bomb,
Landed up in China.

Sound radio and television of their nature bring such songs and a more varied atmosphere of Christmas into millions of homes which might otherwise have to manage on a simpler do-it-yourself scale. Good or bad? Much to be said either way. Certainly the lonely and old, and those in hospital, are served better. And such broadcasts as the Festival of Nine Lessons and Christmas Carols from the chapel of King's College, Cambridge, and of the great community carol services in America and Australia, are jewels in the dross. The royal message of goodwill has an enormous audience round the British world. It originated as a message of goodwill by King George v in 1932 to inaugurate the installation of a shortwave radio transmitter which at last linked up the British Empire: from then on it became tradition. Informative and immediate live broadcasts from out-of-the-way places round the world are a plainly absorbing feature – but a succession of too many faked up studio parties and tinselling becomes quickly indigestible: balancing the whole area of Christmas programmes, with every guest comedian and singer wanting to hop on the bandwagon, proves a usually insurmountable task.

Meanwhile the modern scene gives us newspapers with special Christmas greeting advertisements from football clubs, theatrical persons, restaurants, publicans, laundries and so forth. In big type one finds such messages as: 'Season's Greetings to all soccer supporters from Sheffield Wednesday F.C.' or 'Do-and-Dye Cleaners wish all their customers a Happy Christmas' or 'Vi and Ron of The King Charles, Brondesbury say Happy Times and hope their customers will One Day Recover' or 'Compliments of the Season to all Cats and Chicks from The Hamstrings'. The only moment of relative quiet is found on the great shopping streets on Christmas Day itself, all of them empty as if a plague has taken the town; street decorations still

Christmas card from the Second World War

garlanded across from building to building, the tinsel and the shine still decorating façades like cheap costume jewellery on a plain woman, the plaster reindeer roaring with deader than ever laughter.

Casualties of today's Christmas spirit are reflected in minor ways by the advertising company which pictured an unhappy man weighed down with Christmas presents of ties and socks and asking the world, What am I doing with all these things when I *really* want such-and-such a product? The publishers of this were promptly deluged with letters of complaint from sock and tie manufacturers; one plainly must not hit one's fellow men at Christmas. Likewise an independent television company put out a Christmas card with a vista of snowy rooftops each with a television aerial: not until many had been printed was it pointed out that the pictured aerials were not of a type to receive their particular programmes. And the British post office has run into deeper trouble than this. It commissioned an artist to produce a special Nativity scene to be printed, in colour, on its Christmas-tide air-letters. Special indeed it turned out to be: long after distribution it was noticed that the naked child-figure standing on the Madonna's lap was, without any doubt at all, a little girl. When this was pointed out to the Postmaster General's office, there was no immediate official comment – except for the reported gasp of one of his aides: 'Oh crumbs!'

Such uneasy trip-ropes lie everywhere. But a far more disconcerting reflection of modern manners is reflected in the closing down forever now of certain large and generous Christmas parties in London because of the new extreme hooliganism of young gate-crashers: gate-crashers there have always been, but on today's scale even the fabric of buildings has been torn about. And there was the extraordinary occasion when girls went berserk at a North of England sportswear factory. The mistletoe went to their heads, and they chased male mechanics all over the place yelling for Christmas kisses. Twenty of the girls grabbed an electrician, tied him up, smeared him with lipstick, wheeled him round the premises on a trolley. The manager responded by banning mistletoe from the factory. One of the girls said of the ban: 'It's a bit much when the bosses breathe down our necks.' Some of the mechanics locked themselves up to keep the girls off. Others said: 'I just couldn't escape, the girls were on to me like a ton of bricks.' 'My face was red in more ways than one when they finished with me.' 'I would not like to say where else they got to work with the lipstick.'

At least one may add that the blood ailment medically known as the Christmas disease was named not after a too-festive occasion but after a family of that name: and that in recent years patrons of a Buckinghamshire inn so appreciated the goodwill of their Christmas that they applied to have another, with turkey and decorations and everything else, in mid-summer: there at least, Christmas came but twice a year.

Altogether, though, the most general criticism of Christmas is that of over-doing everything and of the resultant empty purse. But is this a modern complaint?

It was in 1873 that *The Times* carried its first personal message that in future no more Christmas cards would be sent. And a decade and a bit before the battle of Waterloo, long before Dickens and forty years before the first Christmas card, the following letter from a 'Matthew Meanwell' was published in *The Gentleman's Magazine* of 1802:

Mr Urban:

> *Christmas comes but once a year,*
> *Therefore we'll be merry.* – Shakespeare.

By this strange observation, sir, I have been half ruined since the 25th inst. I have a wife and two daughters, and am in a tolerable way of business; but at this season, bills pour in heavily, and credit must be maintained. I hoped, however, after all my Christmas payments, to put by something handsome; but it has all been spent, because *Christmas comes but once a year* ...

Then the wife of the writer of this letter planned a ball and supper, his daughters bought clothes and jewellery ...

Certain of my friends too, men of business, have prevailed upon me to run into some degree of extravagance, by joining them in a few parties of pleasure, as they are called, and which I never do at other times, without a prospect of increasing my own trade, and making profitable connections; but there was no resisting this argument, that *Christmas comes but once a year*, which they strongly enforce by another, *It is a poor heart that never rejoices.* And what man would be supposed to have so poor a heart as not to rejoice once a year? ... reconciling myself to myself, as well as I can, I think how lucky it is, that Christmas comes but once a year!

'*The Same old Christmas story over again*', *by Thomas Nast*

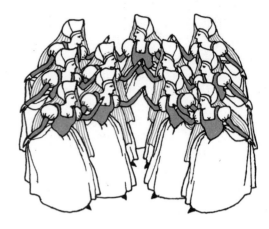

11
Shadow and Joker

A hot Christmas makes a fat churchyard.
SWAN

There is a man who is known as the Maltese Christ. For a number of years he has chosen the day of the Saviour's nativity to fulfil his faithful, mimetic intention of walking on the waters. Each year he is retrieved from the sea half-drowned.

That is the Christmas problem of one human being. And here, far away and nothing to do with him, is a problem faced by others: in an investigation into the conduct of Old People's Homes at Christmas, one of the most poignant factors to emerge had its cause in a familiar process of memory – that as one grows older the immediate and the middle past become confused, whereas the distant days of childhood and of early youth grow brighter and clearer, so much so that pictures or episodes long forgotten shine out suddenly again in the minds of the very aged. Thus, old people tend to remember a great deal about the brightest and most lovable Christmases of all, those passed in the secure light of childhood, and the intervening years are forgotten. The contrast of their comparative isolation from family atmospheres in a Home, comfortable as it may be, is brought closer and becomes harder to bear than at any other time of year.

The Maltese Christ sinks into the sea a thousand miles away from old Mrs Smith yearning for her childhood. Their one connection is Christmas. And together they epitomise all those others whose Christmases are spent away from the general conception of Christmastide, which must always suppose an atmosphere of family and feasting, of general merry-making and the rest of it, so there are those in the shadow, the lonely and the poor,

A Polish szopka *or crib-like construction made in the home and taken from house to house by children singing carols. It is placed on a bench support and used as the background for a puppet Nativity play. This modern example is based on tower motifs from Cracow*

the ill and the old. There are also the jokers in the pack – the odd man out, the eccentric. And one must add to these all those whose work has of its nature to continue through Christmas Day itself – the lighthouse keeper, the hospital nurse, the man with his eye on dials of heat units, volts, seepage. And there are the barred shadows of the prisoner.

And those without even a cell, the homeless and down and out.

A simple and oddly moving poem has been written about a tramp by David Purdy. It begins:

> Once upon some long, long clocks,
> There lived a man who had no socks

and it goes on to tell how this sockless tramp sought warmth in a church, went to sleep, was woken by the arrival of the offertory box, which sent him out again into the cold. The verses end:

> 'Okidoke' said the tramp in a frenzy
> And went outside and caught influenzy.

> A few days later the tramp did die,
> And all over the world no man did cry.

Private and public help for the needy

A wide resonance of loneliness lies in that last line. But now – does such an episode describe any indivisible truth? Certainly it is unlikely, if almost impossible, that a tramp should be turned away from Service in a church. However, in a more general sense it can be said that, while at Christmas or at any other time there are immense efforts made by many organisations to shelter and help those who are helpless and needy, yet at the same time Christmas can be the very worst time in the winter for them. They are anonymous; they cannot all be netted; often they do not want to be. Yet the ordinary places of refuge and occasional warmth are suddenly shut; the library, the museum, the wall of a baker's shop; and as the crowds disappear indoors, all solitary vagrancy becomes, in the open park or at a street corner, both the more obvious and questionable.

Organised help from groups like the Salvation Army are well known to be available, and they do a job of great energy and devotion. But at the same time there come to notice occasions of private help of no small measure. The case, for one instance, of a woman living in the East End of London who opens up her flat each year for people who have nowhere to go, particularly the hard sector of meths-drinkers and drug addicts and the lay-about young. She goes to Soho to find them; they are not necessarily absolutely 'down and out' but very near it, and they certainly have nowhere to go. 'Christmas,' she says, 'is like a road block set up for the rich.' Hard words ... but one may sympathise with someone who is in direct contact with the hard side, who sees her own hard floor giving some sort of rest to the restless, who talks of bitter cases like that of a prisoner released three days before Christmas with five shillings and a pass ticket to London – when eventually he got to the After Care office it was closed for the Christmas holiday. She found him and took him in. On Christmas Day he broke down and cried. 'It was the first Christmas he had been given since he was five years old.' Not, she added, an outstanding case. One of many.

The unusual and beautiful pregnant 'Madonna del parto' by Piero della Francesca

To this, there is too often the half-shrug of a shoulder and the thought: 'These people got themselves into their special trouble – what is the special need for sympathy?' To which, of course, comes a resounding answer sharp with the word goodwill, if not charity. Thus with this woman, who dislikes in particular the sight of a Christmas crib. 'I hate them. So cosy. Christmas, or anything that the originator of Christianity claimed, was the exact opposite to this.' Hard words again, against a strength of sentiment which must do more good than she can account for. But her words are soft in praise of a Soho club owner who realises that many of his clients are oddities who would be left out and lonely on Christmas Day and so, when everywhere similar closes, and though himself over-tired and in need of a break, nevertheless keeps open and gives free sandwiches and drink and pays his staff a heavy extra wage to cope with the Day – which does not end until seven the next morning.

This wide view of the Christmas plight of the not absolutely needy was echoed by a Salvation Army officer. He had many stories to tell of appalling want – but still he saw it as a much wider question. A particularly tragic circumstance, he felt, was that of 'the lodger', the single person renting a bed-sitting-room in a private house. Much too often, he said, such a person is required to leave the house on Christmas Day so that it can be free for the family party. You find them, he said, sitting in bus shelters, or in a shelter in the park, or at the seaside in those wind-shelters on the front. He himself, the officer said, had once been in the same position and remembered clearly walking the empty streets and seeing through the windows family after family celebrating. 'I could see and hear it all. I was the only one who couldn't join in.' So, leaving the redness and the lights of the town behind, there is only the wind-shelter on the front, where the lonely on this one day are lonelier than ever before, with the blank grey expanse of a winter sea for company.

The loneliest day

The Salvation Army's practical work has not, of its nature, anything specifically to do with Christmas, though an effort is made to make Christmas special. Thus there is always a Christmas meal, and presents, and volunteer concerts: and apart from the hostels themselves, the army has a special interest, and on a large scale, in giving presents to the children of men in prison, for this plainly is a time when most of all they miss the father who is away. One of the toughest hostels of all is housed in a disused billiards table factory bought in General Booth's time, and was considered very rough even then, when it had to cater for a thousand men. Five hundred and fifty is the limit now – though still they cannot afford the space for the cubicles they would like – and it is full every night of the year. On Christmas Day the bell rings as usual at eight o'clock and there is breakfast – but then everybody except the sick must leave the building. 'We hate having to do this,' the officer said, 'and I dread the time it's going to be really bad weather.' But it has to be done, for the very simple reason of space – breakfast must be cleared away, cleaning done, and the tables got ready for the Christmas dinner. This is underlined by the fact that, on this day of all days, the organisation sacrifices even its church service – there is no time to

Christmas dinner on board ship, 1875

fit it in. At twelve o'clock the men return to find coloured table-cloths and a proper Christmas meal, and by every man's plate a present of fruit, socks and a handkerchief.

Later in the day there is a concert by volunteer artists from outside, but with specially popular spots by the inmates themselves. This suggests the usual picture of amateur jollity, as in a military camp, or at any local get-together. But the detail can be intensely moving. There was, to cite one instance only, the distressing case of a man who was sent to a hostel from hospital, where he had been treated for very badly wounded feet. He hobbled in on crutches, and eventually his story came out. Far away across England he had been at home watching the baby while his wife was out shopping. He had fallen asleep, and when he woke up had looked at the baby and it was dead. He was so shocked he walked out of the house and had just kept on walking, walking right across county after county for day after day until he had reached London, where he was found with fearfully torn and swollen feet and taken to hospital. At the Christmas concert, this man limped up to the stage and sang, 'My Bonnie lies over the Ocean'.

The spirit of goodwill   In Stockholm there are women Salvationists out in their fur bonnets in the bitter cold, in Geneva they sing to a swing guitar in the rougher dancing bars, in the toughest districts everywhere they are dispensing what must today be a difficult commodity, yet always collecting well-needed *money*. Other organisations, official and voluntary, are at work alongside them. From these, whose list is too long to enumerate and varies from nation to nation, one learns the occasional fact which brings the atmosphere close: that, outside the hostels themselves, it is often difficult to get parcels of food to old people living alone because they are too frightened to open the door, frightened of the dark, frightened of strangers – so that for every door of this kind that might eventually be opened, one must count on some which, against all knocking, remain closed and the occupants foodless. One voluntary worker has an unforgettable memory of the first Christmas meal he brought to a lonely old person – she was sitting all alone in a fireless, shabby, undecorated room before a single place set ready with a knife and fork. The barrenness of that one convivial note of one knife and one fork, and the sense of lonely waiting it conveyed, has remained with him forever. Sad, too, is the fact that many old people who on an ordinary day would have a hot meal brought to them, have their Christmas dinner delivered frozen the night before: the reason, a simple one that for once the voluntary workers have to be at home with their own families. But greater extra efforts are made in other quarters, like a member of a youth club having the quite personal idea of saving up for a bottle of whisky, and raffling it at his place of work for ten times the amount, all of which was turned into food for the old and lonely by adding that most valuable commodity of all, time; not just a charitable few minutes but long slogging hours of extra effort after the ordinary day's work.

The spirit of goodwill, in fact, sometimes boils and usually at least simmers along. It erupts in the expected places and the unexpected. Smallish matters, like the case of a lost Christmas cake, its discovery by an

automobile association, and thereafter its headlong progress across a great mileage of winter roads by relays of the association's patrolmen and its arrival at the Christmas-cakeless owner's door, whereby hearts all round were warmed. And it was at Christmas-time one recent year that police authorities allowed a man awaiting trial in custody to be married. The ceremony involved the time of fifteen policemen and their dog, and at the registry office the law acceded still further to the magic of betrothal by removing the prisoner's handcuffs to allow him to place the ring on the bride's finger.

The general situation of prisoners at Christmas is plainly somewhat of a closed door. Apart from whether some of the prisoners manage of their own volition to walk out through those closed doors, as tends to happen more than occasionally at Christmas-time – because of the longer hours of darkness at this time of year rather than from any generally irresistible wish to join the family circle, or from any perceptible relaxation of the rule of key – apart from such considerations it is difficult to obtain any reliable general information, since what goes on varies from prison to prison according to the governor and the individual inmates. The authorities certainly provide some decorations, and there is a special Christmas meal. Christmas cards are allowed in and out: but personal Christmas presents are only allowed out – impersonally there was the touching case of one group of prisoners saving up from their small allowance to send sweets to all the children of an orphanage, as from Uncle Len, after St Leonard the patron saint of prisoners. Generally it is the character of a few ringleaders who will stimulate from the bleak background a feeling of ephemeral cheer: the governor may organise a tree and a concert and a film show, but it is up to the individual to add to these. Presents are exchanged between prisoners – forbidden and therefore the more fruitful: and small mercies like saved-up tinfoil and coloured paper scraps can do much to make the barren walls glint. One might expect that the mind, contrasting Christmas inside with memories of the outside, would make these days especially depressive: it seems to be the opposite, a little glitter and the old Christmas excitation, and, most importantly, better food, make the period the pleasantest of the year. People who have been on active service will remember something parallel from wartime Christmases, when pretty little made a lot; examining such

Christmas behind bars

memories one will usually find that it was somebody's personal energy which really made the difference.

A more definitely joyful note is struck by a report from the Fanny Bay gaol at Darwin, Australia, which has the reputation of serving 'the best Christmas food in the Northern Territory'. Consequently there is an annual problem of keeping people out.

In any case, in many countries professional criminals outside gaol have a special Christmas problem. This is aligned to a generally held present-day attitude towards holidays – that they have ceased to be a concession but are now a right. So the house-breaker or burglar is faced in summer with the agony of choosing between work at one of his most lucrative periods, with so many houses shut up, and his downright right to be on the beach like anyone else. Similarly at Christmas, known to be a time of deserted warehouses and relaxed watchmanship, and a time also when houses are either left empty for a visit to relatives or overfilled with front-room noise, so again comes the agony, 'Why shouldn't *I* be at home with the wife and kids like the next man?'

The whole question of people who have to work during Christmas is endemically an uninteresting one. Of its nature, such work is usually so important to the public need that it must go on just as before. Unsteadiness of alcohol or any relaxation of convivial high spirits must be discouraged. A sprig of holly on the electric turbine? Mistletoe at the gasworks? The last old puffer to Chattanooga with a bit of a sacred log in the furnace? No. If there are exceptions, the least said the better. We must believe the utilities run on beneath us like running rock. So when one enquires what a lighthouse-keeper's Christmas is like, the answer can only be 'like any other lighthouse-keeper's day', whatever that is like. One may, though, inconsistently add that special food is sent out to the rock, and that local people sometimes get together to supplement this with presents. On reflection, one gets a picture of these particularly isolated men achieving something of the distinction of saints or Holy Men, with a pilgrimage of goodwill plying across the turbulent seas to that hermetical rock, to the sacred marine spire; thereafter comes the ship-in-bottle image of a Christmas tree spiring up the centre of that tall, stone, spray-swept phallus. ... And what, for instance, are the feelings of an imaginative bus-conductor conducting his ghost bus, tremendously full of emptiness, through the plague-deserted streets? He might have much to chew on, or might more simply find a racy Christmas joy in sitting down all the way for once. One never will know the not-much that happens, or what miniature-bottle of alcohol might pass through what sealed lips; it is a matter for the individual and his guarded conscience.

Christmas in hospital Hospitals are naturally in the Christmas limelight, press and broadcasting give us an annual picture of the visits of celebrities to children's wards, of presents piling up, of coloured paper-chains against the hospital white, of the big Christmas tree in the entrance hall. The larger hospitals usually have some sort of dramatic or musical society which puts on a show – pantomime, operetta, revue – at some time in Christmas week, and often an excerpt from this is re-enacted in any of the wards able to digest it. Many a house surgeon has flung on the motley red of old man Claus between snips, and a general effort is made to keep the time as specially cheerful as possible. While the serious work goes on. It must. There is no question. Though the momentous invitation to 'a sherry with Sister' may send its booming whisper through our dreams, it is mostly as mythical as Christmas itself: there are higher jinks among the patients than among the staff, for obvious reasons. And however excitant the crisp of roasted turkey, those who are ill are ill. To put the perspective in its proper capsule, one may quote the mild little story of a woman visiting her upper-middle-aged father in hospital at Christmas. The father had been bedridden for some time and was likely to remain so. The woman was trying to interest him in things, and happened to catch sight of a robin through the window. 'Look,' she said, 'can you see? It's a robin – and do you see – it's standing on one leg! Quite a picture?' Which it was, in its small sentimental way. But the bedridden father said nothing, only looked and looked at the bird. Then, after a long time, murmured: 'He's ruddy lucky to be able to do that.'

One year recently a Christmas party was given in a Yorkshire cinema for forty-eight poodles. Milk, biscuits and chocolate drops were laid out on low tables by the town's civic catering staff, who were in careful attendance. Assumably, a good time was had by all: the atmosphere must have been peculiarly attractive, for an Irish wolfhound was reported to have gate-crashed.

But what of the aftermath? Of Christmas for animals in general? The Royal Society for the Prevention of Cruelty to Animals has strong opinions on the over-feeding of animals at Christmas, and issues a leaflet warning

Christmas Day at the Seamen's Hospital, Greenwich, 1879

against this, and against giving them splinterable bones: and particularly against giving animals to children as Christmas presents. The pup in the pet-shop window may look sad, and a shaken daddy might be asked for a bow-wow – but after the Christmas holidays and the ascent from bouncing puppy-fat to stern doghood with its startling meat bill, the end, at least in England, land of shopkeepers and animal lovers, is far too frequently the execution shed.

In the fourteenth century it was customary in Germany for animals to be brought into church at Christmas-time – cuckoos, hawks and hounds are recorded. But in England the churching of animals does not seem to have been so customary: at least, there is a record in 1570 of trouble in Weardale when a man brought a crow into church and someone else 'put a strawe cross in her mouth, to see how she could flye'. To the minister's reproof, there came the dark and trenchant response: 'It is well if ye doo no worse.'

The usual human wish to make humans of animals proceeds as well at Christmas as at any other time: it is a consistent wish, and only a year or two ago, for instance, a Christmas carol service was held by a People's Dispensary for Sick Animals where seventeen horses, thirty-four dogs, twelve birds and more than a dozen cats formed part of the congregation. An owl, perched on a small boy's hymn book, is reported not to have sung, but to have let out, occasionally, a hoot.

Not so happy is the lot of the goldfish in his bowl. Christmas brings the annual risk of complete disaster. The reason is a simple one. There swims the beloved pet, gloomily moving to and fro between his piece of coral and his grove of plastic seaweed. Why shouldn't *he* have a festive time like all the rest? So into the bowl goes a sprig or two from the Christmas tree, and in the morning he is found dead from resin poisoning. A detail in the holocaust of domestic animal disaster – from the almost sacrificial puppy to the cracker-shocked cat and the budgerigar wreathed gasping in un-familiar cigar smoke. Yet the wild birds outside all receive extra food in their forgotten identity as demons or spirits of the dead, and the sleeping tortoise, wily Greek, knows nothing of it at all – if he happens still to be alive.

A Partridge in a Pear-tree All periods of festivity produce their rogue risks, and Christmas now pre-sents an unforeseen peril for the British peerage. It is all because of that song-game, 'A Partridge in a Pear-tree'. The mass communication media become annually intent on illustrating it; television directors and advertis-ing photographs somehow or other manage to deal with most of the song, even to representing the protagonists of such lines as those containing the three French hens, the eight maids a-milking and the six geese a-laying. But then it comes to twelve lords a-leaping; and annually there is a run on the peerage. Certainly in the last two years lords have been assembled in both a television studio and an advertiser's photographic studio with instructions, m'Lord, to leap and all to leap together, m'Lords. Thank you, now just *once* again. And again....

There is a formidable risk, cruising in the Pacific, of missing Christmas altogether. Your ship may be due to cross the international dateline on the twenty-fifth of December. But a liner can look after this one; the ship's

THEATRE ROYAL
COVENT GARDEN

BLUE-BEARD
BY HENRY J. BYRON.
A GRAND CHRISTMAS
PANTOMIME

THE CENTURY

FOR XMAS

CONTAINING

A SELECTION OF TWELVE REPRODUCTIONS OF THE
WONDERFUL PAINTINGS BY TISSOT ILLUSTRATING
THE LIFE OF CHRIST

A COMPLETE NOVELETTE BY RUDYARD KIPLING
"THE BRUSHWOOD BOY,"—A DREAM STORY

OPENING CHAPTERS OF
"TOM GROGAN," A NOVEL BY F. HOPKINSON SMITH

SECOND PART OF MRS. HUMPHRY WARD'S NOVEL

A CHRISTMAS STORY BY FRANK R. STOCKTON
ETC., ETC., ETC.

calendar brashly skips a day from the twenty-second to the twenty-fourth and on a smiling false and non-existent Christmas Day, under wide Pacific skies to the waving of atoll palm-heads, there is served turkey and sucking pig, baron of beef and the pudding, all as the ghostly ship's engines – which could not, of course, officially exist – drum forward toward the reality of another day. Meanwhile, back on dry land other exigencies come to try the seasonable nerve – each year a minor crime-wave sees the disappearance of the funds of local Christmas savings clubs; American newspaper files show headlines such as 'Santa Claus comes to Broadway on a Crime-wave' with fearful details of stepped up racketeering and over-excited gangland shootings; and there was in America the man dressed as Santa Claus who went into a church and made off with the collection plate – a student of sociology, it turned out, whose duty was to perform a deviate act and write a paper on it. One year, in England, a clergyman was called to a private house to exorcise a one-legged ghost; it had been found to be one-legged by someone laying flour on the floor, thus discovering the not so ectoplasmic but nevertheless inexplicable lonesome footstep.

There is no knowing what can happen at this remarkable time of year. *Historic happenings* Mediaeval history begins by honouring Christmas with momentous royal *at Christmas* events, as if a memory of the ancient priest-king ritual survived in the general consciousness. Charlemagne was enthroned as Emperor on Christmas Day 800, Clovis I of the Franks was baptised on that day in 496, William of Normandy was crowned King of England on Christmas Day 1066 and Baldwin assumed the crown of the Kingdom of Jerusalem at Bethlehem in 1099. However, these were particular occasions; many were crowned on other days, and no particular reverence attached to the Christmastide of 1170, when Thomas à Becket fell to the assassins at Canterbury. At random one may find other irreverences, such as the assassination of Henry and Louis of Guise on the twenty-third and twenty-fourth of December 1588 by order of the King; and on Christmas Eve 1800 an attempt was made to assassinate Napoleon. Nor do the natural elements conserve the sanctities – 1884 saw a thousand people killed in Spanish earthquakes on St Stephen's Day. And so on. Such data, and that Sir Isaac Newton was born on Christmas Day and that Washington crossed the Delaware River at Christmas 1776, are either coincidental or irrelevant, and in the general picture only show that life does and did go on apart from the ordinary celebrations.

That the London *Times* newspaper at last suspended publication on Christmas Day 1913 was a late sign of absolute recognition of the holiday – and on that day a light little domestic note must have echoed in many a home when for once the valet could take a holiday from ironing the paper for Master; though what the Master's frustrated temper might have been like will have initiated yet another of those familiar Christmas battles for peace and goodwill.

More seriously, the real and rightly famous battle of this kind was the truce in the trenches of 1914. Though it was short-lived and never recurred, at least in so spontaneous a form, it symbolises forever the predicament of a

A poster for the Christmas number of The Century *showing a romanticised Father Christmas figure of the period. Designed by Louis John Rhead in 1895*

227

soldier sympathising with a local enemy he must destroy for remote reasons he hardly understands. At that time, it had been made strategically clear that Christmas was to mean no holiday. On Christmas Eve 1914 the Germans launched their first air raid on Britain, making at least its point with a bomb dropped in a Dover garden. The next day, a solitary plane was driven off at Sheerness, and the British retaliated with a naval air attack on warships off Cuxhaven. In another theatre, the Austrians suffered a defeat at Tarnov. And on the western front there was the familiar thunder of artillery and the clatter of machine-gun fire. And then, at midnight on Christmas Eve, allied soldiers in various sectors of the freezing trenches heard a new, less congruous sound – a brass band in the German trenches playing carols. The immediate firing stopped. All around a new kind of silence echoed the richly chorded brass, as if it played from inside its own wide halo of separate, sacred, impermeable frost, yet with the distant world outside still grumbling an ostracised flash and boom of artillery fire – and in that low, hard landscape of torn mud the dual pattern of sounds could be heard as emblematic of Christmas itself, a simple sound of human goodwill isolated against thunderous voices of ancient gods receding.

Christmas in the trenches

The music went on through the night; early next morning there came from the German trenches cries of 'Merry Christmas, Tommy', heads appeared above the parapets, and soon there began that tentative approach to each other of the men themselves, half suspecting a trick, ready to drop or run, officers formulating excuses for retrieving the dead for burial, and perhaps in everybody's mind a certain unspoken confusion bred by the well-believed phrase of that autumn, 'It'll all be over by Christmas' (it was not, that much was obvious, but it *should* have been – something had gone wrong which might yet soon be put right). The whole mood of that long western line was confused – the atmosphere differed from sector to sector, there were cases of Germans being shot by the suspecting French, and of a British regiment firing over the enemies' heads to keep them back. Generally it seems that the initiative for peace came from the Germans; and of these, from Saxons and Bavarians rather than from Prussian elements. This echoes the particular sanctity with which Christmas has always been held in the German heart and home ... all along some sectors of the German line lighted Christmas trees were put up on the parapets of their trenches ... sentimental – but if the sentiment is sincere?

So, where it worked, men for a time shook hands and exchanged presents. Goldflake cigarettes went to Fritz, and Tommy tasted a German cigar, plum puddings went east and German sausage west; a halfway line was agreed on, and on this a football match played, and when a hare was by chance set up, a mutual coursing began on two occasions, Germans and British running together: meanwhile, much talk together of the war and everybody's dislike of it, and there was the singing of nationally popular songs like 'The Blue Bells of Scotland', and of carols. In some parts, truces in daylight were unofficially agreed, and kept, for two days: and in one reported sector not a shot was fired for a week. Reports, though, usually describe the tension felt that at any moment it might end: there was even a

Japanese impression of the attempted assassination of Napoleon, on Christmas Eve, 1800

day when a stray, unintended bullet came across from the German lines, followed a little later by a written apology. In most cases material advantages were taken, bringing up wood and warming matter such as straw to make the future more secure. Both sides watched opposing wire obstacles being improved. No man's land for a time was everyman's. Some days later a general order came from the command that fraternisation was forbidden on penalty of death; love was too dangerous for war. The firing began again, and the silence to which, in one man's words, 'even the murdered trees seemed to listen' was broken, and stayed so.

The history of war shows many cases of stoppage or quiescence over this cold and festive moment of the year, but whether these were dictated by religious or yuletide feeling, or instead by expediencies of weather or policy, is too often too difficult to say: the 1914 episode stands out so strongly because it was plainly a spontaneous sentiment, and well documented by many of the men who were concerned and who happened later to survive. A very different matter, for instance, from the Korean War when a regiment found cigarette holders and whistles and cards hung on trees by the Chinese, with the enticing 'thought': 'Whatever colour race or

'Christmas in Camp', by Thomas Nast, 1889

creed, all plain folks are brothers indeed.' Made plainer by the next message: 'Both you and me want life and peace. If you go home the war will cease.' Centuries before, the Danes did not go home and leave Alfred to the putative peace of his yule: and though the dates of certain Christmas-time battles stick out – Garigliano in 1503, Mincio in 1800 and so on – history shows that there were indeed many cessations of war at this time of winter, and though one suspects that commanders on the whole welcomed a convivial respite for men, morale, morality and themselves, no one isolated motive can be inferred except the very general one that the ancient and powerful excitation of a sunburst in the dark could hardly be expected to die off simply for reasons of an immediate fosse, a passing parados. The whole question is somehow answered by David Jones's Romanisation of the outbreak of love in 1914. Behaviour in the centuries in between is implicitly concertinaed when he hammers the brass tacks of fancy to write:

… On this night, when I was a young man in France, in Gallia Belgica, the forward ballista-teams of the Island of Britain green-garlanded their silent three-o-threes for this I saw and heard their cockney song salute the happy morning; and later, on this same morning certain of the footmen of Britain, walking in daylight, upright, through the lanes of the war-net to outside and beyond the rusted tip-belt, some with gifts, none with ported weapons, embraced him between his *fossa* and ours, exchanging tokens.

Meanwhile the joker in the pack bobs up to astonish us. Though in the diaries of Sir Henry Channon Lady Emerald Cunard is quoted as saying that Christmas is 'only a time for servants', and though Christmas did not stay the hand that murdered the ballerina Harriet Boswell in the gas-lit London of 1872, though everywhere the censorious and tragic proceeds as usual, nevertheless the joker presents such very real fellows of fun as Sir Henry Irving and a friend out to dinner in late Victorian days, and the account that, alone in a hotel dining room, they called for the bill and as soon as the waiter had left to prepare it, went into certain abrupt dramatic action … when the waiter returned he found the gas out, all the silver gone and the window open, showing plainly enough the final exit of these gentlemen of the drama. The alarm was raised, and there was a fine old hullabaloo which Sir Henry and friend only disturbed by one of the neatest entrances in the history of Christmas theatre – on their hands and knees from beneath the all-enveloping cloth and their lair made up of the nostalgic childhood-yearning legs of the dining table.

Matter of a graver kind is furnished by Timothy Haynes, an Irishman who chose one recent Christmas Day to begin his assault on the how-long-can-you-stay-buried-in-a-coffin record. He was duly screwed down and buried – though with air ducts, lights and a telephone – and there, recumbent in a green track-suit in that clean well-lighted place, ended his Christmas Day by beginning to read *Dracula* with an eye yet on his crucifix and bottle of holy water. His diet was the adequate one of lemonade, sweets and mutton chops, his only companion a small pink spider called Cyril. Four

Advertisement from the First World War

231

days and five hours later Mr Haynes was resurrected with a world record, returning from the bowels of the earth in dark glasses.

And so the roster of Christmas activities compounds, with almost rational surprises like the appearance of West German railway terminals plastered with posters in Turkish – for special trains to take immigrant Moslem workers home for the non-Christmas non-feast in Istanbul; and like the kosher killing of turkeys in the Jewish community of east London, when Hanukkah is hovering near to Christmas Day and there is some confusion as to when to eat what – except that, apart from a bird, there always sets in a curious large demand, enough to make a regiment of snowmen, for ice-cream.

The proper values of snow

A taste for ice-cream in mid-winter must be one of the sharpest pointers to our cosier urban age. Going the coal, going the draughts, the mufflers – gone the old exuberance of snow ... people today only like dream-snow, the nuisance value of the real stuff is so much greater with people expecting to get everywhere on the minute. Snow needs tarrying with, trudging through and playing with and looking at. To feel its proper values one must go to such a writer as Colette:

We came back powdered with snow, all three of us – the little bull-dog, the Flemish sheepdog and I ... Snow had got into the folds of our coats, I had white epaulettes, an impalpable sugar was melting in the wrinkles of Poucette's blunt muzzle, and the Flemish sheepdog sparkled all over. ...

The snow for Colette fell in a 'chenille screen of snowflakes like thousands and thousands of white flies' and it tasted like 'a smooth sherbet, vanilla-flavoured and a bit dusty ...' And there was the sheepdog which 'steaming like a footbath ... listens to the whispering of the snow against the shut blinds'. Colette is the writer who sees the year 'sinking toward a winter that was dry, resonant, glimmering with frozen ponds, with snow rosy beneath the sun' as it plunges towards a 'marvellous date, isolated, suspended between the two years like a frost flower: New Year's Day ...'

This is the ideal snow we long for, and against which we can envisage such forgotten protagonists of winter as the reserved Anglican skater in his dark Norfolk jacket scientifically circling and figure-eighting through the entire afternoon round a single orange placed upon the ice, never an eyebrow lifted, hands nonchalant behind back, as if he were warming his posterior at a little fireplace perpetually following him.

Ice is sensed beautifully by Coleridge:

... the infinitely subtle particles of ice which the skate cuts up, and which creep and run before the skate like a low mist, and in sunrise and sunset become coloured; second, the shadow of the skater in the water, seen through the transparent ice; and third, the melancholy undulating sound from the skate, not without variety ...

That was at Ratzeburg; the rink-conscious cold areas of Europe still take regularly to the skate, places that exported all those twirly-whirly, musta-chioed, frogged-jacketed skating masters of old; but in England and other clammy countries the general Victorian exodus to the ice has declined. Nowadays there are other things to do: and so the country skating scene itself – though it still exists – becomes part of the mid-winter legend, something to do with childhood and long ago, exceptional and not the rule.

It was never everybody's experience to skate with a royal family, as was Anne Topham's at the Prussian court of Wilhelm II. There, on the Heiliger See by the Marble Palace, the English governess and her royal charge skated on a roped-off enclosure watched by Potsdam crowds whose weight threatened to break the ice. 'It was very unpleasant to skate in public with royalty,' she has one know. A flash of the personal nature of the old-fashioned Christmas scene follows the skating – in the evening when the princess 'painted and worked feverishly at her Christmas presents'; and then there were difficulties in carol practice with a certain Fräulein von Gersdorff, whose powerful and unusual voice changed abruptly from soprano to alto, throwing the other members of the choir into confusion. 'I thought the altos were weak,' Fräulein von Gersdorff would explain afterwards in that queer deep voice of hers, 'I thought I would help them a little.'

Other white Christmases take other people other ways. There are the thankful who repeat as a joke the old shadowed superstition: 'A hot Christmas makes a fat churchyard'. And there is the physicist who watches the skaters and knows it is all only possible because the massed hexagonal crystals melt by $0.0075°$c for each atmospheric increase in pressure, which alone makes skating possible, the pressure of the skate forming a film of lubricant water – in fact, one skates on water, not ice. And he will muse that ice is birefringent, and ponder on its refractive indices, while

> ... standing at his cottage door
> The labourer thinks of labour scant,
> And sees the haggard hand of want
> Throw shadows on his chamber floor.

as Victorian verses described the annual tragedy of agriculture faced with an iron soil. Snow-shifting was the only silver lining, there and in the city, where snow still means work for the casually jobless. Nowadays extra work in hotel kitchens, too, whether Christmas is white or not, while the waiters above are doing a double stint. Everyone is affected in different ways. Even the public lavatory attendant has his added quota of drunks to deal with, and in one lavatory in London a deserted baby was found wrapped in gift-paper, and in another the attendant reports a sad and secret sound, the enclosed small cry of the dope addict injecting himself – one must assume the pusher has jumped the bandwagon too.

Shelter, the organisation looking for accommodation for badly housed families in Britain, cites the case today of a slum house with five mothers and only one gas stove, and what's the good of a turkey then? At least one can say that generally in poorer places people are looked after better than in years gone by – old people tell their tales of 'nine of us in a bed' and of the unemployed days when even the penniless got into debt and 'they'd throw a brick at us if we went carol singing, so we never went'. Others have livelier memories of the best of the past when 'we all went up Tootin' and danced and got boozed. Kicked up a row in the streets and that ... had a sing-song in the street' – a far cry from the long dark day by the blue light of television.

But television must not be under-rated, it is a companion of extraordinarily great worth to the lonely and chair-bound; it must be so, though in many cases it has also kept chair-bound elsewhere friends or relations who might otherwise have paid a visit. 'It's television that's ruined Christmas as it was,' said one old man, who nevertheless lived with it. However, not so much television but rather the idea of state welfare seems to be at the root of a decline in family visits to the old at Christmas. The woman in charge of an old persons' Home says that added to the general change in the fabric of families living together and sheltering needy relations is the feeling among grown-up children of the old that 'they', the state, will be doing 'something about them'. At one Home in London where half the residents could have gone to visit their married children, most of the old people's families 'didn't want to know', so that in fact only five out of thirty-seven went home from that Home for Christmas.

All such homes vary, but generally a big effort is made to make Christmas Day a different day. The old people cannot go up ladders to decorate, but the staff do much, and there are usually gifts of flowers from outside and carollers or entertainers give up their time to come along in the afternoon. At one Home wine and cider is served, and of course anyone who is able can go down the road for a tot of something special. The tone is set perhaps most deeply by details such as the simple excitement of moving together the usual six-a-piece tables to form a communal horseshoe: and there are telling unspoken matters, such as the absence of any silver coins or charms in the puddings, for fear of trouble with precious teeth. Small presents are exchanged, either bought from savings or sent in from outside, and any relations who want to visit and make the thing go are made very welcome. There is in any case a good communal feeling, so that anybody temporarily away in hospital hopes to be Home for Christmas.

It is a day that many look forward to: but it is also true that most really wish to be home with their families. It is a traditional thought, but one that is often confused with memories of the past. 'Now when I was young...' is the beginning of many a Christmas thought; and perhaps compared with a real return home to a family with modern ways, and with the consequent upset to routine – anathema to the old – they may be better off in their community of memories. Routine is a great panacea for the passing of time, and many still go up to bed as usual at six-thirty on Christmas night.

The superintendent of one Home, who had once worked in a rehabilitation centre for the mentally sick, compared the inscrutable quality of these old people to the demonstrative behaviour of the mentally sick, who were upset by the general excitation of Christmas and by their own associations. But those the old and sane face life as it must come, without much demonstration: perhaps not as serenely as is supposed, but with a sober resignation. When asked where he would *really* like to be for Christmas, one old man, a quite jovial fellow who enjoyed his Christmas, replied in a nice enough, even-voiced, conversational tone: 'Dead.'

Pollock's Toy Theatre, hand-coloured in 1834. The contemporary backdrop is taken from the pantomime Harlequin Jack and the Beanstalk *and shows an old-fashioned holly-wreathed Father Christmas (as opposed to the later and American Santa Claus with a cap) and his wassail bowl*

12

Special Performances

An actor sits in doubtful gloom,
His stock-in-trade unfurled,
In a damp funereal dressing-room
In the Theatre Royal, World.

He comes to town at Christmas-time
And braves its icy breath,
To play in that favourite pantomime

Harlequin Life and Death. w. s. GILBERT

Sweet and joyful, sour and scaring – the many special performances put on to mark Christmastide and the solstice vary between miracle and mystery plays, ancient and modern mummings, ghost stories, Nativity plays, pantomimes and charades. We have already noted something of some of these, and of what is to many people the most moving of all performances, the carol. It would be pointless to print here examples of the words of usual popular carols or of the beautiful French *noëls;* by themselves the words are too bare and need not only their musical setting but also their setting in life, the atmosphere of singing in church or in the winter street, all the feeling of their curiously intimate message. But the carol, along with a few other performances like the pantomime, deserves a short historical word.

The word itself, carol, is connected with the Greek and Latin for 'chorus'. It was also once used more widely to describe things of ring-shape, such as a circle of stones, and in the middle ages it was in general use for a ring dance or song. As a rustic chorus of joy, the carol could then celebrate May or Midsummer or the November fires just as well as Christmas. Bumpkin maids and their men went roistering round in their elected circles, and a fine

A Christmas tree in the Metropolitan Museum of Art, New York, decorated with a fine
collection of eighteenth-century crib figurines from Naples

237

olde tyme was had by all. Later on, the word became much attached to Christmas and quieter songs of wonder, all of which might have been lost to us today had it not been for the passion of several Victorian antiquarians and for the Celtic love of traditional song which had always kept carols alive in pockets of Cornwall and Wales and Ireland.

Origins of the
Christmas carol　　The Christmas carol had in the first place developed in the form of a popularly understood Nativity song as compared with church hymns, which were usually sung in Latin. Once again in the sixteenth and seventeenth centuries the Reformation and the Puritan discouraged such thoughtless revelry, so much so that in the following couple of hundred years carols almost disappeared from England itself – in the 1820s William Hone could write: 'Carols begin to be spoken of as not belonging to this century ...', though he remarked on their continuance in Wales and Ireland. Yet almost at the same time, in 1822, Davies Gilbert published a small *Collection of Christmas Carols* and this was successfully reprinted. It followed the general renewed interest in Christmas traditions, and one can see that, apart from the distant hard core of carolling Cornish and other Celts, the custom never really died in England, only fell into general disuse, being kept half-alive here and there by individual villagers for a mixture of love and money. In 1833 the antiquarian William Sandys published a further volume of carols and French *noëls*, twenty years later Neale and Helmore set a volume of old Swedish songs to new words and musical arrangements – which, incidentally, first gave us 'Good King Wenceslas' – and then again twenty years later, in the 1870s, *Christmas Carols New and Old* edited by Bramley and Stainer finally popularised the carol with church congregations. The American 'O Little Town of Bethlehem' was not written until 1868: and did not become generally popular until twenty years later.

All in all, it took a full half-century for the carol to find general acceptance – and in this we see a parallel with other Christmas customs of the present day which only fully flowered in the late decades of the nineteenth century. The experience in France and Germany was roughly the same. Since that time, the carol as music has become ever more popular, though the mittened and mufflered round of itinerant singing has flagged. Nevertheless, carol-singers for charity still collect useful money – even with a small party singing on a commuting station platform in London, where twenty-five pounds is collected in an hour. And, of course, in America and Australia, very sizeable sums go into the carolling kitty. Many popular carols seem to possess an indefinable quality, something between a lullaby and an anthem but never quite a hymn, which strikes a particularly tender emotion in most people: it may be exact associations that move us so strongly – though nevertheless one feels one would recognise a new song as being 'like a carol'. Yet what is their common quality? How different is the *berceuse* lilt of 'Silent Night' from the major marching air of 'Good King Wenceslas' and its story of the supposed winter walk of the tenth-century Bohemian Saint-King Václav? The most one can say is that two large elements are common – joy and simplicity, of a kind that ordinary people quickly understand.

The pantomime is a British particular, although some of its origins may be found once again in the Roman Saturnalia and later in the Italian Commedia dell'Arte. From these beginnings it went through many different forms until it reached its late Victorian and Edwardian heyday as a fairy-tale performance for the family larded with famous and costly 'transformation' scenes staging fires and palaces, waterfalls and devils' caverns. Today it has degenerated into a semi-vaudeville affair, peppered with blue jokes for an adult audience which still brings its children along. The little ones sit half mystified, or laughing simply because everyone else is laughing.

The word pantomime has a Greek root meaning 'all mime' and in both Roman times and in the harlequinades a couple of hundred years ago no words were spoken – the matter was danced and mimed. The immediate ancestry of pantomime in the form the British know it today is found in productions at the beginning of the eighteenth century. These featured much of the atmosphere of masques and Misrule, with clowning and dancing and topicality and that ancient tendency to reverse the sexual roles of some players – from which we derive the tradition of the principal boy or handsome hero being played by a girl, and comical and elderly female characters being played by men. Through these productions runs the elastic theme of the harlequinade, at first intrinsically and later tacked on to a separate romantic story. Harlequin or 'Frenchy' seems to have come to England from the Paris fairs, and the most interesting factor of his appearance at this Christmas period is that in early days he was not masked but had a blackened smut-disguised face. Here again, then, is the traditional disguise of the mummer, going right back through thousands of years to the pre-Saturnalian old religion of masked worshippers. Harlequin,

'*Preparing for the Pantomime*'

who strove acrobatically with Pantaloon and Clown for the hand of pretty Columbine, was originally dressed in patched clothes and carried a staff. The patches were eventually stylised into the many-coloured lozenge-patterned silk suit, the staff became a bat with magic pretensions, and the smutted face was formalised into the familiar black half-mask which had again the magical propensity of making the leaping, flying, lissom, lozenged figure of this early superman invisible. Harlequin combines the magician of very ancient man with all the topical tricks and whims of the vulnerably human man-in-the-street.

About the middle of the eighteenth century, classical pantomime themes such as *The Loves of Mars and Venus* gave way to folk and fairy tales, and in 1806 *Harlequin and Mother Goose; or, The Golden Egg* arrived at Covent Garden with the celebrated Joseph Grimaldi cast as clown. Clowns are still called Joey after Grimaldi; his popular slapstick equipment featured a red-hot poker (the magic wand again?) and often a garland of sausages (and here one recalls that a garland of sausages round goose or turkey is held to be a substitute for a wreath of sacred leaves). Grimaldi's brilliant career ended with his retirement in 1828, and, soon after this, pantomime entered another phase more richly scripted in rhyming couplets, peppered with puns and topicalities, all-singing and all-dancing, and embellished by those magnificent scenic essays or 'transformation scenes' such as, for example, *Psyche's Bower of Bliss Where Butterflies Dwell*, probably with a butterfly ballet, and, as was then possible, dancers wearing a pair of wings worked by a clockwork box between the shoulder-blades. But pantomime was also 'improving' and managers tried to persuade the moralist father to bring the family by putting on such titles as *Harlequin Grammar*, where the victory of the vowels AEIOU in their encounter with the forces of ignorance was presided over by the Fairy Queen orthography.

Pretty well anything could happen on the pantomime stage, provided the moral outcome showed the triumph of good over evil, beauty over ugliness – only poor Truth went by the board. Reviews of shows in London in January 1870 cite characters assailed by Arabs and left overnight in a forest of banyan-trees to face a host of monkeys; and at another theatre 'troops of Amazons and rose-crowned cupids are represented in combat'. Elsewhere the scene is Constantinople where 'His Lordship ... finds refuge on board a Turkish galley, from which he escapes by boat, and the fair Sophia in a washing-tub. All are made happy at last amidst the rural felicities of Hampstead.'

Meanwhile, it is noteworthy that pantomime titles still mostly carried the word Harlequin in them – thus *The Story of the Beanstalk* features *Harlequin Jack the Giant-Killer* (who also manages to turn into St George, traditional hero of mumming plays); and there are further associations with old magic in *The Gnome-Fly; or, Harlequin, the Nine Dwarfs and the Magic Crystal*. But gradually the part that Harlequin himself played dwindled to nothing, after his long history of usefulness as dancer, mimer, or as light relief after too grandiose a classical piece, or even as an entr'acte to help scene-shifters or to rest breathless singers, and lastly as an epilogue ... a long, long way from

Opposite: *Cover design for* The New Yorker *magazine of 2nd December, 1939*
Overleaf: '*Out for the Christmas trees*'. *An American snow-scene showing the gathering of fir-trees before Christmas, painted by Grandma Moses in 1946*

Dec. 2, 1939   THE   Price 15 cents

NEW YORKER

INFORMATION

the *arliquinades* of Paris, the Commedia dell'Arte and the ancient traditions which underlaid these.

Joey the Clown has been relegated to the circus, where this still exists. It is the tremendous cost of mounting such large productions for a limited season, both pantomime as a full-scale musical show and the Christmas circus, which has forced their general disappearance. However, the theme seems irrepressible: Christmas pantomime has a larger audience than ever before through television, and annually, to larger stadium audiences, the old shows from *Mother Goose* to *Cinderella* to *Babes in the Wood* go on ice. As Richard Finlater has suggested: 'Far from being a moribund entertainment, pantomime is a kind of underground national theatre.' Like any other living art, it will of course change; it will be massed with electric guitars and the Fairy Queen will arrive in a space-craft – but its fundamental release into the realm of magic and its close knitting of the atmosphere of ancient traditions with a richness of human revelry make it a natural fellow of the Christmas season.

Other theatrical pieces have attached themselves to Christmas, like Maeterlinck's *Blue Bird*, and Barrie's *Peter Pan*, and Tchaikovsky's *Nutcracker* – and here again one finds in every case the presence of magic or the superhuman. And special new traditions are still evolving. Thus New York and American television feature *The Play of Daniel*, a mediaeval musical drama based on part of the Book of Daniel and including the episode in the lions' den: the music is of the thirteenth century and played on instruments varying from the vieille to the rebec, the psaltery, the bagpipe and others. Then New York has also put on a dramatic version of *The Miracle on 34th Street* by Valentine Davies, a piece staged in Macy's Department Store

Left and above: *A pair of prints from about 1825.*
'*A Merry Christmas and a Happy New Year*', and
'*The same to you sir, and many of 'em*'

*'The Celebrated Clodoches',
poster for the pantomime*
Bluebeard, *1871*

and built round the figure of 'Kriss Kringle' appearing in reality as the employed Kringle-cum-Santa Claus as a Christmas attraction – an apposite mixture of realism and fairy-tale. There are also in America some pretty devices of a semi-dramatic nature – Charlotte in North Carolina knows 'The Singing Christmas Tree', a choir arranged in a tall triangle and dressed in green capes. They are covered with decorations and tinsel and sing carols, basses at the bottom, sopranos at the top.

Galanty shows   Outside the theatre proper, an atmosphere of wonder used to pervade the old Victorian galanty shows, where a travelling showman projected tales featuring Harlequin and other traditional figures by means of a magic lantern. 'We showed it on a white sheet, or on the ceiling, big or little, in the houses of the gentlefolk, and the schools where there was a breaking-up,' said an old showman to Henry Mayhew. These were often shadow-shows, using silhouetted figures. But later on the cheapness of magic lanterns in the shops and the new coloured slides put an end to the galanty – though these factors brought inside the home their own magic, the bright inked projections of figures which sometimes even moved jerkily into one or two different comical positions. Or there were kaleidoscope effects, with a slide moving round in a truly dazzling manner at the turn of a handle. Primitive motion-pictures indeed – but in the darkened room, with the strange play of bright coloured light, the smoking and 'magic' lantern itself, there was a great atmosphere of excitement at a time when even the appearance in a house of a coloured Christmas annual was an event.

Christmas was a time, too, for shadows on the walls, intimate performances where fingers and thumb made the dark beaked head and the light eye of the Christmas goose, and the arm its long neck. Shadows and firelight again – and there were also sometimes set 'shadow plays'. These involved a strong light behind a sheet and, say, a surgical operation performed with one amateur actor recumbent and another easily slitting his stomach open with the keen-shadowed knife to extract, say, a string of sausages or a giant cardboard cut-out of a heart: all horribly effective. As was also that old illusion the Pepper's Ghost, the transparent image of a hidden actor projected ethereally by an inclined plane of glass and specially

246

directed lighting – a trick of the theatre twice as eerie in the firelit home already excitant with greenery and tinsel and all the other magics of Christmas, ghost stories, toy theatres, kaleidoscopes ... and, as Dickens pointed out, that extra optical excitement or distortion brought about by a lot to eat, the disturbed and waking dream of too much too rich muzzing both the eye and the mind's eye and forever afterwards the memory.

The memory. Here indeed is a special Christmas performance; for remembering Christmas, and especially a childhood Christmas, seems always to bring about a kind of double memory. I do not mean the double eye of the bottle – although *Cassell's Family Magazine* of 1880 has an article called 'Catering for Children's Parties' which tenders the following charming advice: 'Many children will drink water or a little sherry and water ... To my thinking a glass of lemonade is far preferable to *cheap* champagne, and far less vulgar.' No, at least in my own day this was all over, no more of that cheap stuff, not even sherry and water ... and yet, the memories do have some of the quality of piecing together a hard night out, there are the same bright glimpses clearly photographed in a maze of something else momentous yet never quite distinguishable, a peppering of moving shadows, a presence of benevolent nightmare. Perhaps, then, at Christmas the amount of food did have its effect, plus the general bloodrush of nervous excitation ... but one must add another very particular quality, the fact that Christmas of its nature is so allied to past customs and atmospheres and to its inherent celebration of a golden age, that when you try to think back on your own Christmas past the memory does in a shadowy way become a double past, you in the past living another past romanticised from long before.

A period somewhere just before the 1920s, in a world modernised by war but still full of Victorian habits, marks the time of my own first Christmas memories. In an amorphous night-world of dark afternoon light and of the bang and flash and colour of crackers, the first bright fixed picture that stands out is of a cheese. It was a huge Stilton cheese, a fat tan-coloured cylinder with a whitish-green inside veined like marble. A fixed picture, a static cheese? For me it was a cheese also in very slow motion – because it was then the custom to bring out a strong magnifying glass and go through the horrific process of taking a good close-up look at the cheese's own personal population, a host of industrious mites already at work on your next mouthful ... and there indeed they were, crawling and heaving about their greenish world, caught in the act, terribly near the eye yet remote and unconscious of our world above, of coloured paper caps and the smell of port and fruit and the shaded glow of the warm yellow party. Yet in a few seconds they would be inside us! It was indeed disconcerting. Another Christmas spine-chill ... 'Those who are about to die salute thee!' a jollied uncle cried, and we thought he meant *us.* ...

For a child Christmas is looking upwards, at the glittering raised tree, at the table covered with cakes and jellies and fruits, and upwards at the red roaring faces of the grown-ups where all the noise seemed to come from ... one remembers them with coloured hats on, and long paper tongues squawking into each others' faces, and singing and seeming to have more time to laugh and play than usual, but at the same time engaged in their remote grown-ups' party, all dressed up and laughing at a million things indeed above our heads ... while of course we know now that half the time they were appalled by our own noise, and itching at the ignorance of aunts who had given us trumpets and drums, and fearful that we might be sick, and split between a belief that 'Christmas is for children' and despair at our flushed over-excited faces pink with predatory lusts.

*Childhood memories*In childhood there was also a lot of much quieter looking downwards, the long inspection in a quiet corner of new toys, and envy of the toys of others, and concentration on the little puzzles and miniature fireworks that came out of crackers ... and on Christmas Eve there was long and secret converse with the banisters on the bedroom landing, listening to the sound of parcels being wrapped, listening very hard for the chance phrase which might reveal what our presents would be, wondering and wondering what they could be and not a thought for the turkey and all that, the spirit of acquisition getting a firm grip above everything else ... but of course, one then did not formulate ideas about special foods, only relished them when they came, and one did not analyse the effects of decorations, only absorbed them all at once as one big tinsel, one great blaze. Children are punching bags for this 'too much' – they like things isolated, so that their small sharp senses can deal properly with them. Thus the annual pineapple on the table sticks out in memory from anything else, it was isolated by its exotic shape ... and of all the sounds, the sound of carol-singers, because everyone was suddenly quiet and the voices came through clear and unclouded, and of course it was a surprising mysterious sound, for it came from outside in the night.

Moments of dull satiety also seem retrievable from the early years. Too many toys make hard work, the donkey-and-carrot principle takes over, and exhausted by wandering between too many delights one ended up with the familiar childhood groan: 'I've got nothing to do.' So, later in the day, bemused with noise and glitter and too much food, there were long moments trailing the feet about coloured paper streamers littering the dead floor, and with heightened nerves slackening hoping hopelessly that something, *something* would happen. In the end, it usually would. The grown-ups, who must have retired to rest for a while, returned, and there would be the Christmas cake, and ghost stories, and games.

Games! Well remembered indeed. As a shy child, I was very, very frightened of them. All very fascinating, the rules and the mounting excitement and the movement of others – but hanging over everything was the dread of being chosen to step forward alone, to hear one's name called and to have to advance all alone. Not to have to perform or recite, but simply to do something quite impersonal yet *alone* and thus to be the possible victim of titters and ridicule. And there was a game, Postman's Knock indeed, where you had to kiss someone – and this was the most dreadful of all, it was terrible that such a private wish should be made public and there was here the certainty of what should have been a most joyful thing, but directed at oneself was most certainly not, laughter. Also, I can remember standing miserably in a circle in the game 'Poor Jenny is a-weeping' and having my own name substituted for Jenny as they sang and danced round me while I had to pretend to weep with my hands over my eyes – and the mood took right over and I burst into real tears. 'Oranges and Lemons' involved walking beneath the outstretched arms of two grown-ups who chanted, 'Chop, chop, chop, chop, CHOP off his head!' And if the arms came down on you, that was that, again it was *you* who were selected – and whatever nasty origins this game could have had, my own timorous young spirit in its party pants was undoubtedly one further human sacrifice. So – a word of commiseration to all the other millions of shy children for whom Christmas and the party month of January was or is an ominous time, bright with jellies but shadowed too with a dread very like that of the awful dentist's waiting room.

Yet Christmas was good. The proof is not in the pudding but in the fervent anticipation of it, the counting of the crawling days before. It is just that the best of Christmas Day itself all merges into a general brightness, like memories of the earliest sunny summers which you know to have been marvellous but whose very blaze of glory defeats memory: here, in fact, is the blaze of Christmas being summer in winter again. And of the other facets of the affair, the pictures as seen from an adult eye, the angelic faces in church, the gentle quiet of the snow – what do I really recall? Can I remember Christmas church? Can I remember the snow falling? The personal experience is again merged with all the pictures one has seen since, all the books read – did I really experience these things, or are they borrowed impressions? Only a few detailed bright glimpses are sure – of snow I remember only one thing and that too well, wet woollen gloves and the awful ache of frozen fingers. Later, it was different. Adolescence brought me a country Christmas in a really big old Victorian house set in fields of deep snow. Visually, it was perfect. The house had, in fact, been made into

King Bon-Bon and Christmas Cracker chorus, from Punch *1886*

a hotel but this was perhaps a change for the good; the guests were not too many, and it was like a big family gathering on what one imagines to have been a true Victorian scale. So there was the correct setting, and there were all the delights; the only thing wrong was what is wrong with all travel, that fatal fly in the sunny ointment of all exotic brochures – you take your dear old self along too. In this case, my dear young self, a self which thought itself to be much in love with a young lady there, who in turn was totally attracted by somebody else. So the whole Christmas became triangular as a Christmas tree. And thus it was spent. My only consolation is a particular clarity of memory. The sense of melancholy and the lonely, left-out feeling often arrange it so; disengaged, one has more time to observe the landscape. For once, then, I can confirm personally the truth of the huge red winter sun hanging in just the right Christmas card position above the snowline, and of blue woodsmoke rising straight up on the windless air, of snow heavy on the branches moulding multitudinous shapes and of saying the hell, the hell to it all while drinking in its clear frosted beauty with a greater lovelorn love.

An ordinary snow-scene? No, it was indelibly Christmas snow – the enormous strong presence of Christmas, the mounting expectation of the days before and all the other associations, the holly in the eye and the pudding on the breath, could make it nothing else. Just as another Christmas

The famous Lowther Arcade, London, at Christmas-time

250

Day, later on, had somewhere in it a long lonely walk in the streets of an estuary town in the rain, and it should have felt like any other grey drab day with the two waters, salt from the sea and just wet from the sky, unhappily meeting; but it felt not at all like an ordinary day. One knew too well what was going on behind all those lighted windows. The presence of the tinsel and the tree were imprinted on the back of the mind like sunglare on the eye in summer. And so I knew for a while the whole predicament of the lonely at this time of year. Under a dishwater sky the Santa Claus posters and glittering displays in shop windows lost their colour; there was a tattered after-party look about all these things – yet, at the same time as being depressed by them, how I longed to be part of it all.... The shops themselves looked shut forever. The streets were empty of people. Everybody was somewhere else, everybody was with somebody. They were all round their firesides behind those convivial yellow-lit windows, often with their curtains undrawn showing a green tree winking with false frost and further inside the colour and movement, shadows, paper-hats, firelight of family parties. Only I was left out. I think that, at one time or another, everybody must have felt an identical sense of loneliness on a summer's night, passing an open window and hearing the sounds of music and dancing echoing out on the still night air, music of all that doesn't happen, nevermore strains of the song of self-pity.

Yet – on the whole, Christmases have been happy, and, however much the adult hours may have been wearied by ever greater efforts of present-buying, the day or days themselves tend to measure up to the intention. In a way they are like weddings – a serious motive made convivial by people trying to be pleasant and dressed up to ... no, not to kill, but the opposite, to celebrate life. Easy to back away and snigger at all the bourgeois fuss, and at some levels valid – but far more profound to recognise the need for the sanctification of sentiment and the dramatic pleasures of social effort. Best always those Christmases which have copied the Christmas card, those with carols and robins and holly and a family atmosphere and all the older formalities. Although I can well remember one, at a time when I had my first proper house complete with baby, and everything for once seemed right with the world – and we sat down to eat the right turkey in the right kind of red wall-papered holly-trimmed room by the right kind of open fire, the right family sitting round and the right wife entering rightly apple-cheeked from the oven ... and looking round I thought, Heavens it's all *right*, and it's happening to me, and I've even got some money in the bank and passable good health ... whereat, of course, the worm of wisdom rose and said, 'Careful of that warm glow – defences down, this is just the moment when Fate creeps up and delivers a backhander.' And I spent the rest of the day occasionally trembling with seasonable fear. No backhander, in fact, was delivered – but it was another lesson that you take yourself along with you to such festivities, that through all the apparel of Christmas, life goes on. Yet does it? Perhaps I exaggerate. A main purpose of the whole show is to make life as it is usually lived stop for a bit. Among emblems of its regeneration.

The celebration of life

251

Select Bibliography

The following is a list of the principal authorities consulted in the writing of this book. To them and to their authors, the present writer acknowledges his debt with gratitude.

Auld, William Muir *Christmas* Macmillan, N.Y. 1931

Ballam, Harry and Digby Morton, Phyllis ed. *The Christmas Book*
    Sampson Low 1948

Barnett, James H. *The American Christmas* Macmillan, N.Y. 1954

Baur, John E. *Christmas on the American Frontier 1800–1900* The Caxton
    Printers, Caldwell, Idaho 1961

Braybrooke, Neville ed. *A Partridge in a Pear Tree* Darton, Longman &
    Todd 1960

Buday, George *The History of the Christmas Card* Spring Books 1954

Campbell, R.J. *The Story of Christmas* Collins, Toronto 1934

Collins, Philip ed. *English Christmas* Gordon Fraser 1956

Cusack, Frank ed. *The Australian Christmas* Heinemann, Melbourne 1966

Dawson, W.F. *Christmas: Its Origin and Associations* Elliot Stock 1902

Foley, Daniel L. ed. *Christmas in the Good Old Days* Chilton Co.,
    Philadelphia 1961

Gaster, Theodor *New Year* Abelard-Schuman, N.Y. 1955

Graveri, Marcello tr. Markmann, Charles Lam *The Life of Jesus*
    Secker & Warburg 1967

Hadfield, Miles and John *The Twelve Days of Christmas* Cassell 1961

Harrison, Michael *The Story of Christmas* Odhams Press 1951

Hottes, Alfred Carl *1,001 Christmas Facts and Fancies* Dodd Mead, N.Y. 1944

Hughes, Pennethorne *Witchcraft* Longmans, Green 1952

James, E. O. *Seasonal Feasts and Festivals* Thames and Hudson 1961

Kane, H. T. *The Southern Christmas* David McKay Co., N.Y. 1958

MacQueen-Pope, W. *The Curtain Rises* Thos. Nelson 1961

Miles, Clement A. *Christmas in ritual and tradition* T. Fisher Unwin 1912

Nettel, Reginald *Santa Claus* Gordon Fraser 1957

Renan, Joseph Ernest *Vie de Jésus* 1863

Sandys, William *Christmastide* John Russell Smith 1852

Schauffler, Robert Haven *Christmas* Dodd Mead, N.Y. 1930

Thonger, Richard *A Calendar of German Customs* Garden City Press 1966

Wernecke, Herbert H. *Christmas Customs Around the World* The Westminster Press, Philadelphia 1959

Acknowledgements

The author and publishers wish to thank all those who have kindly supplied photographs from their collections, or who have allowed objects from their collections to be photographed for reproduction in this book:

Abby Aldrich Rockefeller Art Collection, 32 *left and right;* Amsterdam Tourist Office, 120 *above;* Australia News and Information Bureau, 171; Phyllis Balestrero, 177 *below;* Bayerische Verwaltung, 178/9; Bettmann Archive, 44, 213; Bodleian Library, 184; British Museum, 16 *above and below,* 22 *above and below,* 150; British Travel Association, 52; Harvey Caplin, 177 *above;* Co-operative Wholesale Society Ltd, 180; Courtauld Institute of Art (from an example in the Royal Collection), 30; Mary Evans Picture Library, 38, 169, 188, 218; Faber and Faber Ltd, 12; Leonard Freed, 120 *below;* Giraudon, 31; Grandma Moses Properties Inc., 242/3; Hallmark Historical Collection, 112, 130 *above,* 131; Claus Hansmann, 13, 14/15, 138, 153, 154, 155; Stephen Harrison, 161; Heal's, London, 186; Kunsthistorisches Museum, Vienna, 85, 101; Siegfried Lauterwasser, 41, 117, 129; Lord and Taylor, New York, 185 *above;* Lord's Gallery, 226; Mansell Collection, 18, 36, 37, 49, 124, 151, 162 *above,* 167, 172; Mexicana, London, 196; Metropolitan Museum of Art, 236; Middle East Archive, 86/7; Erich Müller, 72; Museum of the City of New York, 91; National Museum of Wales, 44; Jack Nisberg, 102; Pollock's Toy Museum, 235; Radio Times Hulton Picture Library, 142; Scala, 137, 216; Staatliche Graphische Sammlung, Munich, 43; Staatsbibliothek, Berlin, 8, 29, 56, 69, 79, 82, 105; Stadtmuseum, Hallein, 84; Otto Swoboda, 42, 51, 88 *above and below,* 132, 185 *below,* 215; Ullstein Bilderdienst, Berlin, 122, 182, 191; Verkehrsamt der Stadt Köln (*photo: Theo Felten*), 118/19; Victoria and Albert Museum, 133, 135 *left,* 225, 245, 246; B.Weinreb Ltd, 244, 245; White House Collection, 130 *below.*

The illustrations on the following pages were taken by J.Freeman & Co. from periodicals in the libraries of the British Museum, the London Library, the Victoria and Albert Museum and the Westminster Public Library:

20, 67, 104, 106, 122, 139, 157, 162 *below,* 164, 175, 176, 198, 200, 201, 202, 205, 209, 223, 230, 239, 249, 250.

The following were photographed from books in the above museums or in private collections: Hans Andersen, *The Little Match Girl*, 189; John E. Baur, *Christmas on the American Frontier 1800–1900*, 93; *The Book of Days*, ed. R. Chambers, 25, 34, 97; Charles Dickens, *Pickwick Papers* (1873), 58; George and Weedon Grossmith, *Diary of a Nobody* (1892), 76, 77; Rose Henniker Heaton, *The Perfect Christmas* (1932), 159, 204, 221; E. T. A. Hoffmann, *Nutcracker and Mouse-King* (1844), 123; Washington Irving, *Old Christmas and Bracebridge Hall* (1886), 55; Clement C. Moore, *A Visit from St Nicholas* (1848), 100; Thomas Nast, *Christmas Drawings for the Human Race* (1889), 70, 109, 115, 145; Douglas Sladen, *More Queer Things about Japan* (1904), 229; Alexis Soyer, *The Modern Housewife or Menagère* (1856), 24.

Special photography was done by Ian Graham, Derrick Witty and J. Freeman & Co. The illustrations above the chapter headings were drawn by Susan Phelps. The publishers would also like to thank James Heard, of Pollock's Toy Museum, for his help with the picture research, and Otto Swoboda and Claus Hansmann, who made available to us their valuable collections of colour pictures.

The following granted permission for quotations to be reproduced: British and Foreign Bible Society, *Neo-Melanesian New Testament;* Jonathan Cape Ltd and the Hogarth Press, *Collected Poems 1954* (Cecil Day-Lewis); J. M. Dent and Sons Ltd, *Quite Early One Morning*, (Dylan Thomas); Faber and Faber Ltd, *For the Time Being* (W. H. Auden) and *Collected Poems of Louis MacNeice*.